# THE LOTUS SINGERS

## SHORT STORIES FROM CONTEMPORARY SOUTH ASIA

EDITED BY TREVOR CAROLAN

## CHENG & TSUI COMPANY

Boston

16 15 14 13 12 11    1 2 3 4 5 6 7 8 9 10

Published by

Cheng & Tsui Company, Inc.
25 West Street
Boston, MA 02111-1213 USA
Fax (617) 426-3669
www.cheng-tsui.com
"Bringing Asia to the World"™

ISBN-13: 978-0-88727-486-2


Library of Congress Cataloging-in-Publication Data

The lotus singers : short stories from contemporary South Asia / edited by Trevor Carolan.
    p. cm.
ISBN 978-0-88727-486-2
 1. Short stories, South Asian--Translations into English. 2. Short stories, South Asian. 3. South Asian fiction--21st century--Translations into English. 4. South Asian fiction--21st century. I. Carolan, Trevor. II. Title.

PR9570.S642L68 2011
823'.0108954--dc22

                        2011002825

Credits:
Front cover illustration: Imagezoo.com
Back cover photograph by Auriel Heron, UFV



Printed in the United States of America

For the Sen Guptas of Cornfield Road, Ballygunge
Friends of 40 Years
*Aum Shri Ganeshaya Namah* . . .

# CONTENTS

v

# ACKNOWLEDGMENTS

HEARTFELT THANKS TO ALL THOSE WHO HELPED WITH this project, most especially to all the writers and translators whose work appears here, and to the original publishers who kindly permitted use of the work. This project could not have been completed without the critical advice and help of Dr. Ira Raja, University of Delhi and La Trobe University, Australia; Urvashi Butalia, Zubaan Books, Delhi; Ritu Menon, Women Unlimited, Delhi; Andrew Schelling, Naropa University, Boulder, Colorado; Dr. Niaz Zaman, National Islamic University, Dhaka, Bangladesh; and Jill Cheng, Cheng & Tsui, whose idea it was. Grateful thanks also to my editors, Alexandra Jaton and Sam Lasser at C & T; Antara Dev Sen, Senior Editor, *The Little Magazine,* Delhi; Anita Rau Badami; Deborah Baker; Jackie Kabir, Dhaka, Bangladesh; Ms. Vidya Rao, Orient Blackswan Publishers, Delhi; Moyna Mazumdar and Devaraj, Katha Publications, Delhi; Renuka Chatterjee, Westland Ltd., New Delhi; Mandy Turner, Researcher, Commonwealth Broadcasting Association, London; Ismail Khilath Rasheed, Male, Maldives; Samir Bhattacharya, *Parabaas;* Jayantara Bose, Srishti Publishers, Delhi; Laurel Damashek, Boston. For their assistance during my research journeys I am indebted to Dr. Yagna Kalyanaraman, Researcher, GM Technical Centre, Bangalore; Rajiv Jai, Panel Member, Central Board of Film Certification, New Delhi; Arpita Das, Publisher, Yoda Press, Delhi; Kalamandalam Vijayan, Director, Kerala Kathakali Centre, Kochi, Kerala; Arushi Sen, Assistant Editor, Yoda Press, Delhi; Rasik Mudkedkar, Goa; Dr. Chandra Mohan, Indian Association for Canadian Studies, New Delhi; Harsh Mohan, Independent Publishers Group, University of Delhi; Ms. Elvira Monteiro, Word Links, Agonda, Goa; Freddy Chakklakal and Subash Xavier, Kochi; Ngudup Dolma, Wongdhen Guesthouse, Delhi; Tuptim the Communications Man at Majnu-ka-Tilla; the staff of H.H. the Dalai Lama Medical Clinic, Majnu-ka-Tilla, Delhi; Mashal Foundation, Lahore, Pakistan; the late Ivan Kats, Obor Foundation, New Haven, CT. A bow of thanks to the Librarians at University of BC, Vancouver Public Library, and North Vancouver District Public Library;

to Perrine Angly, Paris; Stephane and Roselyne Faggianelli, Hong Kong; Uwe Jeske, Heidelberg; Rosita Dellios, Dept. of International Relations, Bond University, Queensland; Rajan Thapu, University of Katmandu, for the Shiva stories; the late Maggie Grey, Bond University; Sylvia Taylor, Director, Federation of BC Writers; Richard Collins, Wales, for the *hiraeth;* Lucila Fadul, Canada Trust; Tejal Chhabra, Sidrah Ahmad and Sam Susanathan for their translation assistance; Christopher Brown, design concepts; and Ron Sweeney, Dept. of English, UFV. *Namaskar* in Kolkata to Amitabh Mitra; Master Asai, Japan Temple, Dhakuria Lake; and for Sam, Didi, Uma, Roma, Bampu, Buri, and the unknown monk. My daughter Erin and wife Kwangshik provided irreplaceable editorial and reading skills. Finally, to my scholarly colleagues at UFV who made it all possible through their generous research support and encouragement: Diane Griffiths, Vice-President Employee Services; Yvon Dandurand, Vice-President, and Brad Whittaker, Director, Research Services; John Carroll, Dept. of English; Satwinder Bains, Director, Indo-Canadian Studies Program; and the ever-resourceful Patti Wilson, Librarian *par excellence.* For all who lent a hand,


*Aum Shanti,*

Trevor Carolan
University of the Fraser Valley
British Columbia, Canada

# FOREWORD

## A STRANGE ANIMAL

SOUTH ASIA IS A STRANGE SORT OF ANIMAL. A LARGE landmass, made up of several countries, some elements of a shared past in history, some commonalities and overlaps in myth, belief, legend, folklore and religion, and yet very different political trajectories in the post-independence period from the mid-twentieth century on.

Putting together an anthology of stories from South Asia is a brave—some might even say foolhardy—enterprise. The skeptics might ask if geography is a sufficient condition to tie such a collection together. Or, questions could be raised about content, about language, about power—most collections that claim to focus on South Asia end up concentrating mainly on India—about representation, and so on. Further, readers may wish to interrogate the very concept of South Asia—at its simplest level, south of what and where, which countries does it include, where does the Middle East end and South Asia begin, should Afghanistan be a part of South Asia or not? Or at a more philosophical level, they may ask what countries as diverse as Nepal and Sri Lanka have in common that enables them to be seen as part of a larger whole.

And yet, there is something, unnameable perhaps, elusive even, but strong and enduring, that links the histories, the presents, the people and the problems of this diverse region. Even just the physical features—or indeed the political faultlines—testify to this; India and Pakistan may on and off be locked in enmity and tension, but their rivers provide ample evidence that there is no escaping their joint present and future. Sri Lanka and Nepal may be thousands of miles apart, but the history of conflict and militancy links them experientially in many different ways.

Further, at a people-to-people or civil society level, the links are even stronger. Activists fighting against big dams, or nuclearization, or violence against women, or repressive laws, or for human rights, have formed formidable links across South Asia, and draw strength from campaigns in each other's countries. Travel further adds to this, despite the many restrictions that exist, particularly between India and Pakistan. Friendships and family relationships add another dimension.

And these are not the only links. A further, complex underlayering is provided by literature, perhaps the most enduring of South Asia's connectivities. Even a cursory look at South Asia provides evidence of a literary landscape that is rich with different forms and languages. Novels, poetry, non-fiction writing, literary narratives, biographies, autobiographies in not one, but many languages not only proliferate within South Asia, but carry South Asian writing to the world. Notwithstanding the importance of print—and more recently electronic forms—the largely oral cultures of South Asia lend themselves to another literary form that populates the region, and this is the story: short, long, told, retold, created in myth, transferred into real life, subversive, innovative, funny, sad . . .

In many ways, an anthology such as this therefore begins with both a tremendous advantage and its opposite. A wealth of stories to choose from, combined with the difficulty of a complex choice: will nationality define choice? Or language? Or class? Or gender? And the categories could go on.

Clearly there are no easy choices. But there are abundant cautions, and one of these, which this particular anthology exercises, is to not allow the "big brother" (or indeed big sister, for India's self-image is that of a motherland) to dominate. Another is to bring the voices that are too often ignored—in this case, Bhutan, Nepal, the Maldives—into the fold; a third is to watch out for language. Perhaps because of the colonial past of most—happily not all—countries in the region, English is predominant and gets more importance than the indigenous languages (it's also the language of social mobility), so it needs particular attention to seek out other languages—something that the editor of this anthology has carefully exercised.

Questions may still remain, and there may well be no satisfactory answers. In the end, any selection of stories, voices, narratives has to be personal, even though the editor may have in his or her mind questions and doubts about precisely the sorts of things that are mentioned above. But no matter how or what, the final decision will come from the reader—and it is to the reader that this volume is now offered, in the hope that she will find here something of the many facets—the concept, idea, and reality—of South Asia.


Urvashi Butalia
New Delhi

# INTRODUCTION

SOUTH ASIA IS A WORLD OF STORIES. STEP OFF AN airplane, arrive by long-distance jeep, railway carriage, rattle-trap bus from the north, or land from a ferry or ship up from the south or west, and you enter into a world of storytellers. Some are wonderful and adventurous, others more slippery or deceitful; there are some who weave other times, other lives within the tapestry of their stories. But always there is a story, and somewhere at its heart, within many layers like the petals of a lotus, is a portrait of oneself.

Forty years ago, flying into Delhi from the Arabian Gulf, a man noticed my fingers tapping to the tabla rhythms of Alla Rakha, the hand-drum accompanist of sitar master Ravi Shankar. An invitation to his home followed and I found myself in a palace unlike anything I'd known until then—a big story. Two days later, the Taj Mahal in Agra beggared what I'd seen in Delhi, but not before a sleight-of-hand artist thinned my wallet amidst a skein of tales about the Taj and the extraordinary characters associated with it. Such cautionary experience, one intuits, is worth the price: I've avoided trickery on the road ever since. Good stories are like this. They may come with a bite, but they give us what we really want as a reader—typically in a way we never quite expect.

My own interest in South Asia began when as a student, I grew up watching the films of Satyajit Ray—his sultry, grainy black & white *Apu* trilogy that offered images of a world apart. Then came a wedding invitation to Kolkata (formerly Calcutta) from travel friends. I was on my way there when I detoured through the palaces of old Hindustan. With the nuptial ceremonies concluded in Kolkata, I took to wandering Ray's Bengal region. A taste of yoga, and I woke one morning with the sounds of the boat traffic on the Hooghly River in my ears. In the fashion of the times—The Beatles had made their way to Rishikesh in the hills a few years previous—I bumped into a wandering monk in the course of his pilgrimage on foot from southern Thailand to the holy places of the Buddha's life in the plains between India and Nepal. We knocked about together and were joined by others attracted to our unlikely twosome—retired scholars of Sanskrit and Pali, Dalits, the lot. Everyone had a yarn to share. It seemed to be the expected price of joining in our travelling gallimaufry.

Later, during further university studies, Chaucer's *Canterbury Tales* revealed that even in the Middle Ages a story was better than ready money when it came to striking up convivial company for a journey ahead. Returned home from my own first ramblings in South Asia, I brought a lot of stories with me. They were, I discovered, the ideal souvenir.

What follows is a compendium of 18 short stories. With a little imagination, readers may sense a kind of journey in their collective voice, a series of recent images and encounters with the "Seven Sister" nations of the South Asia region. As veteran readers, travellers and scholars learn, writers and artists from a specific country or region can offer a kaleidoscope of insights into its daily life and times. South Asian writers are no exception.

As a global audience saw a few years ago with the Academy Awards sweep by the film *Slumdog Millionaire* out of Mumbai, India, our world is changing. More than ever, Asia especially commands our attention. We need to know what is happening in this rapidly transforming region of the planet. As a companion volume to *Another Kind of Paradise: Short Stories from the New Asia-Pacific,* published a year ago by Cheng & Tsui, the editorial approach of this volume has been to locate stories from India, Bangladesh, Pakistan, Sri Lanka, Nepal, Bhutan, and the Maldives with an engaged literary focus. These are stories that talk to us about what is important in the contemporary life of these South Asian societies. As you will find, the collection focuses on a broad horizon of impact issues—on social, gender-based, economic, spiritual, and inevitably, political challenges to cultural orthodoxy as they are presented to us by many of the region's most distinguished storytellers. These are literary voices speaking not from a comfortable distance or from South Asia's far-flung diaspora, but from the home range; they are sure of their ground.

Because the challenge of a foreign language usually cuts us off from reading about Asian cultures in the original, the perspectives that present us with the most insight into new peoples and cultures are often found in good translations, or in stories by native-born writers fluent in English. Works of this nature shape what follows.

We live in a Global Age, and if there is a guiding ethic for our twenty-first century it is that we inhabit an increasingly interconnected world. What is essential to remember is that during crisis periods, humans frequently look for someone else to blame. But this is a dangerous game that cuts both ways, and learning more about each other—and how people of other cultures live their everyday lives—is an effective way of avoiding cross-cultural clashes. This kind of knowledge, however, requires more information than a three-minute evening news clip can provide: it's a matter of *engagement* with the world.

Through heavy trans-Pacific migration to North America during the past 20 years, opportunities have come for most of us to meet new people from Asian societies—through work, business deals, at school, or perhaps through neighbours or a shopkeeper nearby. Within the deeper structure of our growing relationship with Asia, one can also see how South Asian concepts like yoga, meditation, and vegetarianism are quietly becoming part of our own. With the staggering size of its population, it is instructive to remember that the South Asian sub-continent and adjacent area is roughly half the territorial size of the U.S. Within this geography, however, lie the Himalayas, the Sahara-like deserts of Rajasthan and eastern Pakistan, the vast north-central Ganges plain of old Hindustan, the breathtaking southern country of the Ghats and Deccan Plateau, and an undulating line of coastal plains that range from southern Karachi in Pakistan to Cox's Bazaar in Bangladesh. To this, add the island states of Sri Lanka and the Maldives with its fragile sea-level ecosystem that makes it the world's poster state for negative global climate change effects. Within this region—the planet's least prosperous—lives nearly one-quarter of the world's population, more than half a billion in marginal, if not impoverished, conditions.

Despite headline-making political or religious strains, the seven South Asian nations comprise a geocultural region that shares deep history, as well as cultural and social traditions. India and Pakistan, for instance, have had a quarrelsome relationship since Partition in 1947, but also share widespread use of the English and Urdu languages. With their neighbours, they also share economic aspirations and commonalities, including the needs of the poor and of women and girls especially.

Within both Hindu and Muslim patriarchal systems, South Asian women remain vulnerable. Violence and rape are endemic subjects in literature from the region and a furious volume could be gathered around these themes alone. Among women writers there—who, it deserves noting, have courageously refused to remain silent—education and choice are persistently adopted as topics for their ability to serve as vehicles of female empowerment and self-improvement.

The past two decades have seen the Indian novel rise to international stardom with such acclaimed practitioners as Vikram Seth, Arundhati Roy, Amitav Ghosh, Salman Rushdie, Anita Desai, and Aravind Adiga. Modern literature there has been dominated by fiction—though this does not diminish the importance of poets or playwrights in India and throughout the region—and the South Asian novel is top-heavy with male authors. Why this is the case does not have a definitive answer. However, in discussions with writers, translators and publishers from South Asia, one suggestion that arises repeatedly regarding why women excel at writing short stories, even dominating the genre, is that it is probably a case of "available time." Traditional South Asian family obligations loom large here and women are compelled to devote long hours to children, parents, husbands, and often other work commitments. Generally limited in the amount of time they have available to write, women writers, it seems, are becoming modern masters of the shorter form—a situation seen elsewhere throughout East and Southeast Asia. Indeed, readers will note the preponderance of women among the contributors to this present edition.[1]

As a visit to one of South Asia's literary events indicates—book fairs in Dhaka, Lahore, Kolkata, Colombo, Mumbai, Katmandu, Galle, the major Jaipur Literature Festival, or the enormous Delhi Book Fair biennial—the South Asian book trade is well-established. People read avidly and the cult of the author is taking shape here too, as surely as it has in North America or Britain. The widespread and growing use of English means that writers can now be read beyond their own national borders, and translation among regional languages is on the rise. Similarly, other voices are emerging from the smaller nations of Nepal, Bhutan, and the

---

[1] Literary matters aside, it remains a truism that in spite of the social restrictions under which South Asian women may labour, they have confounded the odds and succeeded in rising to high political office more regularly than anywhere else in the world. The list is substantial—Sri Lankan Prime Minister Sirimavo Bandaranaike and President Chandika Bandaranaike Kumaratunga, Indian Prime Minister Indira Gandhi, Pakistani Prime Minister Benazir Bhutto, and Bangladeshi Prime Ministers Khaleda Zia and Sheikh Hasina Wajed.

Maldives, ready to capitalize on the global appeal of English in porting their literary wares to the larger world. Accordingly, a wave of new talent is preparing to take its place on the South Asian literary stage. Many of these younger authors have attended schools in Europe, Australia, New Zealand and North America; subsequently, their interests, values and appetites are simultaneously local, cosmopolitan, liberal, and influenced by consumerism. Add to this the unstoppable challenges of global culture and its fascination with the internet, cell phone technology, and pop music, and one finds that ideas and events that that were unthinkable even a decade ago—individual yearnings of every calibre—are now at the heart of South Asia's developing literary agenda.

With this as background, and with the added phenomenon of global travel, South Asian societies may no longer be as "exotic" as they long were to the West. Yet the human predicament is fully explored in narratives such as Salil Chaturvedi's "Nina Awaits Mrs. Kamath's Decision" with its story of a blind girl in love, or in Niaz Zaman's portrait of a slum-dwelling mother in "The Daily Woman." Readers will also see the emergence of timely, feminist writing from Islamic societies like Bangladesh and Pakistan in tales by Jharna Rahman and Hasan Manzar, with a striking parallel account by Kunzang Choden from the hermetic mountain landscapes of Bhutan. An enduring respect for tradition across religious divides and in changing times survives in Sunil Gangopadhyay's "Virtue and Sin," whereas tradition is given a shaking in Ela Arab Mehta's "Bablu's Choice." Contemporary issues of ageing and the demands of pluralism and diversity are manifest in the stories by Usha Yadav and Mridula Koshy. Surrealism, too, appears in Manjula Padmanabhan's unexpected "A Government of India Undertaking," where the uncanny may be a natural response to the random chaos of South Asia's daily urban experience. Suffering, the poet Auden argued, is something about which old masters are never wrong, and as Mahasweta Devi, a matriarch of Indian writing, establishes with her stinging tale "Arjun," what India's Nobel Prize-winning economist Amartya Sen calls the "durability of inequity and injustice" is also tragically alive and flourishing.[2]

---

[2]See *The Little Magazine*, Vol. III, p. 9, 2009

Stories like these provide us with a keener sense of place and a system of enquiry for understanding how certain characters and their actions may reflect cultural values and traditions, how rewards and punishment are meted out in cultures foreign to our own. They establish the criteria for judging why certain literary works are important to their respective peoples.

With any anthology there are bound to be difficult decisions regarding what is included. Which writers could benefit from more exposure? Indian writers such as Anjum Hasan, Paul Zacharias, and Esther David all deserve to be featured in a collection of this kind, as do Mohammed Hanif and Mohsih Hamid from Pakistan, yet matters of availability, of access to translations, and of obtaining agreements enter into the final equation. Researching strong work by writers from distant places takes patience, time, effort and travel; in the end, an editor winnows and works with what the search turns up. In this respect I am indebted for advice from old and new colleagues alike from South Asia: writers, scholars, publishers, translators, friends, and strangers met by chance in restaurants and in transit all contributed suggestions and made valuable recommendations. What evolved was the decision to simply locate good short fiction—stories that reflect aspects of the current world in South Asia, its conditions of existence, the aspirations of those living there, the changing pressures on everyday life. From this arose the very heart of what *The Lotus Singers* brings to our awareness of Asia. Like the *padme,* or lotus, that grows in cultured garden ponds and scruffy drainage canals alike throughout the region—emerging white and serene, soft blue, or rose-red from the mud and grit of the world—these are the stories of a place and a time within an extraordinary, transforming human landscape. That South Asia happens to be Asia's *other* major world-power region, and which through old, enduring memory may be closer to the West than any other, makes it more than just important. With the vital potentiality of a genuinely "Indo-Pacific" region arising as this century progresses, knowing more about it will become essential generational knowledge. As an early step in this direction, and with gratitude for the years of wisdom she has steadily imparted during the long, slow evolution of this book, I offer it in homage to the great Mother soul of South Asia.

# THE LOTUS SINGERS

## Neeru Nanda   ❀   INDIA

Born in 1953 in Lucknow, Nanda spent her early years there and was educated in Delhi. She spent 12 years as a freelance writer and was Managing Editor of the journals *Indian Interiors* and *Verve*. Her journalistic experience in covering the emergence of India's rapidly rising middle-class, consumer-minded society is a foundational element in her depiction of contemporary life there. While visiting her daughter in New York, an opportunity arose for Nanda to attend a creative writing workshop in narrative voice at Columbia University, and this was followed by her first collection, *If,* from which this story is selected. Her short stories are often rooted in her extensive travels and examine the impact of social privilege on local Indian life. Ruskin Bond, a widely-respected Indian author, has justifiably called Nanda's gritty writing "strong medicine." She studied classical Sanskrit and has said that she admires the writing of Virginia Woolf. She lives in Mumbai.

# HIS FATHER'S FUNERAL

IT WAS BURNING HOT—42° CENTIGRADE!

Shankar's cheeks were scorched and red. With the curve of his forefinger, he wiped the sweat off his forehead and collected the saliva in his mouth to spit it out, just as he had seen his elders do. He squinted up at the round, chubby face of his best friend Veer, and felt secretly pleased that Veer, who was a year older, was walking with him at the head of his father's funeral procession. Shankar was very uncomfortable. His starched, ready-made *dhoti* was poking him in his thin thighs and the sun was burning his freshly shaven head and his bare shoulders.

He moved closer to Veer and asked, "Can't I wear a cap?"

Veer, who was wearing a cap, a cream shirt and khaki trousers, looked over his shoulder to make sure that they were not being overheard, then winked at Shankar and said, "Go ahead, wear it!"

Shankar slyly slid the cap out of the folds of his *dhoti*. Just as he was about to put it on, Veer slapped his hand back and said, "Stupid, you can't. This is not a picnic. Put a big hanky on your head and tuck the ends behind your ears."

"I don't have a hanky," Shankar said.

"Take it from your fa . . . oh!" Veer cleared his throat awkwardly and lowered his eyes.

Shankar looked at him, wondering why Veer had stopped mid-sentence.

It was all right! He himself, the son of the dead father, had not got used to the fact that his father was dead and that this was his father's funeral. He remained silent for a while, then wiping the sweat off his upper lip, said, "I won't be going to school for some time."

"Your hair will not grow back for three months," Veer said with a knowing smile.

"Three months? Did yours take so long?"

"Longer."

The boys shuffled along in silence. Shankar looked at Veer's canvas shoes and then at his own bare feet, collecting dirt on the hot, tarred road.

"What happens when someone dies?" Shankar asked, looking back to ensure that nobody was listening. He saw a mass of white shirts moving towards him. He was reminded of the detergent ads on television where the white was so white it had this haze around it. And in that whiteness Shankar spotted the yellow marigolds and the red rose petals that covered the shrouded body of his father, tied tightly to a wooden platform that rested on his uncles' shoulders. It was hard to believe that inside the new, white sheet lay his ferocious father.

"He's gone! He's dead," Veer shrugged.

"Gone where?"

"I don't know. To heaven or to hell."

"You mean, he won't come back?"

"No. His body will be burnt and it will turn to ashes. How can he come back?"

"Who will burn it?"

"You."

"Me? I can't do it! And why *should* I do it? I didn't tell him to drink and die!" Shankar exclaimed with a shiver. A frightened, uneasy silence followed before Shankar asked, "Did you have to do that for your mother?"

"No. In my case my father had to light the pyre. I was saved," Veer replied raising his eyebrows.

"I won't do it," Shankar said. "When your mother died did she come back?"

"I kept feeling she was around and that she was back. But I never saw her."

"Did you cry when she died?"

Veer did not reply. He looked at his feet and continued to walk.

"Did you?"

"Yes. I had to," Veer mumbled through clenched teeth.

"Why did you *have* to?"

"I saw my sister howl and shriek. It made me nervous. So I ran off to play marbles. My uncle saw me outside Vishnu's house. He hauled me off the ground and dragged me home by my ears, saying, 'This boy has no shame, no feelings. His mother is dead and he is playing marbles.' Then he slapped me and I started howling," Veer said, avoiding Shankar's eyes.

"Did your father cry?"

Veer turned around to look at his father who was walking with Shankar's uncle. Shankar turned too. He saw Veer's dark, tall, obese father and noticed that he had lined his shirt collar with his handkerchief to prevent the sweat dripping down his back. Shankar wished he could do the same. He was not even allowed to wear a shirt. His half-naked body was hot and glistening.

"Did your father cry?"

"I don't know."

"Didn't you see him or were you too busy playing marbles?"

Veer lifted his hand in a mock backhand to Shankar. Shankar gestured back, daring Veer to hit him on this occasion.

"My father is a real actor," Veer said. "When my mother died, he sat down on his haunches, covered his head with his arms and wailed loudly. I don't think he really cried."

They both fell silent. It was just half an hour since they had left the house. They probably had to walk for another half hour. Why couldn't they have taken a bus? Shankar had wondered earlier in the day, but had not dared air his opinion after seeing his mother's distraught condition.

"How did she die?"

"Malaria," Veer replied.

"Do you miss her and feel sad? Did you really cry for her?"

"She used to beat me and she was always so angry that I used to dislike her when she was alive. I used to think she was my stepmother. But you know what?" Veer whispered, leaning towards Shankar, "If one of them had to die, then it was better that my mother died instead of my father."

"Why?" Shankar asked, taken aback.

"Stupid," Veer hissed. "Who earns the money? Father. Who sends you to school? Father. Who buys the TV, radio, food, and clothes? Father. Understand?"

Shankar felt very agitated. He frowned and looked at the road below his feet—falling behind him with every stride he took. His *dhoti* went up and down his ankles and every time it moved, it scratched his thighs.

"Oh God!" Shankar exclaimed, rubbing his groin and wishing he were on the bus that was passing by. "Now what will happen to me? I wish my mother had died instead."

"There would be a different problem then," Veer said, wiser of the two. "Father drinks every night. My grandmother complains bitterly that half the salary goes on alcohol. He talks and sings all night and sometimes beats me up."

"Then what's the difference? At least your mother must have been more loving and must have cooked for you and washed your clothes." Shankar hoped that his plight would turn out to be better than Veer's.

"But my sister does that now."

Shankar resorted to silence. Suddenly, he became aware of what was going on around him. People were covering their heads as they passed the funeral procession. There were some that caught his eye and gave him sympathetic looks. He scowled back at them. This whole thing about his father dying was becoming a nasty affair in his mind. Look at him! He was without clothes, without shoes, without hair on this long, unending road to the crematorium. Anything was preferable to this—even an occasional beating.

"What if your father marries again?" Shankar asked. Veer shrugged indifferently. "Do you think my mother will marry again?"

"Women don't marry again. Only men do. Did Meera, Anandi, and that nice girl down the lane marry again?" Veer asked, looking at Shankar.

"Then who will earn for us?"

Both fell into a reflective silence. Shankar imagined his poor, illiterate mother looking for a job. He shook his head. She was incapable of working in an office and his sister was younger than he was. His uncles? Never! They would not even give a penny. Suddenly, he caught his breath in a gasp and heard Veer do the same. Their eyes were like saucers as they turned to each other, simultaneously, their index fingers pointing to Shankar.

"Me," Shankar said.

"You."

"Oh, my God!" Shankar clutched his head between his hands, sat on his haunches in the middle of the road and broke into a high-pitched wail.

The men walking behind Shankar and Veer came to an abrupt halt and the whole procession slowed down. They were just twenty minutes away from the cremation grounds and the people at the back rose on tiptoe to see what had stopped them. A buzz went down the procession that Shankar had fainted. Before the first buzz reached the last man, a second buzz went down the procession about whether Shankar should be taken inside the crematorium or not. His uncles consulted one another and decided that the procession must not stop, lest the gods get angry with them.

Two of his uncles relinquished their pall-bearer's posts to close friends standing by and marched to the head of the procession where Shankar was sitting on the ground, rocking himself with every wail. They placed their hands under his armpits and lifted his light frame. For a moment, Shankar was suspended between his two squat uncles, his feet dangling. He looked up, in turn, at each one of them, decided that he hated their moustaches and unfolded his legs to put his feet on the ground. He was genuinely upset now. First, they shaved his head, not even allowing him a cap. Now, they were treating him like an errant child, and by tomorrow they would expect him to leave school and start earning. He pulled his arms away from them and continued on his journey to the cremation ground with bigger, sturdier and angrier strides.

Shankar walked furiously and Veer had to run to catch up with him.

"I just had an idea," Veer whispered. "Your mother could marry my father. Then we'll be brothers. We can study and play together all the time."

Shankar's eyes sparkled at the idea. Why not? He would not have to go to work then. "But does your father earn enough for all of us? Could we all manage?"

"We'll manage, my friend," Veer said, slapping Shankar's sweaty back. "Your mother can cook, clean and wash the house for all of us. Then my sister can also go to school."

Shankar thought for a moment, then asked, "Whose house?"

"Ours."

"Ours, meaning yours."

"Of course," Veer said. "If your mother marries my father, then you have to move into my house."

Shankar frowned. He did not like the idea. "Your house is so small. Where would I sleep and where would my sister sleep?"

"We'll all sleep together."

Shankar turned to Veer with angry eyes. He stole a backward glance to make sure that nobody was listening. "If your father beat your mother, then he will beat my mother too."

"So what!" Veer shrugged. "All women get beaten once in a while. It's okay if the husband beats her. But not if another man beats her. Idiot! He will be her husband then. For me, he will be another man. But for her, he will be her husband," Veer said, grinding his teeth.

Shankar didn't like the idea. He mulled over it. There was something that was not right. "But you said women don't marry again."

"That's also true. If I tell my grandmother, she will kill me." Veer lapsed into silence. "Actually she may not. If she gets a dowry she would agree."

"Dowry? What's that?"

"Dowry," Veer said, spreading his hands to explain. "You don't know about dowry? Didn't your parents discuss dowry for your sister all the time?"

"No! What's a dowry?"

"When a girl gets married, she has to take money, clothes, presents and a lot of gold to her husband's house. My father used to tell my mother not to wear her gold jewellery and expensive saris because they had to be preserved for my sister. This way we would have to spend less when she got married."

"But my mother is not a girl. She must have given this dowry thing when she married my father. This time she will be *re*-marrying," Shankar said, pointing an admonishing finger at Veer.

"But my grandmother is horrible. She will not leave her in peace. She will want a dowry, otherwise she will say she can get any other girl, why should her son marry an old widow with two children? I've heard her say all kinds of horrible things, even to my mother. It used to make my mother cry and that is when she would beat me up."

"So what about my mother? If she has to pay your father and grandmother to get married, then she can also get another man. Why should she marry that ugly, drunken toad of a fat father of yours, cook and wash for a dozen people and get beaten at night?" Shankar said, his eyes flashing.

Veer stopped.

Suddenly he lunged at Shankar and both the boys fell to the ground. Veer straddled Shankar, held him down by one shoulder and punched him with the other hand. Shankar moved his head from side to side to avert Veer's punches. Then he clutched Veer's hair, and with his other hand, caught hold of his throat. They rolled on the ground, punching, pulling and kicking each other. Soon they were both covered with grime and dust. Anger burned their skins and drove them to hit and hurt each other with greater force.

Once again, the procession slowed down and Shankar's uncles, near at hand, started hollering, "Hey, you two! What's the matter? Can't you behave yourselves for one day?"

Veer's father ran hurriedly to the front of the procession, and picking up his son by his collar, gave him one whack on his bottom. He pushed him roughly and said, "Shame on you! He has lost his father and you are fighting with him? Do you know what that means? What was the fight about? What did you say to him?"

"Nothing," Veer said, trying to free himself from his father's firm grasp.

"Can't be. Come on, what did you say to him?" Veer's head jerked backwards as his father gave his hair a tug.

Shankar's uncle, who was roughly holding onto Shankar's arm, said, "Never mind. Let's proceed."

Quite suddenly and unexpectedly, Shankar piped up, "He called my mother an old widow whom no one will marry."

Maddened, Veer replied, "He called my father a fat toad."

"He wanted dowry for marrying my mother to his father."

"You liar. I never said that."

"You did! You did. You even said that your . . ."

"Hey! Hey! Stop it!" Shankar's uncle gave Shankar a light slap. "Is this a marriage hall or your father's funeral? What nonsense have you two been talking? How can you even talk of your mother's marriage? We are not even of the same caste. And widows do not get married again."

Shankar and Veer, who had been glaring at each other with flared nostrils and heaving chests, suddenly looked at Shankar's uncle blankly.

"What did you say? Caste?" Veer's father asked. "I come here for my friend's funeral and you talk about caste? What is your wife's caste for that matter?"

"I had a love marriage," Shankar's uncle said.

"Oh, really! So none of the rules of caste apply to you. Is that why your father-in-law had to give you such a fat dowry? Don't you dare talk caste to me. I wouldn't marry her, even if you came begging to me with a fat dowry."

"Oh yes, you would! Such is your caste." Shankar and Veer were listening intently. These were things they had never heard before. They were now privy to an adult world.

Veer's father was in a rage by now. Shankar's uncle was being arrogant and dismissive. Shankar, at that moment, was ashamed of him. He looked at Veer with innocent, apologetic eyes, and then looked away. He heard his uncle's voice as if from a distance. "You want to bet on that? In front of all these people gathered here for a solemn cremation?"

Shankar saw Veer's father glaring at his uncle for a long time. "If it hadn't been a funeral, I would have rubbed your nose in the ground for saying that. You have lived in Bombay for two generations and you talk about caste like a bloody third-rate villager. I'm leaving. I'm too low—just an ordinary trader—to attend this high-caste, blue-blooded funeral. You come to my grocery store and we will settle scores then. And if all your debts aren't paid by tomorrow then I'll break your bloody legs. And you, Veer, if I see you playing with that scholarly Shankar again, I'll wring your blooming neck, do you understand?" He spat viciously just a foot away from Shankar's uncle's leg and, dragging Veer by his forearm, started walking away from the funeral procession. After a few steps, he turned back and, tapping Shankar's uncle on his shoulder, said rather grandly, "Now that Shankar's father has died such a noble death, leaving behind him unheard-of riches, Shankar might need to earn for his family. Send him to me, I'll give him a job."

Suddenly, Shankar did not want to be an adult. He did not want to spit like his uncles, nor line his collar with a handkerchief, like Veer's father. He wanted no part in this wilderness of death and marriage, caste and dowry pay-offs. He did not want his mother married off to some toad. All he wanted was to play marbles and cricket with his dear friend Veer. He wanted to be in school forever. He looked up at his uncle and felt scared of him. Scared of the power of his decisions now that his own father was dead. He wished his father had not died. However nasty he had been, at least he had made sure that Shankar got food, clothing and education.

Shankar looked again at his father's dead body, wrapped in a white sheet, covered with rose petals, and feeling a huge sense of loss, burst into tears.

## Mahasweta Devi  🌼 INDIA

Mahasweta Devi is one of India's most renowned writers. Born in 1926, her parents were members of the literary community in British colonial-era Dhaka. Following Partition, she moved to West Bengal in India and studied at Visva-Bharati University at Santiniketan, originally founded by Rabindranath Tagore. She later completed her Masters in English at Calcutta University. Devi began writing at a young age, and contributed short stories to a variety of magazines before her first novel, *Nati,* was published in 1957. Among her more than 60 books are the masterpiece *Hazaar Chaurasi Ki Maa* (also a film), *Rudali, Bioscoper Baksho,* and *Chatti Munda O Tar Tir.* Devi is known for her writing about the lives of ordinary men and women, as well as for her firebrand activism on behalf of India's economically repressed Adivasi tribal people. In 1996 she received India's highest literary accolade, the Jnanpith Award. Her work has been translated into half a dozen foreign languages.

# ARJUN

*Translated from Bangla by Mridula Nath Chakraborty*

*AGHRAYAN* WAS ALMOST OVER AND THE MONTH OF *Poush* was just round the corner. It was not cold enough yet for the sun's warmth to be welcome.

The ripe paddy crop in Bishal Mahato's farm had been harvested the previous day. All day, along with the harvesters and casual grain pickers, Ketu Shabar too had been collecting the leftover grains of paddy in the fields. Now, in the foggy twilight, he needed a little liquor to warm him and to relax his aching body. The desire was sure to remain ungratified, but, he told himself, there was no harm in fantasizing.

Originally published as "Arjun" in Bangla in *Dainik Bartaman,* 1984. This English translation by Mridula Nath Chakraborty first published in Meenakshi Sharma ed. *The Wordsmiths,* by Katha, 1996; and in *The Bell and Other Stories,* by Katha, 2000, New Delhi.

His wife, Mohoni, was not with him. She came to the fields only when he was not around—Ketu was frequently in and out of jails. His offence: cleaning the jungles for the paddy crop.

It was no use trying to reason with Ketu Shabar about this. Ram Haldar gave him the job and Ketu did it. Haldar collected the profits from the felled trees, and Ketu and others like him went to jail. But what could he do? All that mattered was the four-piece at the end of the day— be it for chopping down a tree or chopping up a man. In fact, it might be easier to chop up a man! Why hadn't anyone asked him to do that? wondered Ketu. He might even earn four whole rupees that way! But he quickly corrected himself—"I didn't mean it seriously, of course."

Ketu does not ever question his predicament. If you were born in the Shabar tribe of Purulia, you *had* to cut down the trees. And you *had* to go to jail. It could be no other way. If one Ketu was in jail, and something needed to be done, Haldar could always find another Ketu. Nothing lost—except that the woman in the house had to go looking for work.

The last time Ketu had been jailed for cutting down the trees of the Forest Department, Mohoni had gone out looking for work. And who knows what happened . . . In spite of the inevitability of the situation, Ketu couldn't face the prospect of returning to an empty hut. No wonder the mind and the body demanded liquor. A little intoxication, a little oblivion . . .

Lost in reverie, Ketu was suddenly confronted by Bishal Mahato. "I have some work for you," he said.

"Is it about the votes, *babu?*"

"No, no! I'm not worried about that. The people will have to elect whoever I nominate, won't they?"

"Hanh, *babu.*"

"Well? What did Ram Haldar tell you?"

"The same thing that you said."

"And what was your reply?"

"Just what I told you."

"What kind of an answer is that?"

"I am just a fool, *babu,*" said Ketu.

"Never mind. There is something I want you to do. Are you interested?"

Ram Haldar and Bishal Mahato belonged to different parties. But for Ketu and his companions, they were two of a kind. One had to appear dumb whenever they were around. Both these deities had to be pleased, if one were to make a living in this area. But who among them would dare to say "No" to these party members? Haldar and Mahato too knew that the Shabars were indispensable—they held the world record for jail terms, after all.

Now, Bishal Mahato had indeed managed to arouse Ketu's curiosity. Elections were round the corner. Bishal *babu* had been busy, attending meetings, giving speeches. So if the matter didn't concern votes, what could it possibly be? Whatever it was, it must be something shady.

"You have to cut down the arjun tree," Bishal said.

"Why, *babu?*" Ketu was startled.

"Just do what I say."

"Please *babu*, I've just come out of jail, *babu.*"

"If I wanted to send you back, would you be able to prevent it?" asked Bishal Mahato.

"No, *babu.*"

"This is not like one of Ram Haldar's contracts. Only through his illegal operations do you land in jail. Who'd dare to arrest you if I ordered the removal of the tree from the main intersection at the government road?"

Ketu's mind went blank. He had never thought about it, but it was true. You worked for Ram Haldar and you promptly got caught. That meant another trip to the jail. But Bishal *babu's* word was law. He actually ran the country, you know! So, who would send you to jail if, under his instructions, the shady tree no longer stood at the government road?

An idea flashed through Ketu's mind. *"Babu,* are you making a *pukka* road this time, to ensure the votes?"

*"Pukka* road? Here? Ketu, you must be mad! It has not happened in thirty years. And it won't happen now. No, I need the tree."

"A full-grown tree?"

"Yes, the whole arjun tree."

"And how would you transport it?"

"Ram *babu's* truck, what else."

It was as if the clear sky, the pure, cold air and the Santoshi Ma *bhajans* blaring out on the cassette player were prompting Bishal Mahato to speak the truth. It was that magical hour when earth bids farewell to the day and twilight disappears into the arms of night. The wind carried the smell of ripe paddy from the fields of Bandihi. But Ketu was oblivious to all that. Mahato's request had stunned him. It was as if a huge stone had been placed on his chest. This is what Chandra Santhal must have felt when, during the Harvest Revolution, they had pinned him down with a half-maund measure. That weight . . . frightening.

Bishal Mahato and Ram Haldar belonged to two different parties. But only in word did they represent opposite camps. One conducted the *panchayat*, the other ran the sawmill just outside the borders of the district. If one ordered the arjun to be cut down, the other happily provided the transport to carry it away.

Hai! The tree couldn't be saved. It was the only surviving relic of the Bandihi jungles from the *zamindari* era. It still evoked memories of the past in the minds of Ketu and his friends. When the jungles were not jungles in name only, the Shabars had been forest-dwellers. Gone were those days when they scampered off like rabbits into its dark depths the moment they heard or saw a stranger approaching. Was that why they had been identified as Khedia Shabars, in the census records? The elders of the tribe still revered the arjun tree. They believed that it was a manifestation of the divine. Now Ketu was to be responsible for its death!

"Yes, *babu*. I'll cut it down," Ketu Shabar said. He stretched out his hand for ten rupees. What a strange evening this was. He was even given what he had asked for.

"Go, go drink," Mahato said. "You won't be able to manage the job on your own, so get all those just released from jail. I'll see to it that you are all taken care of."

Ram Haldar's business did not stop with one or two trees. First, he put up posters, "Save the Forests," then vandalized the jungles. Hands that wielded the axe were rewarded with torches, wrist watches, gleaming radios, cassette players, cycles, and of course, unlimited quantities of liquor. Each according to his capacity and capability. But the fallout was that whether innocent or guilty, the Shabars were repeatedly persecuted by the Forest Department or the police.

Mahato's offer was much more promising. Who else would offer them so much?

"Very well, I'm going to the town now. For a meeting . . . I must get some posters. How on earth can one conduct a campaign without wall-posters?"

"Get some for me too, *babu.*"

"Why, do you have a wall to stick them on?"

"No, no, *babu.* I'll spread them out on the floor when I sleep. Then I won't feel the cold in my bones."

"All right, all right. See that you cut down the tree in two or three days. I'll have it removed when I return."

"The arjun tree, *babu?*"

"Yes, yes, that one. Of course, it will be like the death of a *mahapatra*, a noble soul . . ." the monkey-capped, sweater-clad Mahato muttered as he disappeared into the foggy darkness of the night.

Ketu was deep in thought. He went to look for his friends—Banamali, Diga and Pitambar—to see if they could offer a solution.

Since he was carrying liquor, they welcomed him warmly. All of them had wielded the axe. All of them were just out of jail. He who wields the axe goes to jail—that was the rule of the land. Just as it was understood that Ram Haldar would get palatial mansions built in Purulia and Bankura. That was fate. So what could they possibly do to change the order of things?

"Let me think," said Diga. Among them, Diga was treated with a little more respect. He had actually attended four whole days at the non-formal education centre! And learnt the alphabet too.

The four Shabars drowned themselves in thought and liquor. During festivals and weddings, they went around the arjun tree, beating their *dhol-dhamsa* drums. After a certain wish had been granted, the tribals made the ritual sacrifice of their hair and buried it under the tree for good luck. Hadn't Diga's father said that the tree had medicinal properties?

Drunkenly, Pitambar exclaimed, "Even the Santhals come here during the *Badhna Jagoran* for the cow dance."

What a predicament! Cut the tree, you go to jail; don't cut the tree, you still get jailed. What is the Shabar to do? This prosperous village of Bandihi sits where once the jungle used to be. Now it falls under the jurisdiction of the Forest Department. But of course the Shabars don't have any claims to it.

After much contemplation, Diga said, "So why should we alone take the blame? Why should only Shabars get trapped in a false case? I'm going to tell the others. After all, they too revere the arjun. What do you say?"

Who knows how long the arjun had stood at that intersection. No one had really noticed it all these years. It was as if the tree had been there from time immemorial and would be there for time eternal. But now, all of a sudden it had become enormously important for everyone. As if it was a symbol of their existence!

The Forest Department did not control only the jungles, but the fallow land too. So where could the Shabars go? They had simply begun to wander from place to place. Wherever they saw a green patch of jungle land, they would settle down. Then the jungles would start disappearing. The fallow land would be sold off. Once again the Shabars would be homeless.

When the arjun had been a young tree, the Shabars had offered prayers to it before going on hunting expeditions. Now that it was mature, how grand it was! A shiny bark, the top touching the sky. On full-moon nights, the tree and moonlight seemed like one. During *Chaitra* and *Baishakh*, its spread of leaves provided such shade. It meant so much to them. That arjun at the crossing . . .

Pitambar asked, "For how long has the arjun been guarding us? That one tree is the entire jungle for us. And our few families, the children of the forest. Now Mahato wants that very tree?"

"What can we do? Everything belongs to Bishal *babu* and Ram *babu.*"

"Till we had built our huts, we lived under the arjun. Only later did Mahato give us the land to build our huts . . ." went on Pitambar.

Diga put in his bit: "Didn't the Santhals come to it for shelter and consolation after Haldar had burnt their shanties?"

One by one, they began to recall stories about the arjun tree. Each one realized that their lives and fate were inextricably linked with that of the arjun. Society and the system had continually persecuted, exploited and almost obliterated this handful of tribals from the face of the earth.

Now the same fate awaited the arjun tree, the last mute symbol of their existence.

"Bishal *babu* is going to town. We must collect the cash from him before he leaves," said Diga.

"You will cut the tree then?"

"Five people should be enough to do the job. We'll ask for one hundred rupees, what do you say?"

"You may have to go to jail."

Frequent visits to the jail and constant exploitation by society had taught the Shabars to mask their true feelings and intentions. One face was presented to the Mahatos of the world, while the other one remained hidden. In the days of the British, the Shabars were the only ones who could be relied upon to set police stations and checkposts on fire. Today the *babus* were dependent on them, for these same Shabars performed the all-important tasks of land encroachment, crop theft, disposal of corpses and clearing of government-owned forests.

So who would be so dumb as to go to jail for cutting one single tree?

Diga gave a shrewd, cunning laugh. "You don't worry about it," he told the others. After all, he knew the alphabet, had been to the jails of districts as far apart as Jamshedpur, Chaibasa, Medinipur and Bankura.

Bishal *babu* was assured that by the time he returned from the town, the job would be done. "Go and conduct your election meetings with an easy mind. Give us the money. When you come back, you'll see that the tree is not there."

"Make sure that Ram *babu* doesn't get a hint of what is happening."

"Why, isn't he giving you the truck?"

"Yes, but he'll still create a big fuss. Also, take care that no one outside the district gets news of it."

"We'll see, *babu.*"

On the surface, politicians hoisted different flags, but underneath, they were like sugar in milk. No conflict of interest when it came down to brass tacks.

Bishal *babu*, you have taught the foolish Shabars many a lesson, haven't you—what they call non-formal education!

The leaders of the two opposite camps abuse each other in public meetings. The cadre members do not understand all this. Abuses, petty quarrels and occasional bloodshed are all part of the political system. There is bound to be some dispute over the arjun too. But then, how many people would really support Ram Haldar? The entire village was under Bishal Mahato's sway.

❧ ❧ ❧

"A trip to the town really becomes frenzied," thought Bishal Mahato. "On the way there are speeches and gatherings at the public halls and bazaars to be attended to. In the town, so many chores have to be taken care of. Get the moped light repaired, buy a new lantern, a shawl for the wife, some medicines . . ."

Satisfied with his trip, Bishal Mahato was returning to Bandihi. The problems of votes had been taken care of. Oh god! When would they build a proper road to the village? Nengshai, Tetka, stream after stream, and then the descent down the bamboo bridge. After that, the tortuous way through slippery paths and uneven roads.

But as he neared the village, his head reeled.

Against the backdrop of the deep blue sky, the majestic arjun tree stood with its head held high—like a guardian of the village, keeping vigil from its lofty post. Once upon a time, this land used to be guarded by hundreds of leafy sentinels. One by one, they have all gone, leaving no trace. Only the arjun is left now. Alone, to guard this devastated, neglected, humiliated land of his.

Unbidden, a proverb flashed through Bishal Mahato's mind: "The leaves of the arjun tree are like the tongue of man."

All around boomed the sounds of the *dhol-dhamsa-damak* and the strains of the *nagra*. An agitated Bishal Mahato rushed into the village. A huge crowd had gathered around the arjun. Its trunk was covered with *aakondo* garlands.

Haldar was standing at the perimeter of the crowd, holding on to his bicycle.

"What happened?" asked Mahato.

"The *gram-devata* has made them do it," answered Haldar.

"What? Which ill-begotten fellow says so?"

"Diga had a dream, it seems. You paid him money in the dream and instructed him to build a concrete base around the trunk. People from all the tribes—Santhal, Khedia, Shohish, Bhumij—have now gathered to make their offerings."

"To the *gram-devata?*"

"Yes, and the crowds have not stopped coming. There is practically a *mela* on. We'd thought these fellows were fools. But they have made fools of us, Mahato!"

Bishal stepped forward to taste the full flavour of his defeat.

What a stupendous crowd! Ketu was dancing away like a maniac, going round and round with his *dholok*.

Bishal was suddenly afraid. This tree, these people—he knew them all. He knew them very well. And yet, today they seemed like strangers.

Fear. An uncomprehending fear gripped him.

# Salil Chaturvedi ✿ INDIA

Salil Chaturvedi lives with his wife in New Delhi. In December 2009 he, along with a crew of three, sailed a twenty-foot sloop from Mumbai to Goa to draw attention to accessibility issues for disabled persons. Salil himself was partially paralyzed in an accident in 1984 and uses a wheelchair. He has represented India in the Australian and Japan Open Wheelchair Tennis tournaments and has also worked as an actor on the children's television show *Galli Galli Sim Sim*, the Indian remake of *Sesame Street*, where he plays the role of Jugaadu, a disabled garage owner and a friend of the Muppets. Salil writes short fiction and poetry and has won top honours at the British Council/Unisun Short Story Competition, 2007, and was Asia region winner of the Commonwealth Broadcasting Association's 2008 Short Story Competition. Currently, he spends his time planning his forest garden that he hopes to set up in Goa, and is passionate about leading a low-energy, sustainable lifestyle. He blogs at salilchaturvedi.blogspot.com.

# NINA AWAITS
# MRS. KAMATH'S DECISION

IT WAS SUNDAY AND NINA LAY IN BED, LISTENING to the morning. *Shlick ... shlick ...* she heard Granny shuffle to the toilet at the end of the corridor. A little later, Granny flushed the toilet and cleaned the outside of the bathroom with the broom ... *swishhhh ... swishhhh ...* where she would've dribbled a little. She then dragged her feet back to the bedroom and, lying down, asked Jesus for some help with her incontinence, which meant it was about six o'clock.

Nina heard the *chuga-chuga-chuga* of the motorcycle as it idled past her window. That would be Ophelia's brother going to the milk booth on his newly acquired "Bullet" which he rode on the slightest of pretexts. The motorcycle reminded her of Ramesh's voice. She thought of him now and smiled. Ramesh had got her again last night, at the end of Chapter Three where he had slipped in an "I Love You, Ninu," accompanied with a long, dramatic sigh. It was an old novel that she had heard before, but she hadn't remembered the love phrase waiting to ambush her. He was such an actor!

Suddenly Nina turned serious. The argument had spoiled it all. Since the argument she had stopped giving Ramesh any new novels to record. She still followed her routine with the old ones, though. Every night, after giving the dogs their post-dinner snack (fish bones that disappeared in seconds), Nina dug a small hollow in her pillow for the earplugs, put a tape in the Sony Walkman gifted by Francis and listened to a novel in Ramesh's delicious motorcycley voice. She loved the way he used his voice to bring colour to the characters, especially when he took on a falsetto for the female parts.

BHO-POO, Bho-Poo, bho-poo, bho-poo, bho-poo . . . the poee vendor careened past Nina's window, honking his way up the incline, towards the houses near the river, from where he'd return in about twenty minutes. His horn was like a morning alarm for the koels. Within minutes the air was bubbling with rapid calls of koel-koel-koel-koel-koel! topped with a shrill, elongated koo-oooo, as if asking, How was that? "That was excellent," Nina responded, nodding her head. She could hear some koels in the distance, too. She guessed they were perched on Mrs. Pinto's mango trees. "Do koels all over Goa wake up at the same time?" she wondered. "Is Ramesh listening to them as well? Mrs. Kamath must also like koels? I wonder if any koels are born blind."

Still in bed, Nina imagined herself as a koel flying over the forests of the Western Ghats. Starting from Gujarat, she flew south over the wide placid waters of the Narmada, then glided low over the morning fresh waters of the Godavari, flew over Goa, skimming the glassy surfaces of the Mandovi and Zuari rivers, climbed up again, over the slopes of the Sahyadri mountains into Karnataka, finally settling on a Gulmohur tree in her cousin's house in Mangalore. She covered this sub-continental journey in less than three minutes, and all the while she could hear the koels ringing in the Sunday morning. "That was fun," she thought, "and I don't even feel tired. Flying is such great fun!"

Nina really missed being a Coppersmith Barbet on Ramesh's scooter. The twenty-minute ride was the most thrilling part of her day. She struggled with the scooter as it went up the hill and then she dived downhill in free flight, the wind whistling by her face. She experienced every dip and elevation in the road as unexpected eddies. She slid crazily around curves and swooped through traffic, this way, that way, one hand always on Ramesh's shoulder telling her which way he was going to turn.

One morning, he had raced his scooter on National Highway 17, calling out the speeds: "Eighty . . . ninety . . . ninety-five . . . ninety-eight . . . *hundred!*" She had squealed with pleasure, telling him to slow down, but "I can't! I'm a Peregrine Falcon!" he had said. "I'm diving for the kill!"

After that, he had claimed that he had set a world record for the fastest Kinetic Honda on NH 17. Just then they had been overtaken by a bright-red Kinetic Honda driven by a young boy who wore a red-coloured vest and a big smile. Ramesh had had to revise his record immediately. His was now the fastest speed for a *silver-coloured* Kinetic Honda. Later, Nina wrote a poem about her experience:

She teeters, totters, twitters in alarm!
She discovers freedom at the tip of her arm,
Have you seen a bird discover flight?
It's pure delight, it's pure delight!
"It reminds me of *The Parliament of Birds*," Ramesh said.
"*Parliament of Birds?*"
"*Parliament of Birds.* It's a book by a Sufi mystic. Fariduddin Attar, I think. The birds represent humanity and the hoopoe represents the Sufi saint. I'm not sure, but I think *The Canterbury Tales* are based on this book. There are thirty pilgrims in *The Canterbury Tales*, right? And there are thirty birds in *The Parliament of Birds*, so . . ."

The koels had quietened considerably now. Nina heard the resonating *hoop-hoop-hoop* of a coucal. "Think of a crow wearing a rust-coloured jacket . . . a stylish man-about-town type," was Ramesh's description of it. She waited for *her* special coucal to hoop under the window, like it used to every Sunday morning. But it had all changed since the argument.

"No, I couldn't find anyone else!" she had heard Ramesh screaming at the top of his voice that day. She had pulled her hand away from the doorbell just in time. She had stood outside his flat, her back against the wall, listening with every nerve. At first she thought of leaving, but when she realised that the argument was about her she stayed on.

"Just look at you. Hale and hearty, nothing wrong," Mrs. Kamath was saying. "Why do you have to go marry a blind girl? If your father were alive, he'd never allow this. Have I ever stopped you from anything? But a blind girl! We'll be the laughingstock of the entire community. It was alright till you two were friends. I thought you were helping out the poor girl. But this is going too far! A blind girl, imagine. What's wrong with Mashelkar's daughter?"

"Ma, you must be blind not to see Nina's qualities. She earns twice more than Rekha, so she's quite capable of looking after herself. Anyway, money is not the point. Can't you understand a simple thing? I love her!"

"Love! I'd heard love is blind, but not blind like this. I'll see what happens to your love when you have blind children. Besides, they are Christian. Why can't you marry in your own religion, forget caste . . . that's asking for a lot these days!"

"Are her parents blind? She works in a bank . . . a *nationalised* bank. The government thinks she is good enough, why can't you?"

"Stop shouting. The government does charity . . . I don't have such a big heart. Besides, the government is not your mother. Nobody voted for me to be your mother. All the time I'm thinking only what's good for you. Okay, she has a Class-A job and a degree from the University but there is more to life than that. Ask me, I know. No one gives a degree for raising children and running a house. That's what life is about, not college degrees. *Deva* . . . it's all my fault . . . I should have seen it coming. All those trips seeing birds and I never knew that you were both becoming love-birds. Yes, you're right, I am blind. Foolish me!"

"Whatever it is, I've made up my mind, Ma. It's Nina or no one else. I'll give you two months to think about it!" and Ramesh had stomped off into his room. The blood had drained from Nina's face and she had started trembling. As Ramesh banged the door to his room, the novel slipped out of her hand.

*Chee-which-which . . . chee-chee-which-which . . . chee-chee-which-chee-chi!*

Nina smiled. Her favourite singer had joined the morning line-up. Here was a bird that could sing. "She looks like a proud opera singer, with a bloated chest," Ramesh had described it. "She knows she's good and likes to show off. She even wears a kind of black-and-white overcoat, with white edges—you could say she's formally dressed."

Nina followed the intricate tune of the magpie robin closely. The chirping got more strident, gaining intensity as the bird believed more in itself with each note that fell right. "Why can't Mrs. Kamath believe in me the way Ramesh does?" Nina thought. "I wonder how long she will take to make up her mind. Oh Jesus, can't you make things all right? It's gone on for too long. I can't take it any more, Lord. Please, make her see some sense. Please, please, please, sweet Jesus, show her the way. You know that I won't run away even though Ramesh speaks of it, you know that, don't you? You must know that. I'm not a girl that will bring shame to my family, or his. I ask just a small favour, dear Lord. You've been good to me, nothing to complain, but, please make her decide quickly. Show her the way, Jesus, and I'll abide with the decision. It'll be your decision. I'll accept it, I swear I will. Oh Jesus, help me build my nest, please, that's all I ask. It's a small thing for you."

Nina stretched her arms behind her head, her fingers searching for the glazed glass of the window. She traced the crack in the glass with her fingers right till the edge, where it met the rusted metal casing. Just below this spot was the latch to the window. She lifted the latch and pulled the window open. Then she held the metallic grill, feeling the deliciously intricate floral pattern. With the cool morning breeze came the sounds of *be-quick-be-quick!* The bulbuls were up! "That's right," she thought to herself, "tell Mrs. Kamath to be quick." As she thought this, the bulbul changed her call to the longer *be-careful . . . be-careful.* "Hey, you aren't allowed to say two different things," Nina admonished. Then she remembered the time when Francis, then a young boy of twelve, had gifted her a toy whistle. When you blew into it, the breath went through a tiny container of water and produced a bubbly trill that sounded just like a bulbul. Francis had a knack of picking out the most interesting things. Last month he had sent her a speech-reading software that read out everything on a computer screen. The voice had an American accent, though, and she wondered if she could get Ramesh's voice on it. She had asked Francis about it but he had been excited about other developments.

"Ninu, there are some freaky things happening here . . . just found out that somebody's planning to set up a Call Centre where blind people can send in photographs. The people at the Call Centre will describe the pictures to them!"

"What? How do you mean? Send pictures? How?" Nina asked.

"Using a phone camera, silly. They're expecting blind shoppers to use the service for things like finding out prices of products printed on cartons, or just to find out what the sky looks like. All for a fee of course, but just imagine someone waiting at the end of a phone line to describe the world to you!"

"Will I be able to use it here?"

"It's just a phone number so I'm sure you can call too, but hey, listen, it's just an idea right now . . . will take some time to happen. How's Ramesh?"

"Fine."

"Any decision yet?"

"No, not yet. But let's see . . ."

"I'm telling you that witch will never decide. You guys should just go ahead and . . ."

"Shut up!"

"Oh, I forgot, she might end up being your mother-in-law! Better start doing some self-defence courses, El Niño. If you want I can send you some instructional material from here."

"I'll talk to you later . . ." and Nina hung up.

"Say hello to ma and pa . . ." Francis managed to squeeze in.

Nina heard the metal squeak of the gate. She followed her father's footsteps as he climbed the three steps to the veranda, the tea cup rattling in the saucer. The dogs followed him excitedly, panting noisily. She heard father pull the cane chair. He then switched on the fan and . . . *puk!* . . . took out his glasses from the plastic case. He started reading the newspaper.

*Tuk-tuk-tuk! Tuk-tuk-tuk!*

Was Ramesh also listening to the barbets? Was he remembering that special day when she'd been out in the veranda, mimicking the bird?

"That's a Coppersmith Barbet," he had called out from the road. It was the first time they had spoken to each other. They'd got talking as if they'd known each other for the longest time. Then he had started dropping her to the bank on his scooter.

"Early bird catches the worm," he said, the first time he gave her a lift.

"So that's how you think of me . . . a worm!"

"*Arre,* no, no! I was thinking of it the other way around. You're the bird . . . a Coppersmith Barbet . . . I am the measly worm. And I don't mind being eaten by you."

"God, what dirty thoughts. You must really be a worm to think like that!"

But she had waited for the worm every morning. She waited for the scooter to come to life as her father read the newspaper in the porch, sipped his tea loudly. As soon as she'd hear the scooter she'd kiss her father, pick up her handbag and cane and start descending the steps to the gate.

"What? Ramesh is on his way?"

"He'll be here in a moment, papa. I don't want him to wait."

"How do you know he's coming? He could be late today?"

"The same way I know when you're reading the editorial, papa!"

That was something her father wondered a lot about. Papa was such a fool. It was simple, really. He read the paper quite energetically, constantly commenting on the news, but when he reached the editorial he would fall silent and his foot would start shaking. "What does the editorial say today, papa?" she'd ask when she heard the slipper slapping against his soles. Mr. Coelho would look up with a start. "Bu . . . bu . . . but . . . how do you know?" he'd sputter before reading it out to her.

*Sweeeee . . . sweeeee . . . swit-zizi!*

The first purple sunbird of the season! That was surely a good omen. Was Jesus trying to tell her something? The squirrels were chattering excitedly on the semal tree now, which meant that the sun was hitting the tree-tops. Nina knew what was coming next. Usually the tinkle of Mrs. Kamath's prayer bell lasted just a few seconds, as she said a casual "hi" to her Gods before rushing into her daily chores, but today she was really going at it. Nina waited for it to stop but the prayer bell went on and on. *Ting-Ting-Ting-Ting-Ting-Ting-Ting-Ting!* It rang powerfully, drowning out everything else. Nina sensed Mrs. Kamath's resolve. "Our Father, who art in heaven, hallowed be thy name . . ." she started saying the Lord's Prayer.

The prayer bell had stopped ringing, but its sound still reverberated in Nina's ears. She was saying the Lord's Prayer for the fifteenth time when she heard the *hoop-hoop-hoop* of the coucal just outside her window.

## Kunzang Choden ✻ BHUTAN

Kunzang Choden is Bhutan's best-known writer internationally. Born in the year of the dragon, 1952, in Bumthang, Central Bhutan, she received her primary and secondary education in Darjeeling, India. She studied psychology at university in India and sociology in the U.S. at the University of Nebraska. She has since worked as a teacher and, later, in development for the United Nations Development Program in Bhutan. She began writing in the 1990s and in 2004 published *Folktales of Bhutan*. A year later, her partly autobiographical novel *The Circle of Karma* arrived to put literature from her small, little-known Himalayan nation onto the world stage. Acclaimed by critics abroad for its rich portrayal of daily life in this beautiful, remote part of the globe, it has been translated into English, Dutch, Turkish and French. Since then, Kunzang has continued to research and write on Bhutanese oral traditions, folklore, and—as her story here indicates—women's and social issues. Kunzang Choden has represented the Royal Government of Bhutan at conferences internationally and lives with her husband in Thimpu, the capital of this small, thriving Buddhist nation.

# I WON'T ASK MOTHER

WHENEVER YESHIMO HAS SOME SPARE TIME SHE goes to stand at the edge of the hill to look down at the school. She looks longingly at the children in their uniforms with their backpacks filled with books. She envies them. They are the lucky ones. Yeshimo thinks that it is too late for her now, she is already eighteen years old and cannot go back to school. Who starts school at eighteen? But she did go to school once for a whole year. She was in kindergarten in that very school she looks at every day. She remembers her first day. Her mother had accompanied her that day. She had been excited and yet nervous. There

29

were so many children she had never seen before and everything was so new and so strange. She had a knotted feeling of anxiety in her stomach and her heart had pounded in excitement. She had looked forward to going to school ever since her parents had told her that they had decided to send her. She remembers feeling the crisp new uniform rubbing against her legs as she walked and the pinch of the new shoes on her little right toe. She recalls her mother standing in the distance with the other mothers with a broad smile on her face as the children were made to stand in lines. Then a teacher came to the front of the assembly line and finally called out her name, "Yeshimo," and she was taken to a room full of children. She looked around the room and saw all the children in their new uniforms. They were all about her own age.

Yeshimo's year in school was an uneventful one. Most of the time, the children memorized the alphabets in English and Dzongkha. They sang and danced a lot. By the end of the year she had also learned to write her name in bold blunt letters in English and delicate curvy letters in Dzongkha. Now she recollected little of what else she had learned, it was such a long time ago. Sometimes she shut her eyes and tried to recall some of the songs she had learned and she often found herself humming the melodies, but she could not remember the words.

Yeshimo had to leave school the year her mother's health had suddenly taken a turn for the worse; that was just after she had completed kindergarten. Her mother needed her daughter in the house as none of the boys would be of any use. "How can a boy do a woman's work of running a house and caring for a sick mother?" mother had reasoned loudly. Her parents said that it was enough if they had three educated children in the family; after all, her two older brothers were already going to school and her younger brother too would be joining once school re-opened the next year.

Mother was never a healthy person; she was always ailing in some way. She suffered from terrible spells of dizziness and had to stay in bed for days at a time. She moaned loudly. When she moaned like that everybody had to be very quiet and they had to whisper when they talked and walk on tip-toe, for any noise aggravated mother's dizziness. In between her groans they heard her crying in a trembling voice, "My miserable karma. Why am I so wretched?" She tried desperately to hold herself still even when she was already lying immobile in her bed. The movements were in her head. Father got impatient and threatened to leave his family and go away. But they all knew that he could not go, for where would he go to? He was a simple man with a severe speech impairment and could not talk without slurring and stuttering. He also had a bad leg that made him limp. He had nowhere to go to. It was an empty threat. He simply said these things out of desperation because when mother fell ill he had to stay home to attend to her and his work in the field fell behind. The situation was not new for Yeshimo; her life had always been marked by these events—mother groaning and trying to hold still, father threatening to leave and the boys getting ever more uncooperative and boisterous. She saw all these problems but there was little that she could do to change anything so she simply said, "I am not sure what to do. I will have to ask mother." The declaration of not knowing what to do freed her from the responsibility of doing something to change the situation.

Her mother was not afraid of father leaving the house but she was terrified that her daughter would meet a man and move out with him and leave the family. Without Yeshimo she would never manage on her own. Just thinking of this made her dizzy. Her head would spin and she would feel nauseous. She tried to take control of herself, she would not dwell on this fear, instead she would assume the rightful authority of a mother over her daughter. So she warned her every day. "Daughter," she called. Yeshimo immediately knew that when her mother called her "daughter" rather than by her name it would be the repetition of the monologue that she thought of as "let mother tell you." She felt her body grow tense and dullness spread through her head. Yet as a dutiful daughter she knew she had to listen to what her mother had to say.

"Be careful daughter, you don't know what it means to be a woman. We are not like men. We have to be extra careful. Before you realize what is happening you will have a string of children around your neck. Look at me struggling from dawn to late night for you children." She breathed deeply. "And before I know, all of you children will leave like visitors who just came for a meal." Earlier she always added the phrase, "Like the visitors who come for a meal, they will simply shake off the food crumbs from their laps and be gone." Whenever mother said this Yeshimo could not help smiling. She thought of the departing visitors actually shaking off the food crumbs in their kitchen—rice, bits of vegetables and dust. Mother had explained to her that it was just a way to say the visitors may enjoy a meal in a house but they may never know the actual problems in the house.

It pained Yeshimo to see the look of dejection and bewilderment on her mother's face when she said, "That's enough mother. Don't repeat the same things." Yeshimo's interjections came as such a shock that mother stopped midway through her sentence, suddenly looking lost and confused. Anyway Yeshimo had not yet met a man whom she fancied. How could she leave her family, with three brothers still in school, a father who was not like other fathers, smart and able bodied, and a mother who suffered from such sudden illnesses?

She worked hard but her mother was slow in her praises and too quick to point out her failings. Every morning there was chaos in the house. First the boys refused to get up when Yeshimo got up to clean the house and prepare the food. The boys never helped her—they always had homework to finish or tests to study for. Mother found endless chores around the house, all the time complaining, "And all these nameless jobs that take so much time." Father went to attend to the cattle after he had burned incense in the incense burner, a daily ritual he performed without fail. Yeshimo thought that all these tasks outside the house at least gave father some respite from the chaos and confusion in the house every morning. The boys squabbled and shouted at each other until mother smacked the one nearest to her, and scolded Yeshimo, "Look daughter, they have to go to school. Give them food quickly and send them away. Why are you so late today?"

Yeshimo worried that the neighbours would hear all the commotion and begged them to be quiet. Lowering her own voice to a whisper she implored, "How disgraceful! What will the neighbours think of us? Please be quiet." She imagined the neighbours saying, "See, that's how uneducated people behave." Nobody seemed to hear her. As much as she loved her brothers she resented the fact that she had to interrupt her studies so that they could go to school. She hoped that the least that they could do for her sacrifice was to do well in school and get good jobs. She worried when they did not study. She got up extra early on the mornings when they had exams to be sure of waking them up to study. When they failed the exams she rebuked them, getting emotional and teary. She was becoming like her mother in the very ways that she disliked, like repeating herself in long self-pitying monologues, "Why don't you study harder and do better? Look what happened to me. I could not continue school and now I am stuck here in the house without any prospects for a future. Look at my friend Chimme—she is working in an office and has a good salary. Do you know that she even bought a TV with her salary? She has the prestige of working in an office; she has a place in society. Do you want to be like me?" But she did not mention her other friends who studied up to class ten and were now unemployed. They had not found jobs anywhere in the government or in the private sector. They had applied for every job advertised that indicated minimum qualification as "class ten." Many of them were still in Thimphu waiting for job opportunities.

Finally Yeshimo was all alone in the house. The boys had left for school—they would only come home briefly for lunch at noon. Father had gone to plough the field and would come home later. Mother had to go and see a sick friend in another village and she would return home only in the evening. As usual when going to see a sick person, mother packed the customary basket full of uncooked rice and half a kilogram of butter. She took Amul butter instead of Bhutanese butter. "Thanks to the Indians I do not have to mess with cutting and measuring butter these days," she said each time she put a packet of Amul butter in her basket. She also took a dozen eggs. As she prepared these gifts she continued to give her last instructions in her usual monologue. Mother's words faded into the background and Yeshimo only heard the songs from a recent movie on her radio. The sad love songs filled the room and penetrated her heart. She felt a mysterious longing. Just before the door shut she heard her mother's last words, "*Ya*, don't spend too much time listening to the radio and daydreaming. There is work all around you waiting to be done."

Yeshimo smiled absently for she could see what had to be done. Everywhere she looked she saw more work but it seemed like mother felt compelled to tell her each task that needed to be done, even the obvious ones like cleaning the house and washing the dishes. In fact, it appeared like Yeshimo made no decisions at all, she just did what mother told her to do. Every day, the breakfast utensils had to be gathered and washed and the house cleaned. The used cups and plates were lying in a circle around the electric rice cooker and a pan of chili and potato. The family members usually sat in a circle on the floor to eat their meals. The boys always ate fast and carelessly, talking and fighting all the time. They had scattered rice everywhere. A cup of tea had been knocked over, leaving a trail across the room.

Yeshimo took down the big aluminum bowl from the shelf and systematically placed the utensils in it, stacking them one on top of another. After she had put away the pan and electric rice cooker she carried the aluminum bowl to the tap outside her house. She crouched on the concrete floor under the tap and began to scrub the soiled plates and cups, dabbing the scrubber in a bowl of dissolved Surf washing powder. She had forgotten to ask mother to buy a new bar of soap for washing the dishes. They always used the black bars of soap; they were cheap but very good. Surf was good but sometimes left a smell on the utensils, especially if they were not rinsed well. So Yeshimo made sure that each utensil was rinsed thoroughly under the tap. The water splashed down from the leaking tap and she felt the wetness soaking in through her clothes. She put the washed utensils back into the bowl to let them drip dry in the sun. She stood up and soaped her hands. She spread out her fingers and inspected them. They were covered in soap suds. "How would these fingers look on a computer keyboard?" she mused and smiled. Then she rinsed her hands and tried to shake off the water from her clothes. Just then she saw her neighbour, Jangchub Choden going to work. She had joined school a year after Yeshimo and she had dropped out in class eight. But her uncle in Thimphu helped her to get into a computer training course and then helped her to get a job immediately in a government office. "If only I had continued school and had a well-connected relative in Thimphu to help me to get a job I wouldn't be here," Yeshimo thought with a sinking heart.

Every morning at about this time she saw Jangchub Choden going past her house. Today she was wearing a new *kira* again, Yeshimo noted.

She was wearing a pale blue one with a dark blue blouse and a trendy jacket with a large floral pattern. She really knew how to dress, taking care to coordinate colours, Yeshimo thought, with a sense of admiration and a growing sense of envy.

Jangchub Choden had worn her *kira* so long that the hem swept the ground as she walked. As she passed Yeshimo's yard and had to cross the overflowing drain, she gracefully pulled up her *kira* above her ankles and crossed the drain nimbly. She looked up suddenly and saw Yeshimo looking at her. Jangchub Choden's lips which were darkened with brown lipstick parted into a smile of greeting. Yeshimo smiled back at her but her eyes were focused on the high-heeled shoes that Jangchub Choden was wearing and admired her as she daintily maneuvered herself over the uneven cobbled stone pathway. Staring absently, Yeshimo let her usual chain of thoughts run in her mind: "If only I could have continued school, even if I don't have a well-connected uncle in Thimphu I would have worked and worked hard and done well enough to be going to an office instead of cleaning up everybody's mess. I would not have to do all these 'nameless chores' in the house day after day." She looked up and saw Jangchub Choden disappearing around the corner, her small hand bag swinging from her shoulders.

Yeshimo had a pair of high-heeled shoes once. Her cousin in Thimphu had sent her a pair which fitted her perfectly and they were just the right colour, her favourite, a pale brown. But she could not bring herself to wear them: "I cannot wear these shoes, these are for girls who work in offices and not someone like me."

"Mother what do you think? Can uneducated girls wear high-heeled shoes?" she asked. She had a tube of lipstick, a pale pink one, she had self-indulgently bought one day in the market. She had gone to buy rice and cooking oil when she saw the tubes of lipsticks lined up in the glass counter. She had stood there for a long time in front of the counter, indecisive, asking herself repeatedly, would mother approve? Then suddenly, she had said, "I will take this one" and pointed to the palest pink shade. Mother had breathed heavily, sighed deeply and frowned when Yeshimo showed her the lipstick but she had not said anything. Yeshimo wore the lipstick only on special occasions and felt self-conscious all day. She could not behave like an educated girl. How could she possibly work in the garden and the fields with lipstick and high-heeled shoes?

Yeshimo was wearing a pair of flat plastic shoes and stood with her legs apart in the soil she had dug. She dug the hardened soil in the garden and spread the manure she had carried a few days earlier from the cattle shed and sowed the mustard greens just as her mother had instructed her to do. She knew exactly when and where to sow the seeds but as always she had waited for her mother to tell her. As she worked in the garden she kept the window of the kitchen open so she could hear the radio. She could listen to the radio all the time when mother was not in the house. Mother complained that when the radio was on it hurt her head and made her nauseous. She prepared another bed but before she could sow the radish seeds the boys were home from school and demanding their lunch. Fortunately she had already heated the leftovers from breakfast and called out, "The rice is in the rice cooker, the vegetable is beside the hearth and there is fresh tea in the flask." Covered in dirt and manure she did not want to go into her kitchen which she had just cleaned and washed. She could hear the plates clattering for a while and then the boys were gone as suddenly as they had come. She continued to work in the garden for some time. Finally she took off the wrap which she wore over her *kira* to protect it while working and then after dusting herself she washed at the tap before she went into the kitchen to eat. She had hoped that she could eat with father but there was no sign of him as yet. Something had delayed him. Perhaps the ground was too hard for the plough; he could not work fields at the same time as the others because of mother's illness. She ate lunch by herself.

Her friend Chonzom had invited her to come to her house to watch TV in the evening. She hadn't told mother as yet. Just the thought of telling her mother made her feel tense and uneasy. She could see her mother, looking at her questioningly: "You went to see TV just the other night. What's there to see again and again?" She asked this each time Yeshimo sought permission to go to watch TV in Chonzom's house.

"Mother, the program on the TV is different every day," she could hear herself explaining.

But today she was not going to explain the same thing again, she would cook dinner early and she would just ask father to tell mother that she had gone to Chonzom's house. That way she would not need to wait for mother's questions and her reluctant permission.

Just before sunset she heard her father coming home. She could hear him chanting his mantra, "*Om Mani Padme Hung Hri.*" Because of his stutter only she could recognize the holy syllables he chanted. To the others his chants sounded like nonsensical words. She felt a pinch in her heart, the same kind of pinch which she felt whenever she overheard the people calling him "the dumb lame." She loved her father, he tried so hard. She had listened to him come home many times and she knew exactly what he was doing without even looking. As usual he would go to the tap to wash his gum boots, brushing off every speck of dirt from them. Nobody could understand why he washed his gum boots every day only to go out into the mud again. She knew that he would then put them over the wooden fence pole for the water to drip. He would want his dinner soon. So she threw a few more pieces of firewood into the hearth to cook the vegetables quickly. The boys had already come home, and they were taking off their school uniforms. Even before greeting them she was scolding them, "*Ya, ya,* don't leave your clothes everywhere. I don't want to hear you asking me where this or that is tomorrow morning when you are dressing for school . . ." she stopped suddenly for she had heard these same words before, these were not what she wanted to say to them, these were her mother's words. Mother was speaking to her, she was not talking to her brothers. It was her mother's habit to repeat herself, not hers and she had repeated these words every day.

The boys were carefully hanging their clothes on the hooks and looking at her irritably. Her youngest brother muttered, "Why do you always say the same things? We know what to do."

"Father, please tell mother that I have gone to Chonzom's house. I may be late. I will probably eat dinner with her so don't wait for me to eat."

Father tried to say something without success so he just nodded languidly.

A few minutes after she had entered her friend's house even before they had switched on the TV the electricity went out.

Chonzom shone the flashlight to look for a candle on the shelf and lit it. "The electricity will come back; today is not our day for load-shedding."

They waited and waited; the lights flickered on for a second and then there was pitch darkness again. Yeshimo looked out of the window and saw darkness everywhere. "I think the electricity will not come back on. There are no lights anywhere. There must be a major problem," she said as she sat on the floor.

They decided to wait and see. The girls sat by the candle-light, drinking tea and eating roasted rice. They talked and laughed as they waited for the electricity. Yeshimo suddenly asked her friend, "How does it feel to have a job outside the home?"

"Well, I went to school for eleven years so I feel happy that I got a job. It would have been humiliating if I didn't get a job. I can't imagine how my parents would have taken it. Worse still, what would the neighbours have said? I feel really lucky."

"Do you like your job? I mean what kind of things do you do in the office?" Yeshimo's eyes were shining in the dimly-lit room. She could barely wait to hear her friend's answer.

"I am doubly lucky to get a job and have a good boss. He is kind and understanding. He just lets me be; he neither scolds me nor overworks me. There isn't that much work either. I work on the computer when I have to. But we all have to stay in the office whether there is work or not. I also answer the telephone calls and I am in charge of the photocopying machine. All sorts of people come to use that machine all the time. I told you the boss is very kind and lets everybody use the machine. But since the machine broke down some months ago I have been spared from that job. I have plenty of peace and quiet these days." With a playful smirk she added, "I hope the machine never gets repaired."

"Please tell me more. What else do you do in the office?" Yeshimo asked. There must be other interesting things that her friend was not telling her.

"There is nothing much else. It's nice to sit in an office, to have the *bukhari* blazing on cold winter days. My colleagues are very nice and we sit and chat a lot whenever we have no work and we chew *doma* and drink tea. We take turns to bring *doma* to the office every day. That reminds me tomorrow is my turn. Then, what else? I can't think of anything special that we do. It's easier working in an office than working at home, that is for sure."

Yeshimo imagined her friend operating all those machines. How important she must feel! She had felt so proud when she had cooked rice in the electric rice cooker the first time. The rice cooker was the only machine she could operate.

"Then, at the end of the month you get the salary," said Yeshimo dreamily.

"It is different but who do you think does the housework for me anyway? I still have to do it. I still have to cook and clean and wash my clothes. Come on, you have seen me working in my garden during the weekends. Going to work in an office does not mean that I don't have to do work at home."

"I suppose you are right but it is still better than being stuck in the house like me. No salary, no prestige, just doing nameless jobs day after day. My mother always tells me that before I realize it I will have a string of children and then I will be tied down for the rest of my life like her. My mother is such an unhappy person. I am afraid I will become like her." She had never said this to anyone. In fact she was surprised that she even verbalized this fear, for she had never allowed herself to think of this. "So I will always be an illiterate unhappy person just like my . . ." her voice trailed off.

"You can attend the adult literacy classes. They are conducting classes in the school every evening," Chonzom suggested.

"How will that help me?" Yeshimo was puzzled.

"You will not think of yourself as a useless illiterate person after you attend these classes. You will be able to read and write. Once you can read you will read about all sorts of things and about people everywhere."

Yeshimo was not persuaded. "You are crazy, how can I go to school now? It will be so embarrassing. You know how old I am."

"Of course you can still go. There will be so many other women attending the classes. Some of them are even older than you. Why should going for literacy classes be embarrassing? You can try and see for a few days and if you don't like it, they can't force you to stay."

Just then the electricity came and Chonzom immediately switched the TV on. The Bhutan Broadcasting Services (BBS) was just giving the reminder of yesterday's news headlines in Dzongkha and concluded with yesterday's weather forecast. Bumthang got the BBS program a day later by post on a cassette. Chonzom changed the channel and they watched something else. But Yeshimo could not concentrate on the TV for she was still thinking of the adult literacy classes. Chonzom's eyes were glued to the programme. Riveted by the popular Hindi serial, she just hummed and nodded when Yeshimo tried to talk to her. Yes, she would try to do something on her own. She would start attending the classes from tomorrow onwards. She had decided for herself. She would not always wait for mother to tell her what to do. "I will not ask mother," she heard a voice in her head say. She felt her heart beating excitedly like on the first day she went to school many years ago. As she made her way home, walking over the cobbled stone path with the help of a flashlight, the childish tune of the alphabet ABCD . . . came to her lips. The powerful experience of making a decision for herself made her feel free and she hummed the tune of the nursery rhyme all the way home.

## Sushma Joshi ✿ NEPAL

Sushma Joshi is a Nepali writer and filmmaker. Born in 1973, she works out
of Kathmandu. She is well-travelled and spent her early years at school near
Darjeeling before moving to the U.S. to attend Brown University. She later
went to graduate school in New York at the New School of Social Research,
where she earned an M.A. in anthropology. Joshi's literary skills were polished
during several summer workshops at the Breadloaf School of English in
Vermont. Her writing has been published in *Utne Reader, Ms. Magazine* and
*Kyoto Journal*. She founded and edited *Reproductions,* an online journal affili-
ated with Harvard University. Her awards include a MacArthur Foundation
Fellowship and a Rockefeller Foundation Bellagio Centre Residency in Italy.
She has also appeared at the Ubud Festival in Bali. Her books include *Art
Matters,* a collection of art criticism, and the story collection *End of the World,*
which was longlisted for the Frank O'Connor Award.

# LAW AND ORDER

BISHNU LOOKED OUT OF THE WINDOW OF HIS CELL
at the Police Headquarters in Tangal and saw the garden of the neigh-
bouring house. The garden was planted with neat rows of red tomatoes
climbing up their vines, small bunches of spinach and broccoli, and on
the sides he could make out bushes of wild *aiselu* berries. It reminded him
that he was hungry. Very hungry.

Six months ago, he had tried to get recruited to, and been rejected
from, the British Gurkha Army. Everything he had strived for, the long
hours he had run around the hills to build endurance, the weights he had
carried, the hours of training he had done to strengthen his body and
train his mind, seemed to have been a colossal waste after this rejection.
His parents were dejected. He had lost his one chance to go to a foreign

country, to Hong Kong perhaps, or Singapore, or Brunei. He had lost his one chance to get a British Gurkha pay and pension, and become wealthier than all the rest of his village compatriots put together. If he had been accepted, he could have built a house in Kathmandu bigger than the Laptan's bungalow. He could have married the Laptan's daughter. He had passed all the tests, except for one.

The recruitment flyer, which had been posted outside the Pokhara camp, said the basic requirements were:

1. Age 17½ to 21
2. Minimum height of 160 centimetres
3. Minimum weight of 50 kilogrammes
4. Chest circumference of 79 centimetres with minimum 5 centimetres expansion
5. No applicants needing eyesight aids will be accepted
6. Generally good oral hygiene, with up to two fillings, false teeth or a single gap

Bishnu had spent the last three years in preparation, even hanging from a tree for half an hour every morning to raise his height from 158 cm to the required 160 cm. He had made the first cut—out of twenty thousand men, they selected 370. Bishnu's heart had beaten with delight when he heard about it. He had been so certain he would be selected.

For four months, they tested him. He ran around a mountain with stones on his back. He lifted weights. He even let the men open his mouth and check his teeth as if he were a dumb animal. The running was the hardest. They made him, along with two hundred other men, puff up and down hills with huge sacks filled with rocks on their backs. He cheated and took a little rest behind a hill, but he thought it prudent not to mention this to the barking man who administered the test. They watched with binoculars. But he had always been good at eluding the eyes of authorities since a boy. They never caught that brief flicker of a moment as he sat down before he started to run again, right behind that hill, which they did not bother to watch because it was too small to merit attention. Almost a hundred men fell off in that race up the mountains.

Then there had been a physical exam. They checked him from head to toe, making him open his mouth as if he was an animal for sale. Then, after he thought he had passed the toughest tests, they made him ride that damned horse. And that was what had done him in. He had never ridden a horse before in his life, having grown up in the hills. "Advance!" the recruiting officer barked at him. The horse, a big prancing brown monster, was as startled as he was when he got on top of it. It started to move below like a quicksand of leather. The horse's back was broad but he couldn't hold his balance. Increasingly panicked, he tried to adjust his weight and hold on to the reins. The horse, sensing fear, panicked and started to run. He fell, but his foot was caught in the metal stirrup. The horse dragged him for fifty spectacular metres to the edge of a field, before finally coming to a panting, foaming halt. His back and arms were rubbed raw by being dragged through the ground. His crotch was rubbed raw from trying to sit on the horse. He had never felt more frightened in his life—his thoughts centering less on his near-death experience than on the permanent damage that might have been sustained by his balls from this particular colonial test of his manhood. After limping off the recruitment area, he went home and slept for three days. On the third morning, he checked his private parts. He was so relieved to know that his balls were intact that he didn't mind that the two front teeth had been knocked out by his vigorous fall. The black gap on his top row of shining, white teeth could not be restored, the local hack at his town informed him.

Of course the British recruitment team did not offer any compensation for his injury—why should they? It was a "Come and be tested at your own risk" trial of bravery. All of the men who came, came with the full knowledge and acquiescence that they were going to be put through the toughest tests in their lives. The brave Gurkhas, after all, had to live up to their global image as brave, ruthless and completely fearless soldiers—and how could you be a brave soldier if you started to whine about a tooth that got knocked in?

All twenty thousand men who put in an application wanted to get in. They all desperately longed to wear that hat, that khaki green felt hat with the dark-blue *pagari* folded in six folds around it, with a shiny aluminum cap badge on the left. The elastic strap was always firmly under the chin, so the hat, tilted stylishly to the right to touch the right ear, would not fall off. The dark blue outfit, which a trooper had brought back from Singapore, was called the Number Three. "The sleeves are rolled down when the sun sets, and rolled up when the sun rises," one of the boys who had come to be recruited informed Bishnu importantly. This ritual had appeared, to the listening men, to be the height of military rationality. They had all trained hard, keeping the image of the blue outfit and the green felt hat in mind. But they came knowing that more than a third would be rejected. Many would leave with various levels of injury. Well, Bishnu had lost his teeth. At least his balls were still intact, that's all he could say.

So now Bishnu had a gaping hole where his front teeth used to be. But that did not stop the Police Force of Nepal from recruiting him when he had showed up one fine summer day to put in his application. "If we started rejecting everybody with a couple of missing teeth, we would have no recruits at all," the man behind the counter assured him cheerfully, when Bishnu pointed out that his front teeth were missing. The dental hygiene in the Nepali hills was not the most efficient or sophisticated, and some of the men in the police force were missing a tooth here and there. Besides, Bishnu, bored with waiting in line for hours, had just done a perfect parody of Bhuwan KC. Like a dazed, lovestruck hero, he had thrown out his arms as he sang in a deep falsetto:

"*Timi nabhaye, jindagani kada sari cha. Feri pani mero kehi gunaso chaina.*"

(My life is like a thorn without you. And still I have no complaints.)

The recruitment officer did not like Bhuwan KC. More to the point, they had a band in the police force that was in need of musicians, and the officer thought that Bishnu might be able to contribute his musical skills. "Do you play an instrument?" he asked. And indeed, Bishnu said that he had, since childhood, played the *madal*. A few minutes later, a *madal* materialised like magic, and Bishnu gave the officer a demonstration. Using both hands, he pounded out a pitch-perfect melody on the horizontal drum. The officer, bored to tears by men trying to bribe him with a couple of jars of homemade ghee or some other equally trifling gift to get their sons admitted, was rather entertained. He thought Bishnu would make a good addition to the police force.

"Thankyousirthankyousirthankyousir!" said Bishnu, saluting the man five times before he walked out.

The training at the Police Academy wasn't easy but not as physically formidable as the military training of the British Gurkhas. Bishnu soon found that he had become very popular among the men with his *madal* and his parodies. Still, he could not forget that he was going to be a mere *chowki hawaldar,* instead of a British Gurkha soldier.

After his training, he was sent straight to the headquarters in Naxal, where there was a community police station. The headquarters was located behind high brick walls. The large square compound, bordered by Tangal on the east, the road to Nagpokhari on the west, Gairidhara on the north, and Naxal on the south, was heavily guarded on all three entrances. Inside, Bishnu was awed by the massive red Chinese brick buildings. A large red flag with the sun and moon waved in the yard. He had noticed the policemen, shirtless, in their vests, whistling to women from cell windows that overlooked the road, but had never imagined he would himself be there one day.

Bishnu shared his concrete cell, decorated with four narrow pallets, with two others, Bhola and J.B. They were from Dadeldhura and Dolpo, respectively. They both had strange accents and different versions of the Nepali language, respectively. Bhola, who had smooth curving eyebrows, a straight nose, and a ferocious gaze, talked like a man straight out of Bhanubhakta's epics. J.B. also had an epic feel about him. He spiked his sentences with what Bishnu learnt was Dolpoli and Tibetan. He had a round forehead, furrowed with two deep lines in the middle. His eyebrows curved downwards, where his eyes, wise, omniscient, seemed to take in all the comings and goings of the hundreds of men at the headquarters. Two deep lines ran from his nose to the edges of his lips. When J.B. smiled, his mouth opened to reveal a set of perfect white teeth.

The officers had braids and a row of medals hanging off their chests, tied to colourful ribbons. The new recruits had plain uniforms without any medals or braids or ribbons or badges. "Well, at least they provided the uniform," Bishnu consoled Bhola, who was sadly eyeing his nondescript uniform.

The cell, small, plain and unadorned, had grey cement walls. Bishnu sat down on his wooden pallet and looked out of the window. His window, a square like that of a jail cell, looked right into the neighbour's garden next door, where vegetables grew in neat rows. The whole garden, awakened by spring rain, was in bloom. Bishnu blinked, and looked inside again, and saw the plain, unwashed grey walls of his room.

Below his bed was his *rashun*, a ration canister of cooking oil, three kilograms of rice, a couple of litres of kerosene and about half a kilogram of yellow *dal*. It was parboiled rice, and stank like humid socks trapped too long inside wet shoes, but at least it was rice. His salary, in crisp, green hundred rupee notes, was given to him at the end of the month. He was so overjoyed by his acceptance that he sent five hundred to his parents, so that they could buy themselves a goat and celebrate.

He spent the remaining thousand to buy a kerosene stove, a bunch of spinach and potatoes, and twelve bottles of alcohol. The majority of those bottles were emptied in a drunken spree the third night with Bhola and J.B. Four bottles of Mt. Everest whiskey and four bottles of *Khukuri* rum were ceremoniously emptied. Before they knew it, they had blown their first month's salary on a drunken spree that lasted throughout the night and left them with raging headaches, bleary eyesight and official warnings.

"No drunkards in the police force!" the officer barked at them at 5 a.m. sharp the next morning as they stumbled out of bed with raging hangovers. He had heard about their exploits and come to warn them. This kind of behaviour was not to be tolerated. Of course all the officers drank, but that was another matter altogether. "Dump those bottles in the garbage truck, and don't let anybody see you. And from now on, be warned! If I catch you again in such a drunken state, all three of you will be kicked out of the police force!" his voice hammered into their skull until Bishnu wanted to get down on his knees and plead: "Sir! Stop, stop! Please don't make so much noise! My head is about to burst . . ." Instead, he hung his head and prayed for the rant to end until the officer stormed out of the room. Bhola, in total misery, staggered to the end of the room, and put his forehead against the cool wall. Bishnu started to sing in a small voice: "*Fero pani mero kunai gunaso chiana . . . And still I have no complaints.*"

That day, the Superintendent made them jog around the track for two hours more than the rest of the force. The three went around, over and over, three disgraced policemen, and scapegoats for the purpose of teaching the police force a lesson. J.B. jogged around doggedly, seeming without a loss of pace. Bhola, fearsome eyes glaring at every spectator who dared to watch his misery, panted and puffed, sweat pouring down his back. Bishnu, bow-legged, squat, and flailing his arms like a fish out of water, elicited a smattering of laughter and applause as he went careening wildly down the track for the umpteenth time.

Bishnu's headache went away by the end of the week, but not his perpetual hunger. They had been well-fed at the Police Academy—in large, heaping servings of rice, *dal,* yellow cabbage and potato curry, doused in too much salt and turmeric. Once a week, they ate meat. But headquarters was different. The mess where they ate never served satisfactory food. Bhola, who had drank considerably less than the other two on their night of celebration, had saved his money and now used it to cook special delicacies. In the morning, he made eggplant, the aroma of which gave Bishnu and J.B. a terrible grumbling in their stomachs.

All through that first month, and the next, Bishnu was aware of hunger rumbling inside him. As he marched with the rest of the platoon, as he met his supervisor, as he manned the booth by the Tangal gate, he felt a gnawing in the empty space inside his stomach.

There was always something besides rice to eat in his own home in the hills. His village was small, his house even smaller, small and red with a grass thatch roof, but they had never gone hungry. His parents kept a buffalo or two in the backyard, and the milk flowed day and night. His mother had a garden next to the house, and grew succulent green spinach, soya bean and pumpkin to add to their diet of corn and millet.

Bishnu felt like he was starving at the end of fifteen days. The parboiled rice was simply not enough. Looking at the stolid faces of the men around him, he wondered how they survived. Or did they know of some other way of getting food that he didn't know? By the end of the month, he knew all the tricks of the trade. Or almost all. Here's what people told him:

1. Steal from the officers' mess. This was a dangerous and often futile pastime, but reckless and foolhardy souls had been known, over the years, to do it.
2. Intimidate the storekeepers who sold the most basic delicacies and promise them protection in exchange for: a bowl of *momo,* a plate of

*aloo tarkari*, a pack of cigarettes, a few bottles of beer. This was the most popular and most productive way to keep yourself well-fed.

3. Get your family to send you the basics—fermented spinach, bamboo shoots, dried bean paste nuggets, dried meats and fresh vegetables were often spirited in like contraband, carefully hidden away from the prying eyes of the other men and guarded with zealous attention. This was the most common method of getting a little home-cooked food along with some protein.

Bishnu, who had sent off an urgent request to his parents for food supplies, knew that there was one more way to get food that his fellow policemen had not thought of. Sitting on his hard wooden bed, he could glimpse, morning after morning, tantalising glimpses of his neighbour's garden. He sat by the window and watched the pretty girls pass in and out of the top floor of the massive yellow bungalow. They came out to sew or read their English novels with the bright, shiny covers. It was rumoured that one of those girls was a pilot who flew her own plane. Rich motherfuckers, he thought. His cell, located on the highest floor, had an uninterrupted view of the bungalow and the garden that the other policemen could not see. He could see the women as clearly as he could see the vegetables, and he could not tell, as he salivated, which one he wanted more.

The last couple of days, Bishnu had started to see the long lines of green soya bean, the wild rows of spinach, the fierce green hearts of tomatoes in his daydreams, just as he had started to see that girl in the red *kurta* who appeared on the roof in his dreams at night. He wanted that girl in his bed in the same way he wanted that cluster of ripening tomatoes in his mouth. Her breasts gave him the same undefinable sensation as the red buds of the strawberries peeping, tantalisingly, from below the soya bean plants. At night, his dreams started to get confused, and as he became hungrier, he dreamt that the girl in the red *kurta* had transformed into a long, elegant stalk of radish that he pulled out of the earth, brushed off, then munched raw, eating her slowly, bit by bit, the damp earth still clinging to her body, and she had a cauliflower for a heart, and inside her there were two ripe tomatoes, also to be savoured, slowly and with great caution. At the last moment, he felt his tongue slide into a pit of seeds that he had to hastily spit out of his mouth because her insides were a big pumpkin and slimy and had started to rot . . .

But the smell was similar to the smell of the pumpkin that Bhola had started to cook on his stove, and it was time to get up. Bhola was guarded these days—after that one drinking spree, he had decided to keep to himself and not share his food or thoughts with his fellow policemen. Bishnu swung out of bed, sluggishly pulling on his clothes over his underwear. "J.B., how high do you think is the wall?" he asked. The wall separated the headquarters from the road outside. The police force was strictly sequestered within the compound. The architecture was designed not just to keep out criminal elements, but also to keep in the police force. The gates opened for the officers' vehicles, and for their morning jog, but it was difficult to leave without being apprehended.

"A steep fall. You could break a leg," said J.B. He blinked and sighed. "Don't tell me I didn't think about it."

"Those tomatoes are driving me crazy." Bishnu flexed his fingers on the edge of the window.

"And the women! The women." J.B. was the only man who could make an innocuous statement sound that crude.

"Have you seen that little one in the red *kurta?* She was wearing golden anklets the other day," J.B. said. "I saw her in my dream last night."

"Have I seen her!" Bishnu said. "Have I seen her. I must have eaten her about ten times by now."

The wall was about fifteen feet high, built of stout, orange Chinese brick. Bishnu, who as a boy had climbed every tree in his village, knew he could scale up and down the headquarters' wall without a problem. The yellow bungalow, where the garden grew, was surrounded by a wall that was not quite as high. But the wall was adorned, at the top, with triangles of broken glass. It glinted like an apparatus of pain—a torture strip—in the sunlight. "I don't know if I would survive that glass, J.B."

"You would be taking a chance with your balls," agreed J.B. "What about the gate?"

The gate was high, painted a rusty red, and had long, iron spikes, designed to deter miscreants, on top. "Those spikes," said Bishnu. "They would not be too comfortable to sit on."

"Well, *Dai*, it's your life. Your equipment." J.B. looked at the mirror and patted his hair into shape. "I am going to sneak down the road and get *sukuti*. The man who works there happens to be a cousin."

Bishnu felt jealous. He could often catch a drift of smoke floating into their room on a windy day, laden with the smell of roasting, juicy flesh from the barbeque shack down the road. Damn, his mouth was watering just thinking about it. He wanted to ask if he could come as well, but innate modesty held him back. J.B. was taking a risk leaving the compound. Guards and dogs roamed HQ. Bishnu was not sure if he would want to add another person and increase his chances of being detected.

"When do you plan to go?" he asked with curiosity.

"On Saturday," said J.B., without hesitation.


The next day, Bishnu made up his mind. He would scale the wall and raid his neighbour's garden. He would do it that night. Not the next day, not the day after, but that night. It was the darkest night of the month and therefore the easiest night to get in and out without being seen. He would show them that he, Bishnu Bahadur Bista, could feed himself as well as anybody else.

Bishnu's mind raced as his face and body reflected a practiced calm the whole day. He did his exercises in perfect order and did not draw a reprimand or a rebuke. When all the men retired to their own rooms, he lay down on his hard wooden bed and shut his eyes.

"J.B., I am going out tonight."

J.B., who had thought Bishnu was asleep, was caught by surprise. J.B. was taking advantage of the unexpected absence of Bhola, who had taken a few days off to take his pregnant wife to the hospital, to peer out of the window and catch a glimpse of the girl next door. He jerked his head in guiltily. "Where to?"

Bishnu rolled out of bed and joined him at the window. He pointed to the yellow bungalow.

"You're going to risk your life?" J.B. asked. "You know they have that Alsatian dog, don't you?" *Al-shishun,* he said, making the dog sound like stinging nettle. "The one that howls all day long?"

"And keeps you awake all night long. I know."

"May death take that dog soon so I can get a good night's sleep. But doesn't look like it's going to die soon. He gets fed better than we do. I see them dumping chunks of meat in his bowl every morning."

"Yes," Bishnu said. "Have you noticed that its howls always comes from one place at night?"

"So?"

"This means it is caged." Bishnu put on his best shirt and took his flashlight in his hand.

"What you need is a winged apparatus. One that will fly you straight into the garden." J.B. had a fanciful imagination. "Don't yell for me if you get stuck on those walls."

"Besides, I will see the girl. And I would not miss that for anything in the world."

J.B. looked at him and sighed. He was feeling the same way. He sat there at the window and imagined Bishnu and the red-*kurta* girl walking hand-in-hand down the beds of cauliflowers, singing the police anthem.

"*Dai!*" He gave Bishnu a slap on the back. "Good luck." The two saluted each other, and then Bishnu disappeared.

The policemen on guard gave him a sharp glance, but he walked with such confidence they didn't ask him where he was going. Vehicles were passing by on the road outside. The ancient shrine of Ganesh was just outside, and Bishnu thought about the elephant-headed god briefly before scaling the wall. The wall was steep, but he was short and quick and gifted with the skills of a born climber. Nobody saw the apparition of a man appear in ghostly shadow above the wall, and then drop below noiselessly.

Bishnu sauntered down the road, an ordinary pedestrian, enjoying his casual midnight walk. He walked to the barbeque shack that J.B. had talked about and saw the huge flames and smoke coming out of the hut. People were drinking and shouting and having a good time. Damn, it smelt good. Too good. He wanted to go in and say hello to the cousin and assure him J.B. was going to show up tomorrow and perhaps solicit a plate of meat on the side, but he knew this was not the right time.

Bishnu doubled back and walked towards the bungalow. A polished brass plaque was nailed outside. The lettering was inscribed into the metal: "Raniban Residence." The windows were darkened. He had noticed, in his most prudent moment, that one portion of the wall had less glass protruding from it. That glass could be avoided with a deft catapult.

Flanks tensed, sinews tight with tension, Bishnu climbed up the wall. Soon, he was precariously balanced, his crotch directly on top of a shining sea of broken glass. Unless he lost his balance, there was no reason for him to sit on the glass. That is the moment when the dog, alerted by the malignant presence of an agile nocturnal vagabond, started to howl.

Bishnu had heard the dog howl before. But he had never heard it quite this close up. The barks promised instantaneous dismemberment to the unseen intruder from a maw slathering with foam and fury. When the dog took a rest, it was for deep-throated growls that seemed to emit from a predator with talons and sabre teeth, not a specimen of the canine variety. Thank God the beast was caged!

A sharp stab of pain on his hand told Bishnu he had not paid attention. A drop of blood fell from his cut palm. But fear left him as he slid down into the garden. He looked up, wondering if he could see J.B. still standing by the window. And sure enough, there he was—a tiny figure leaning out pensively, a cutout figure in the square of the big, bare building. This is how the women must see us, Bishnu thought, and for a moment he was aware of the alienation of his own existence.

Bishnu, in the interest of anonymity, decided not to wave and attract attention. The lush growth of the garden beckoned. Here were the tomatoes, laden with the reddening fruit as he had dreamt. They smelt more pungent than he had imagined. Here was the corn. He felt the scratchy leaves in his hands and caressed them, before finally uprooting one, two, three, the smell of recent rain humid in his mouth as he bit into one. He wondered if he should make his getaway as quickly as possible, in deference to the dog who was now keeping up a steady howl. But the fresh carrot in his hand was too enticing. He brushed the earth off, then bit into it, ripping off the green top and chomping it up, just like he had done in his dreams. The carrot tasted perfect—bitingly sweet and succulent. He smiled in satisfaction, and threw the stub of the carrot towards the dog's cage. Then he was among the broccolis. He chose a green heart and broke the clunky neck off with the deftest of movements. Nobody would even miss it. A little further on were the soya beans, peskier to harvest, so he stuffed a few into his mouth and chewed them raw while he ran amuck among the scallions, picking here, there and everywhere. Then he was in the corn again, and he had to pick an armful of succulent cobs—the dog's barking was steadily getting formidable, and he wondered if he should go before they let it out—but then the fresh chilli appeared, and he could not resist stopping and picking up a few spikes of green fiery fruit.

By this time his plastic bag was full. He was halfway towards the exit when he saw the light come on in a window above. A loud and irritated voice yelled, "Ruby! Shut up!"

Ruby, taking his master's voice as encouragement, barked even louder, his barks splintering into the night like pieces of audible glass. Bishnu, clutching his *khukuri* knife with sweaty fingers, wondered if he would have to kill the dog if they let it free. "I guess I would have to kill it," Bishnu thought, imagining the dog plunging out of its cage to sink its teeth into his throat. Should he make a dash for it? As he hesitated, a girl appeared at the window. She was an apparition, dressed in a white night-dress. He could see her breasts rise and fall with her quick breathing. "What's going on, Papa?" she said, peering out.

"Don't know."

"You would think we would not have to worry about burglars."

"Why?"

"We are next to the Police Headquarters, after all."

Bishnu almost laughed. He loved the passion in her Kathmandu voice. She was a divine being, a hundred times more adorable upfront. The universe, studded with bright stars, was wondrous and magical. J.B. doesn't know what he's missing, Bishnu thought.

"Should we let Ruby out?" Bishnu could not move. Could he choke the beast with his bare hands before it attacked him? He imagined himself, caught at the throat by that immense dog, his hands still clutching his plastic bag of vegetables. "Vegetable-stealing policeman caught red-handed and eaten by Guard Dog," the headlines would run in *Kantipur* the next day. His parents would kill themselves from shame when they heard about his untimely and undignified death.

"No." The father appeared to like speaking in monosyllables.

"He seems to have calmed down. The barbeque shack upsets him, all those drunks," the girl said. The voices got quieter. A few minutes later, the light was switched off. The voices of his owners seemed to have calmed Ruby, who emitted low rumbles, but had stopped barking.

With one deft movement, Bishnu threw his bag of vegetables across the wall. He heard it land with a soft thud in the dust outside. He scaled up the wall. As he climbed, he could see the shards of glass coming into his field of vision. His palms were slippery with sweat. He did not trust his legs, trembling with stress, to do the highwire manoeuvring required to vault over the burglar-proof wall. "You could lose your balls," he could hear J.B.'s voice in his head. At the last moment, he lost his nerve. "I would rather climb the gate than vault over this glass," he thought.

Bishnu grabbed hold of two spikes at the top of the big gate. The tin gates, to his mortification, swung back and forth, wildly, creaking like a child's swing. Damn, that dog was starting to howl again! "May death ferry you down the river," Bishnu cursed.

In his haste and nervousness, Bishnu sat on a metal spike. The pain seared him. All he could think of at the moment was to get off the gates before he either got shot by the police or eaten by the dog. How could he have deluded himself into thinking this was easy?

He was down. A soft thud. He felt his crotch, stiff and sore, but there was no time to examine himself for injuries. He grabbed his bag of vegetables and made a sprint across the road. As swiftly as he could, he climbed over the Police Headquarters wall. He hid behind columns, skirted empty water drums, and avoided the severe look of the King and his family in the portrait hung in the vestibule before reaching his room.

Bishnu sat there by the window, feeling his wounds with one hand. "Hurt?" J.B. emerged from the window, where he had watched Bishnu's every move.

"You can't make an omelette without breaking a few eggs." Bishnu's other hand slipped among his treasures for one perfect vegetable to eat. His hands slid around, feeling the slippery edges of tomato, the hairy skin of corn, the rough edges of the cauliflower's heart. He picked out a handful of soya bean pods, and popped them open in his mouth. The raw beans tasted like home.

"Well?" J.B. asked.

"I have enough vegetables to last us a week, if you provide the roast chicken, J.B.," Bishnu said. "But damn, I almost lost my balls doing it."

J.B. laughed a short, staccato laugh. "I bet you got to see the girl, huh?"

"She was in a white dress. The most beautiful girl I have seen in a long time."

"Well, Bishnu, you missed it!" said J.B. "After you went across that wall, that girl started to take off her clothes, one by one, like she didn't even care if we were all looking. So I got to see her, as naked as the day she was born, standing right there by the window. Swear to God!" he said, bent over double from laughing.

"I had a field day in that garden." Bishnu was annoyed by J.B.'s story. He was jealous, that was all.

That night, they had fresh corn, and the night after that, tomato and chilli *achar* to go with the roasted chicken that J.B. brought back from his cousin's shack. The night after that, they ate the cauliflower, fried with some potatoes, and on the last day, they peeled and ate the last remaining radishes, spiked with chillis and coriander.

Bishnu savoured every bite of his meal. He knew there would be no more vegetables tomorrow. He would have to go back to looking at the garden through his window, seeing yards and yards of fresh vegetables and fruits that would be as unreachable as the girl on the top floor. As J.B. put out the light, Bishnu pulled his scratchy blanket up to his chin, and closed his eyes. A sudden vision of fields of tomatoes shimmering and transforming into hundreds of dewy women in red *kurtas* swam into his consciousness like a surreal hologram.

"J.B., I realise it now. The hunger of your stomach you can always satisfy with a cauliflower and a tomato, but what about the hunger of your mind?" he mumbled.

"Only an idiot would try to satisfy the hunger of his mind," J.B., half-asleep, took a few moments to respond.

"But your mind demands satisfaction," Bishnu insisted in a drowsy voice.

"It's not possible, *muji-jatha*. This is no time for philosophy. Let me sleep." And soon the gentle snores of J.B. filled the room.

Bishnu, pausing to watch the hundred women of his fantasies, had one of those lucid thoughts that arise in one's consciousness just before that sweet slide into sleep, the awareness that his mind would always be roving over unreachable landscapes of desire, leaping from luscious fruits to beautiful breasts, from the sensual smell of summer sap to the breath of a real live woman, and there was nothing he could do to satisfy them all. They would always remain half-dreamt, half-imagined, half-seen, half-felt. As his teeth sank into the tomatoes, he wondered if sleep was the only realm in which the desires of the mind were fully satisfied, or whether even in sleep fantasies of the mind rose and took on impossible proportions. Or perhaps, he thought confusedly just before he fell into a deep sleep, his mind was the only place where women could mutate to the fullness of a fruit, and the pungent ripeness of summer juices, and move from human to plant and back again with no discernable boundaries, and all of this was just as real as the long, mournful howling of that damned dog outside.

## Hasan Manzar  ❧  PAKISTAN

Hasan Manzar is the *nom de plume* of Syed Manzar Hasan. Born in 1934 and a physician by profession, he runs a private psychiatric clinic in Hyderabad, Sindh, where he is settled. Writing in Urdu, he has published several collections of short stories, a novel entitled *Dhani Bux Kay Baitay*, and work for children. He has also translated literature into his native Urdu. Manzar's style is noted for its social realism. His literary concerns reflect current social and political influences, as well as the ambivalence human beings can demonstrate when confronted with moral or ethical dilemmas. His story collection *Khaak Ka Rutba* won the Academy of Letters's Moulvi Abdul Haq Best Book Prize in 2007, and his work also appears in *The Penguin Book of Classic Urdu Stories*.

# EMANCIPATION

*Translated from Urdu by Muhammad Umar Memon*

IF THERE IS ANYTHING IN LIFE WORTH HATING, IT is hatred. And that's been true with me—always. Long ago, my father and my mother often flew into a rage over my failure to hate certain people; later, my in-laws.

My husband and I were returning from a ritual bathing in the Ganges. My in-laws knew why we had gone there. They knew that I was barren and they hoped that a few drops of the sacred water might help me get pregnant. But my husband and I knew well that the visit could not help us. My husband cared a bit too much about religion, otherwise he would not have set out at the mere suggestion of others on a costly pilgrimage to the Holy Ganges; he was far too shrewd to dump money into a worthless enterprise. Perhaps he believed in miracles.

As for me, I've always loved the Ganges. I still do, with reverence. In fact I love all rivers, not because loving rivers is in my blood, but because rivers have informed my childhood.

Travelling by train between east and west we passed over the Ganges many times. Each time, just before the arrival of that moment, my mother would sit up tense with anticipation, her fist full of coins. Each of us also held some change in our hands. The moment the bank of the Ganges appeared in view, the women who sat in the middle row in the compartment would move over to window seats. My mother had never been negligent in this matter. She always took a window seat, even if that meant sitting out and waiting at the station for all of us under the open sky till midnight.

I enjoyed every part of this journey and felt particularly joyful when the train crossed a bridge. But the joy of crossing the Ganges was in a class by itself. The orange iron girders suddenly rose to high heaven and, just as swiftly, swooped back down, reverberating with strange noises. Just then I would think of all the kids in our city who had never seen a bridge sway in this manner. They could not have been more unfortunate!

Through this echoing rumble would rise the piercing whistle of the locomotive, as if paying its respects to the Ganges, like the women in our compartment. Precisely then the coins would hit the iron girders with a clink and then plop down in the waters below. People in other compartments would also toss fistfuls of coins. I would poke my head out of the window and look back at the long line of compartments behind ours, straining to figure out which among the outstretched hands belonged to my father. Once, though, when a coin ricocheted off a girder and hit me on the head, I jerked my head back inside. I never again stuck my head out. If we happened to be crossing the Ganges in the daytime, I would content myself with peering at the boys who lurked, half-submerged, in the water below the bridge, ready to dive and retrieve a falling coin.

I knew my younger brother always managed to wedge a coin or two between his fingers so that it wouldn't fall. This was our mutual sin against the Sacred Ganges, mine in that although I knew about his deception, I chose not to snitch on him. In principle, I should have hated him for it, but I could not. I was powerless.

Often when the train crossed the bridge at night and I slept, mother would shake me violently to wake me up. The river always looked different at night. The iron girders raised and lowered their heads as always and the river below appeared perfectly calm. Every once in a while, though, the edge of a wave gleamed momentarily in the light of the moon; sometimes the moon itself seemed to have descended into the waters; and often the light from a bonfire filtered through the groves on the river bank. I would let my head, heavy with sleep, rest on the window sill, dimly aware of the clinking coins as they struck the girders and dropped into the water.

But that was a long, long time ago. On the night I am talking about, I sat alone in the compartment. We were returning from a pilgrimage to the Holy Ganges. My husband—my Lord Husband was in one of the compartments ahead of mine. He disliked the idea of women travelling together with their husbands in the same compartment, otherwise he would not have abandoned me all alone.

After bathing in the Ganges I was feeling a gentle warmth throughout my body; the cool night air blew over me and made me dizzy with sweet inebriation. We were four or five small stations away from our town and still had an hour or two to go. I was in no particular hurry to get home. I had no children waiting for me; as for my in-laws, they were waiting less for me than for the vessel in which I carried the sacred Ganges water and which was now my sole prized possession. But he who was bound to me by the sacrament of marriage, he, I knew, would treat me like a stranger as soon as we reached home. He had repeatedly told me that too much closeness with his wife interfered with a man's contemplative life. He certainly had reached the age when contemplation behooved a man.

I do not hate life. Yet, in spite of my youth, I had become thoroughly bored with its unmitigated monotony. At home, there was nothing enjoyable for me to do, nor were there any books I would have liked to read. You don't expect to recite the *Bhagwad Gita* day in and day out.

At some small station the train came to a jolting halt. My eyes fell on the ticket checker outside. Outfitted in his black uniform he stood leaning against the lamp-post, his eyes riveted on me. An old-style kerosene lamp, with the name of the station inscribed in three languages on its square shade, burnt palely on top of a post. In its dim light, I could scarcely see the ticket checker's face. The train made a scheduled stop at this station at night out of sheer formality, for hardly anyone boarded the train here, even in the daytime.

My husband wouldn't be impatient to check up on me. We had been married for three years, and he had long ago passed the stage when he could be expected to come rushing to inquire about his wife every time the train stopped.

I glanced at the ticket checker, then at the vendor, and then at the dog sleeping under the vending cart. After I had checked the name of the station, my eyes grew heavy with sleep. My body was still warm after bathing in the river and the night air was pleasantly cool.

Dimly through my drugged senses I heard the guard whistle, the engine pump out a few quick jets of steam with a piercing squeal, and the ties hitching the carriages together groan as the train moved out at a snail's pace. Then I must have dozed off. When I woke up with a start, the train had moved quite far from the station and picked up speed, and the ticket checker was bolting the door from inside, his back to me. I don't think of myself as an atheist; still, I didn't think it necessary to invoke the help of the holy water I had with me.

That snatch of sleep must have been the longest sleep I ever had. Just as the end of sleep signals the end of night and the arrival of a new day, so on one end of that sleep lies the dark night of my life's story and on the other, its new dawn.

Instead of sitting up in alarm, I just lay there and through my barely closed eyes watched him approach me almost without a sound. He was in his mid-thirties, of stout build, with a fair complexion—perhaps, for that reason, quite handsome by some standards—probably a native of the northwestern region. When he had come quite close to me, I pulled myself up suddenly and asked him boldly, "What?" To appear undaunted by danger, even if there were any, I gazed out the window unperturbed.

Until a woman looks directly into a man's eyes, he doesn't know quite how to use force, like someone poised to attack but unable to find the pretext to do so. My nonchalance disarmed him so completely that he asked nervously, "Ticket!"

I knew my husband had our tickets, even so I started fumbling in my purse absent-mindedly. And then I looked at him with questioning eyes.

"Never mind," he said, forcing his eyes into those of mine, as he grabbed the upper berth with both his hands and bent over me, blocking all possible avenues of escape.

Hatred for my husband washed over me like a tidal wave. Abandoning me to my fate, he must now be sitting in the men's compartment without a worry, supremely satisfied with his great piety. He had no right to expect anything from me now—absolutely none. But women do not lay waste to their homes out of hatred for their husbands.

The vessel of the sacred water lay some distance from me. I looked at the emergency chain helplessly. There was no way I could reach it, at least not without a scuffle. And there he was, looking at me in a manner calculated to captivate me with his strong, masculine beauty.

Suddenly, as I sat surrounded by him, a scene from childhood came rushing back to mind. I was travelling by train with my mother. At some time in the night, the train pulled into a small station somewhere in the East. A haggard, breathless peasant forced his way into the jam-packed women's compartment to help his wife disembark. The couple gathered their baggage—a few large bundles and some tin canisters—and began offloading it from the carriage. The husband grabbed their small boy, climbed down, sat the boy on top of a bundle, and climbed back up. Just then, the train started to move. We all heard the boy's pathetic screams as he sat in the darkness at a station which didn't even have a platform.

The husband was in a fix: should he jump off the moving train or stay aboard with his wife? Somebody suggested pulling the chain, which they did, repeatedly, first the wife, then the husband. But the train, unaffected by their misery, chugged along. The woman began to wail, the husband comforted her, "Don't worry. We'll get out at the next station, rent a bullock-cart and go back. Why are you crying? Surely somebody will take care of the boy till we get there."

I did not resist, which encouraged the ticket checker to sit down beside me. The strong scent of eau de cologne wafted into my nostrils. He seemed to have doused his chest rather generously with it just before entering the carriage.

I felt his hand crawl slowly across my bare back and fall on my other shoulder. The speed of the train had not dropped, nor could the familiar sound of changing tracks, which usually announced the arrival of a station, be heard. I felt the weight of his body over mine. Through my fogged senses I managed, God knows how, to say, "But I am not clean!"

At that level of intimacy force was altogether unnecessary, and so was violence. He laughed and got up to go to the opposite seat. In that split second, when his back was turned to me, I made a dash for the chain and pulled violently at it, just as the peasant woman had done. The ticket checker's last, unfinished sentence, "Where do you . . ." cut off in a hurried, nervous "Stop! Don't do that!"

He jerked at me, trying to pull me away from the chain.

The sound of the train coming to a sudden, grinding halt rose in the deathly, dark jungle—a sound evocative of the clanking of chains as they were shaken off the body of some prisoner. The ticket checker threw himself on my feet.

I was crying. My hands were still clutched to the chain. I heard voices approaching us outside in the darkness. He entreated, "Please forgive me. Please don't tell them anything. For God's sake, please . . ."

At that moment he who was so strong, tall, fair and—perhaps—quite handsome, looked utterly miserable, so pitiable in his venial helplessness lying on the floor; even more pitiable than I had felt myself to be just a short while ago.

"For God's sake . . ."

For a moment I felt the same hatred writhe inside me, which my educated parents had always encouraged me to have, and which my Lord Husband and his parents had always considered a part of religion.

Then the sound of the door being forced from outside was heard. The inside door handle turned, as though by itself. The ticket checker got up, slowly dusting off his uniform. The struggle had ended for him.

I peered into the darkness outside. I knew this area. Further down where a feeble light filtered through thatched huts was the place where I had often seen peacocks pecking at grain during the day. Give or take half a mile, but no more. But why was I thinking about that? Really, such a thought could not have been more out of place!

The railway guard and police escorted the ticket checker out of my compartment. Both of us were doing our best not to look at each other. The sound of heavy boots crunching the gravel by the tracks could be heard for some time, and then the train started again.

I was ready to do anything, just anything; but what I could not do was to cry on my husband's shoulder. His shoulder would have been a lifeless object for me to rest my head on and cry. Sitting opposite me he may have looked like religion incarnate, but to me he was no more than the god of hatred; a man who could hate others, singly or collectively, by calling them Muslims, because they belonged to this country or that, because he assigned them to a despicable caste; and who could also hate a lonely and vulnerable person like myself because I was incapable of producing in my stony heart an emotion as delicate as hate.

What could he be thinking? I wondered. Being disgraced? But if he was disgraced I was hardly to be blamed for it. A certain satisfaction, because my assailant was, as my husband had suspected all along, a man of another faith? Or, perhaps, brooding over the poison which would continue to spread inside him; what if that abominable barbarian has succeeded in what he had set out to do?

When I next saw the ticket checker he was handcuffed. He was under arrest at our station. A sudden desire to go up to him and smell his chest overwhelmed me. But I restrained myself, fearing I might break into laughter. Instead, I buried my face in the handkerchief, as one about to cry does.

After a brief interrogation the case was entered and we were allowed to go home.

That pious visit to the Holy Ganges changed the course of my life.

My husband assumed an attitude of chilling aloofness and silence. My mother-in-law treated me like a *Shudra*. Whereas earlier I could denounce certain Hindu customs with impunity, I could no more. Even if I had criticized the outmoded practice of female self-immolation, it would now have been interpreted as an ill effect of my Western education. I even avoided going anywhere near the home altar which had the image of one of the gods. For one night, after a protracted silence, a question echoed in the darkness: "Did he touch you?" And then I heard a long gasping sound. They were words that betrayed a long-festering doubt, a doubt that could only now accept some reassurance.

I had already been subjected to the interrogations of the judge and the officers investigating the case, to which was now added this accusation, rising through dark silence. Certainly this was not my own conscience reproaching me; that poor voice was silent. There was nobody with me in the room except my husband; and my conscience slept peacefully like an innocent child. My husband lay so far away from me that even if we had extended our hands we could not have possibly touched each other. Suddenly, I was overcome by the desire to break into laughter and ask: "That's *it* then. Your Lordship has been agonizing all this time over whether someone has touched me with the same intention as you once had yourself?"

Even now when my eyes fall upon an ad for used cars and the words "Owner Driven" or "One Man Driven" come to view, I am suddenly reminded of someone exhaling a long, gasping breath in the darkness and of my totally unnecessary reply, "No. No one has ever touched me except you. I am unblemished."

A little while later I heard my husband turn over in bed and snore. His snores sounded like "*Hare Om.*"

One winter day we were sitting in the sun in the open veranda. I was knitting a sweater. My mother-in-law was rubbing oil into my husband's hair. My father-in-law was ensconced in his rocking chair reading the newspaper. The next day I was scheduled to appear in court. At every court hearing my in-laws, all of them, felt they were being disgraced somehow; as their daughter-in-law would now have to get into a *tonga* and go to court where she would be asked about criminal assault, rape, and other indelicate matters. And as I was subjected to these questions, my husband and father-in-law would sit through them with their heads bowed in shame. They would try to stay the farthest away from me, so that the world would know that the law of their religion was infinitely more important to them than the law of the court. No matter how the court ruled, as far as they were concerned I was no more than a beautiful, expensive glass object, which, once broken, is allowed to remain at home, but which can scarcely be used again.

To break the silence, my mother-in-law asked my husband, "You never did finish telling me about that yesterday."

"About what?"

"You know, you were telling me about your friend who was forced to go out of business—remember?"

"Oh, well, he had a quarrel with his partner."

"I already know that. But when your friend was setting up the shop he found only mountains of good in his partner, didn't he?"

My husband looked at me, as though I were expected to know the answer.

"No good can ever come of these people," my mother-in-law observed. "Never!"

By now my father-in-law had stopped rocking in his chair. He lowered the newspaper and looked at me over the top of it with questioning eyes.

I could not have been more absorbed in my knitting than I appeared. But finding everyone staring at me, I scratched my temple with the knitting needle and tried to say what they wanted to hear from me: "Your friend should not have gone into partnership with a Muslim in the first place. That was a mistake."

The colour of suspicion turned a shade darker in their eyes.

I continued, "Muslims simply cannot be trusted. Never!"

I heard the echo of my thoughts: You are telling a lie.

My father-in-law quietly got up from his chair, left the newspaper on it, and stepped into the backyard garden. My mother-in-law, remembering some unfinished work, hastened to the kitchen; and my husband settled down into his father's empty chair and began browsing through the newspaper as he rocked gently.

I knew they thought I was lying. Yet, in those days, I found myself saying only those things that pleased them: how ridiculous the customs of Muslims were, how deplorably unclean they were, how at one of my Muslim girlfriends' houses everyone walked right into the kitchen with shoes on. Like everyone else at my in-laws', even I started calling the despotic father-in-law of my husband's sister "Aurangzeb," the most fanatic Muslim ruler, because he was an utter kill-joy, who enjoyed hurting people indiscriminately and went after them with a vengeance.

But when my sister-in-law showed up one day at our house and I asked her half in jest, "How's Aurangzeb-ji?" nobody found it funny anymore. Perhaps the joke had gone stale, or had become out of place.

My Muslim girlfriend still came to see me occasionally. On such visits, I tried not to talk with her alone. Instead, I would make her sit within earshot of my mother-in-law. If, during our conversation, she slipped in an English word, I made sure that my next sentence included its meaning in Hindi. If she asked in English, "How is it going?" I would reply in

Hindi, "Who knows how many more times will I have to appear before the court yet."

After talking in Urdu for a while, if she inadvertently used an English word, say, "witchcraft," I would say, "I don't believe in this *jadu-tona* stuff. Maybe they do."

"They" stood for the Muslims—of course. At the back of such unnecessary clarifications loomed, perhaps, my fear that in spite of the calamity, by letting me continue meeting with this Muslim friend, deep down in their hearts my in-laws had consigned me to the category of the irreligious or as someone contemplating conversion to Islam; or if not that, then surely as ready to run away.

But on such occasions my mother-in-law invariably managed to leave the room. My husband, if accidentally he came into the room, would ask an unnecessary question—such as where he could find a particular book—and then exit right away. He hated us both.

One day I told my Muslim girlfriend, "There are always two elderly men with my assailant at court hearings. Both give me the creeps."

"Must be Gog and Magog."

"One of them resembles my assailant quite a bit. He is the same height, the same build, the same fair complexion. The only difference is that he has a beard."

"Must be your assailant's father."

"And the other man, who is even more suspicious, always waiting for an opportunity to stare me in the eyes, he also has a beard—who could he be?"

"Your assailant's father-in-law. Who else?"

"Can't be," I said, categorically. "I think I have seen his father-in-law. He must be the same man who was trying to comfort my assailant's wife by calling her, 'Daughter! Daughter!' That was when she saw her husband in handcuffs for the first time and started crying. Some woman! I don't know if I could have cried had I been in her place."

"She must be crazy."

"Strange thing, though, is that she was looking at me accusingly instead, not at her husband; as though I was the one who should have been handcuffed, not her husband."

"A husband is always innocent in the class she comes from. Surely you know that."

Besides a few custodians of the law, there were just the five of us in the courtroom: my husband, me, the ticket checker, his young wife, and the wife's father.

Even on such a shameful day the three stuck together. Perhaps they were thinking that I was solely to blame for this misfortune. Perhaps the wife thought I had falsely accused her husband, or even if he had in fact assaulted me with criminal intent, so what? The offence was not grave enough to warrant his being imprisoned.

The father did not have the heart to see his daughter in tears, nor the wife to see her husband in such straits. I had the curious feeling that this incident was no more meaningful to them than algae spread over the waters of their life, which they preferred to tear away so as to drink again from the limpid waters beneath.

They wanted to settle with me out of court, were willing to pay the damages if I could be persuaded to say that being all alone in the compartment that night I had panicked at the sight of a man and pulled the chain out of sheer nervousness.

In the eyes of my assailant's wife I saw an earnest entreaty. I also saw scorn and accusation in those eyes, but what I did not find was the slightest trace of the kind of feeling a woman is expected to have for her husband under such circumstances.

To settle out of court, to offer a bribe, to apologize, or, if need be, even to destroy me—they tried every method. At least they were unswervingly united behind a common purpose.

But for our part, it was as if an animal had died in the pool of my life and that of my husband. With every passing day, the dead body—bloated, decaying, deformed—rose to the surface. To drink from such foul water was out of the question.

After the first two court hearings, in which my assailant appeared accompanied only by his father-in-law and his attorney, and which ended in adjournments, suddenly, at the third one, he appeared with a crowd of supporters who had flocked from God knows where. Broad-chested, young and old men, who looked so much alike: matching turbans with black skullcaps poking out of the center; the same silver and gold chains dangling from gold and silver buttons in their lustrous black velvet waist-coats; the same fresh, rosy complexions; and the same baggy *shalwar* trousers flapping in the wind as they walked. Even their sandals looked curiously alike. Only their ages and the presence or absence of beards and moustaches made any difference at all.

Those two elderly men were part of this crowd.

The two would bring things to eat, and would try to feed them to the ticket checker whenever they had a chance. Unlike my assailant's wife, they didn't feel sorry for him, but neither did they seem to feel any apprehension over the bleak future which awaited him. They would offer him advice all the time and steal side-glances at me whenever they could. I could do nothing about it, except cover my head even more securely with the hem of my sari and try to hide myself. As it were, I had to fend for myself in the court; no one was there to sustain me in my ordeal. In a manner of speaking, for me at least, the trial had ended that fateful solitary night after I had pulled the chain. More than this, I neither hoped for, nor cared about.

Before the crowd of my assailant's supporters materialized, I heard a rumour that a telegram had been sent to his village and his relatives were about to arrive. Later on I came to know that one of the two old men was his father and the other some accomplished Muslim holy man. The latter looked fearsome, and always seemed to be mumbling something. He had a ridiculous moustache; it was trimmed so that it began about half an inch above his lip. His beard was red, and so was the hair that streamed down over his neck from underneath his turban, like a horse's mane.

In the courtroom, this old man tried to cripple me with the piercing intensity of his eyes. Once in a while, finding him absorbed in meditation, I would sneak a look at him. The strange thing was that underneath his hairy appearance, he did not differ much from a Hindu sage—the usual *rishi munis* I knew. Both have a kind of tranquil fire in their eyes. He had been especially summoned to help the ticket checker out of the mess he had created for himself. Before answering a question, the ticket checker always looked in his direction for an approving nod.

My Muslim girlfriend later told me that this old holy man was an adept in a special charm, one that is read while the throat of a black rooster is slit. Nobody is allowed to eat the rooster, and it has to be buried while still writhing and fluttering. When I heard that, an unknown fear made me involuntarily touch my throat.

"And what does he recite in the charm?" I asked, trying to drown my dread in a laugh.

"Oh, he just asks for succour from *Bhagwan,* or, let's just say, from your *Bhagwan's* Muslim counterpart."

"Does he help?"

"Certainly."

"Even in a case like this?" I asked. "I mean even people like my assailant?"

"Surely you don't mean to say that evil people have a separate god to ask for help, do you?" my friend scoffed.

I was living like a perfect stranger at my in-laws'. Once it occurred to me to end the episode where it had begun. Why not make another pious visit to the Ganges? But then I thought that for that purpose, the river in our town was just as good. Almost every year it provided peace to some agitated soul or another.

One morning in the month of *Baisakh* I went to the bridge over our local river. Below, by the bathing ghat at the edge of the water, I could see women's yellow and red saris. Children sitting on the bank were skipping pebbles and rocks in the water. A few boys were bathing directly below the bridge, their black shoulders glistening above the water in the morning sun. With no particular reason I extended my hand over the guard-rail and waved it as though I were throwing something into the water. The boys at once shouted, "*Mataji! Mataji!*" and began paddling around in the water.

The memory of my dead mother came to me. I also remembered my brother—the thief!—who was now living in Germany, my sister who was in the U.K., and my father . . .

The breeze over the bridge was cool and comforting. I took all the change out of my purse and threw it into the water coin by coin. With every falling piece the boys plugged their noses and dunked their heads into the water, emerging seconds later with the same coin which they showed to me in their triumphantly waving hands.

I returned home in the afternoon, without having bathed in the river, and went straight to my room.

I don't know who came up with the saw, "There are as many versions to a story as there are mouths." But he must surely have come up with it centuries ago in a courtroom. Based upon events and statements piled one on top of the other, the story that finally emerged was far lengthier and different than the actual experience I had gone through within the space of a few moments that night. When the prosecution went into details of my college days, my religion-preserving husband just sat there dumbly. And his father took a deep breath as though his worst fears were being proven true today.

The ticket checker maintained that: (1) it was true that he was standing against the lamp-post, but he was simply filling out the routine papers there; (2) it wasn't true that the lamp-post was located directly opposite the women's carriage; (3) when later the train started to move he did see a young woman emerge from one of the carriages toward the tail part of the train, but whether this woman was beautiful he could not have guessed at all; (4) he suddenly felt as though the woman wanted to commit suicide, so when the carriage passed in front of him, he grabbed the handlebar on the door and climbed aboard the footboard, and entered the carriage as he pushed the woman in; (5) the woman was crying inconsolably at that time because, as she said, her husband was thoroughly fed up with her and, along with her in-laws, unhappy over her inability to bear children; and (6) the woman had even told him that she had once before attempted to kill herself, and if, after her present visit to the Ganges, she again failed to conceive, it mattered little whether she lived or died.

Some of these statements were in fact true. For instance, it was true that I was barren. It was also true that during the course of the trial I had often been seen strolling over the bridge, instead of bathing in the waters below it.

But the testimony of the railway guard proved inconclusive. It failed to establish that when the train stopped the ticket checker was struggling with me to keep me from jumping off the train and had managed to pin me down on the floor and clamp both my hands. That Muslim guard had seen me hanging on to the chain, all right!

The case was dismissed. The ticket checker and I were both honour- ably acquitted and came out of the court. My husband and his father were terribly unhappy; if not for my sake, then, surely, for their religion's sake, they had badly wanted to see the ticket checker sentenced to prison.

I stood outside the court building—abandoned, friendless, unwanted—while my assailant walked away surrounded by a crowd of well-wishers who had joyously garlanded his father and the holy man. For a moment I imagined a scene: some people are digging a pit with worshipful reverence. The ticket checker places a big black rooster in the hands of the holy man, and then in the hands of the ticket checker's father, a long knife. The saintly figure mumbles something inaudible. Suddenly I see a jet of blood shoot from the rooster's slit gullet, followed by a long rasping breath. Seconds later a flutter of wings and the black, lustrous wings themselves go down the pit and disappear under the fine, yellow dust crumbling over them. The men slap down the dirt with their hands and then stamp upon it with their feet.

Quite as suddenly, I returned to my senses. This was the exoterica of religion, part of its fascination and appeal.

✤ ✤ ✤

The river was muddy. Big round patches of oil floated here and there on the surface. The shadow of the bridge trembled over the water on the downstream side. Once in a while a tugboat passed by, or the loud whistle of a ship was heard. *Ghon-on-on.*

An empty beer bottle came floating in the distance. I picked a coin, took aim, but stopped. The bottle was too far away.

A little while later an empty beer can, thrown off the bridge or from one of the ships, came floating our way. I took aim with a coin and hurled it as I said, "Amstel."

"No, Heineken!" she said from behind.

The coin hit the can with a clink. The can swirled and the name bobbed before me for a second. Triumphantly I said, "See, it's an Amstel!"

Both of us laughed. Sitting on the grassy bank we often played that game, especially when it wasn't misty. And this evening was glorious. On both banks of the river, European, Asian, and African children were running around on the grass and rolling down the slopes, while their mothers sat in the mild sun and read newspapers, or just peered through their binoculars to watch the ships come in or go out. A few infants had fallen asleep in their strollers.

"Another round—shall we?" my West Indian friend asked.

"No, that'll do for today," I said. "I've got to cook supper for the children as soon as I get back home. My husband is on call tonight. And since today is my lucky day, I hope the phone won't ring every five minutes for him to rush to the hospital to take care of some drunkard."

Getting up from the grass, I said, "Your score is four, and mine seven. The river swallowed five of your coins and two of mine."

She also got up, dusting grass off her slacks, and said, "You're a perfect marksman. I just can't believe it."

"Can't believe what?"

"That you still don't eat meat."

"That has nothing to do with eating meat," I replied. "I have been throwing coins at targets in the river all my life."

## Kunthavai ✤ SRI LANKA

Kunthavai is the pen name of Era Sadadcharadevi. A widely-respected Sri Lankan author who writes in Tamil, she is noted for her politically charged fiction, particularly her short stories. Originally from Yaalpaanam, she lives in Thondaimanaru, Jaffna District, in northern Sri Lanka, which suffered greatly in the recent secessionist war led by Marxist rebels. Kunthavai's story here depicts something of the dreadful challenges faced by common people during this 25-year-long period of civil strife in which nearly 70,000 people died. Among the first group of Tamil medium graduates of Peradeniya University, Kunthavai has since worked as a teacher. Her works include the collection *Yogam Iirrukkirathu* (Fortune Remains).

# THE DISPOSSESSED

*Translated from the Tamil story "Peyarvu" by A.J Canagaratna with Antara Dev Sen*

THERE WAS A TENSE SILENCE IN THE BOAT. IT WASN'T like the people didn't speak at all, but almost as if on cue, they would fall silent every now and then. Sivaranjini knew they were all thinking about the same thing—the abandoned houses, the wells and gardens. They, too, had left behind onions tied up in bundles and hung in the shed. They should have sold the crop soon after the harvest. Some carters had even come to their garden plot, wanting to buy, but they had turned them away. The price that the carters offered would hardly cover their investment, Mahendran had said. So the onions were brought home and spread out to dry. Men were hired to tie them up in bundles and they were hung up in the shed, with enough room between them for air to circulate. Prices would go up by the end of February. But the fighting had broken out before that.

73

They had had to flee, leaving everything as it lay. They had hired a tractor to plough the land, bought manure, planted the crop, hired a water pump every three days to irrigate the plots and frequently sprayed pesticides. Twenty-five plots of farmland planted with onions had all gone to waste! The more they thought about it, the more unbearable it felt. If only they had sold the onions to the carters, even at their prices. At least they would have got their money back. They would have lost just their sweat and toil.

From the other corner of the boat, Sivaranjini heard the wailing of a child, and its mother trying to pacify it. She gently stroked Amuthan, who was lying in her lap. As she wiped away the water from his wet body, she prayed that he would not catch a chill. How would she get medicines in the place they were going to, Kilinochchi? She had heard that there was a shortage of medicines and drugs even in Kilinochchi's only government hospital.

The sea, as if unable to bear the boat cleaving its body, showered them with water again and again. Everybody was soaked. At first, Amuthan had been thrilled by the water leaping into the boat and was full of laughter. But he was worn out now, and hungry besides. There was less than half a pound of sliced bread in the zippered leather bag. It was a rare commodity, bought in a shop at Chavakachcheri the day before. But whenever she tried to feed Amuthan the bread, he said, "I don't want it." The last attempt was when they were on the Kilaly seashore, waiting for this boat. Watching the darkness swallow up the crimson sky in the west, she had tried, unsuccessfully, to persuade him to eat. They didn't want to eat the bread they had bought especially for the child, so they had saved it up carefully.

Amuthan was hungry, though. Apart from two cups of milk made from Anchor powder, he had had nothing all day. But he was very obstinate. He didn't like bread and this loaf was somewhat stale anyway. In the mornings, he would only eat string-hoppers with just a few mouthfuls of *sothi*, the coconut milk and onion soup. If they had biscuits, he might have had some.

But the biscuits were finished. The last packet had run out on the evening of the third day. They had been trudging for some time and had sat down on a dry spot under a tree by the side of the road. Then, perching the pot of water on some stones, they had lit a fire of dry leaves to boil their tea.

"The army is getting closer. Everyone must leave the village," the announcement over the loudspeaker said. Languor and irritation overcame her. "How many times must we run like this? I'm not going. I'll wait here for a bomb to kill me. You take the child and go," she had said haughtily, sitting obstinately still. Mahendran had hurriedly gone out and bought whatever he could get before all the shops were either emptied out or shut. He had bought tea, sugar, milk powder and biscuits. "The neighbours are locking up their houses and getting on the road," he said. It was only then that a sense of urgency seized her. She managed to cook rice and a *sambar*-like *dal* curry in the midst of packing their bags. She ate part of it as if they were having a proper lunch, and brought along the remainder in the terracotta cooking pot.

That food had lasted them until the following afternoon. Seated under the shade of the thatched roof of a locked shop, they had eaten the last handfuls of that meal. But Amuthan had not eaten then.

The next day, they heard that someone was selling *dosais*. Indeed, under a thatch, they found an old woman selling hot *dosais* made of wheat flour for fifty rupees. They bought one, but Amuthan merely nibbled at it.

When they ran out of biscuits, Sivaranjini had given Amuthan milk powder mixed in water from the flask. Now that was finished as well. This piece of bread was all that was left.

The people in the boat were still silent.

The roar of the engine picked up. The waves beat against the sides of the boat and frothed. The sea breeze blew constantly. Wearily, she closed her eyes.

Behind her eyelids, crawling people appeared, so many that they blocked the street. Their belongings tied up in gunnies and bags, dragging or carrying their children, these people moved slowly, in family groups. She could see them only dimly through the rain, harsh as wires, trudging through the mud and sludge.

Sivaranjini's closed eyes also saw her own suffering as she walked. The mud stuck between her toes, causing unbearable irritation. Her husband was walking ahead, carrying Amuthan in one hand; with the other, he held the handlebars of the bicycle loaded with their things. She dragged herself along behind him, every step absolute agony.

She opened her eyes wide and resolved not to shut them again. The sea looked black and dense; the sky seemed to rise from the sea and curved overhead. In the dim light of the waning moon, clouds the colour of ashes spread across the sky. If you looked up, they seemed to hang low and motionless, filling the eyes. She imagined how it would look if a red and yellow helicopter appeared, its blades hissing, against the backdrop of the dark sky.

She remembered that the night they had left home and were resting under a huge tree, a helicopter or a bomber had been flying in a northerly direction, red against a black sky, firing round after round, raining fire from the sky. It circled again and again, firing. Though they knew that it was not targeting them, they had felt a sense of fear, not entirely devoid of aesthetic pleasure, at the spectacle.

After it left, they were too frightened to sit under the tree. They pushed open the door of a compound behind them and went into a house. There was no room to sleep indoors, for it was chock-full of people. They spread out a bedsheet in the compound and lay down. But every time they heard an aircraft engine, they picked up Amuthan, grabbed the bedsheet and ran for cover, hugging the wall of the house. They didn't get a wink of sleep that night.

The helicopter that had missed them that day would not let them off so easily if it were to come today, she thought. It would definitely swoop down and drop a bomb or two, or it would dip and strafe them with fifty-calibre guns. Everyone, except those whose bodies were shattered by the bombs, would have to jump into the sea.

One night . . . it might have been the third day, when they were sleeping in the stone-pillared hall of a temple, they had woken up in a panic. After washing their feet at the well, she had applied ointment to the cracks on her feet. Finding room to stretch out, they had slept in the *mandapam*, secure in the belief that they would not bomb a temple. She was startled awake by a sound that almost shattered her eardrums, to find the people around her shouting in utter confusion. She got up drowsily, groped for Amuthan, picked him up and ran out. Later, they learned that a shell had fallen on a house by the temple.

When she returned to the place where she had been sleeping, it was occupied. She didn't have the heart to start a fight with the poor, tired souls who had stretched out and fallen asleep. She sat in the little space she could find and spent the rest of the night with Amuthan in her lap, thinking of the child who had been killed when the shell hit the house.

The next night was also like that. They slept under the portico of a locked house, which was quite comfortable. At midnight, though, a heavy downpour flooded the balcony. She had to stand in a corner, carrying Amuthan, who slept with his head on her shoulder.

When she thought about it, they hadn't had even one night's sleep since they left home. Last night, they hadn't closed their eyes at all. They could have slept in the school hall, where they had managed to find shelter. But the memory of a child's body floating under Kaithady Bridge, which they had crossed during the day, kept sleep away. Added to that was the memory of the child's mother, wailing for the child who had slipped from her hip. Four or five people were holding her against the parapet wall. Had she tripped as she was crossing the bridge, because she was just too worn out? Or had she let go of her child under the rush of people pressing her on?

At dawn, she came to a decision. She knew what she had to do. She couldn't keep Amuthan here in the midst of all these dangers. Whichever part of the Jaffna Peninsula they moved to, war was sure to dog their footsteps. They couldn't flee from place to place as long as Amuthan was with them. His safety had to be assured.

They had to leave Jaffna and cross the lagoon. There was no other way out. The mainland was quiet now. For the moment, at least, fighting would not break out there. True, this decision did not seem entirely right; something niggled at the backs of their minds. If they left now, would they ever be able to return?

At dawn when they came out of the school hall, they found people cramming themselves into the trailer of a tractor. They got in as well, knowing of no other way to reach the shores of Kilaly Lagoon.

They had been told the boat journey would take only three hours. Weren't the three hours over yet? But part of her wished that they wouldn't reach shore. She would have been happier if they could go on travelling like this, at sea.

As time passed, she felt increasingly uneasy. She didn't want to think about what they would do once they got there. Oh, God! What could such a multitude of people do there?

As if on cue, a point of light appeared and gradually grew bigger. For a moment, she wondered whether the light was meant to guide their boat in. She had heard that some boats had followed the wrong beam of light and ended up near the Pooneryn naval base.

Now, the light fell full on the sea. Beyond the edge of its beam, beached boats loomed black. The helmsman stopped the engine, picked up a long oar and stood on a plank. They heard the sound of the oar regularly beating the water. The boat manoeuvred smoothly, avoiding the small rocks near the shore. The helmsman is clever, she thought. Some boats, which had already deposited their passengers on the shore, turned back and sailed past them.

The boat touched the shore and the passengers got off, one by one. Mahendran picked up the child from her lap, and she too got up. She felt giddy and had to hold on to the gunwale. Must be hunger. All of the previous day, she had had only two cups of tea. She stepped into the water and stumbled. She held on to the gunwale and planted her feet firmly. Mahendran, who was still in the boat, handed her the child and asked her to take care. The seawater washed away the mud, soothing her cracked feet. Slowly, she walked out of the sea.

The boat's passengers had got together again on shore. The strong sea breeze dried their clothes, heavy with salt water. After he had brought their belongings, Mahendran carried their bicycle ashore. Again, he loaded their meagre goods onto the bicycle. They started walking away from the shore, the cycle wheels and their feet sinking into the sand with every step they took.

The light they had seen from the boat lit up only the seashore. The sky must have been overcast. It was pitch-dark and the trees loomed like *pootham* monsters.

They looked for space under the trees that lined the path. People were sitting under every tree they passed. They walked on and finally found a place for themselves. They spread out the bedsheet, put Amuthan on it and lay down beside him.

When Sivaranjini woke up, it was morning. Her husband and child were still asleep. Her body ached. Would her head start spinning if she got up? she wondered. She had no idea what they would do now. The boughs of the tree could serve as a roof, but where would they find food? Who could feed so many people?

She got up slowly and walked to a thicket behind the tree. On her way back, her legs gave way. She sat there, buried her face between her knees and, in her helplessness, she wept. Mahendran woke up and tried to console her, saying, "Everyone is going through the same thing."

By the time she had cried her fill, Amuthan woke up and reached for her, calling, "Amma." She picked him up and hugged him tight. Then she took him behind the bush and carried him back after a while. Rubbing his face on her shoulder, he whined, "Amma, give me some bread."

Hurriedly, she set him down beside her and opened her shoulder-bag. She tore off a piece of bread, strewed some sugar on it and raised it to his mouth. When she saw him eagerly opening his mouth to eat it, she felt that sense of helplessness return. Her fussy child, who was so choosy about what he ate, who would eat only four mouthfuls of string-hoppers and *sothi*, was eagerly eating this tiny piece of stale bread! She wanted to cry again.

When he had eaten the little piece of bread, Sivaranjini tore off another piece. And then she felt someone's eyes on her. She straightened and looked up. It was the child of the family that shared the space under the tree with them. He stood there, staring at the piece of bread in her hand. He was about Amuthan's age. Three-and-a-half years old—four at the most.

She tore the bread into two pieces and with her eyes, she invited the child to come and take one. Without any hesitation, the little boy came up and took what she offered. His mother must have seen this, for she looked like she wanted to say: "Why all this?" But she said nothing, just stood there helplessly.

She still had two pieces of bread. That would be just about enough for Amuthan, she thought. The piece she had held in her hand was gone. As she took out another piece, she felt a pricking at the back of her head. She turned.

Another child, the child of the family sheltering under the next tree, was peeping over his mother's back, looking intently at the piece of bread in her hand.

## Manjula Padmanabhan ❦ INDIA

Manjula Padmanabhan was born in Delhi, but grew up in Sweden, Pakistan and Thailand. An artist, illustrator, cartoonist, playwright and novelist, she has illustrated 21 children's books, and has had a long-running cartoon strip, *Suki*, in the *Sunday Observer*. Her short stories are marked by an unconventional humour; however, critics have observed how themes of alienation and marginalization play a large role in her books. Her futuristic play *Harvest*, about the sale of body parts and exploitative relations between developed and developing countries, was selected from more than 1400 entries in 76 countries for the Onassis Prize in 1997. Her publications include *Getting There*, a semi-autobiographical novel about a young woman illustrator in Bombay; *Kleptomania;* and *Hot Death, Cold Soup*, a collection of stories about moral awakenings that range from murder mystery to science fiction. She lives in Delhi.

# A GOVERNMENT OF INDIA UNDERTAKING

ONE MORNING I SAW A BALLOON SELLER CROSS THE street and vanish round a corner. I say "balloon seller," but he was more than that: against the bleakness of the city, its bone-grey buildings, its ragged people, its rubbish heaps and hidden rats, he had appeared as if from nowhere, a vision of youth and delight. High over his head swayed an immense bouquet of pink gas balloons, a hundred or more of them, alive, crowding together, bouncing apart, bright pink, bright with white specks. The balloon seller strode briskly along under their gay and thronging mass and, in a twinkling, had slipped from view, swallowed by the city.

So swiftly had he appeared and disappeared that I felt it my duty to run across the street and confront him again, if only to confirm the vision. But he was nowhere in sight. I wandered in and out of various little lanes and streetlets and caught nothing of him, no hint or sign that he had ever passed that way. It was on this pretext, looking for the balloon seller, that I entered a narrow gully with short squat buildings crowded one athwart the other and saw a sign which read: "Bureau of Reincarnation and Transmigration of Souls—A Government of India Undertaking." It was neatly hand-lettered in white paint on varnished wood, and contrasted strangely with the crumbling wall onto which it had been nailed.

I stood back to take a second look at the building, but no, it was just like all the rest to look at. Bleached, flaking paint, gaping doorway revealing a dark uninviting interior, a flight of worn wooden steps. There was a faint smell as of a bakery, or a urinal, perhaps. I stepped inside and noticed, once my eyes had adjusted to the gloom, an ancient *chowkidar* dozing on his wooden stool to the side of the door. Further in, a neat little peon sat at a small desk, staring with fixed purpose at its surface. It was covered with various objects: pencils, matchboxes, empty cigarette packets, an old glass ink-well and a paste-pot disfigured by successive encrustations of paste, and all of these arranged as for an obstacle course. I drew closer and saw that it was for the shiny cockroach scrabbling about erratically, trying to reach the crumb of food dangled by the peon just beyond the reach of the insect's questing feelers. I saw too that the creature's diligence would not be rewarded: down the leg of the desk, six of its brothers had been left to wriggle to their deaths skewered with government-issue straight pins. I watched in fascination, not daring to disturb the peon at his sport, to ask him where I should go and whom I should see in the Bureau of Reincarnation. But he anticipated me and said softly, not looking up from the desk, "Tea in fifteen minutes." I took this to mean that I should climb the flight of stairs, so I did.

Hardly had I reached the first floor, but I found I had joined a queue. That is, I arrived at the landing and was brought up short against a flesh-coloured room-divider which had a sign pasted on it which read, "Q this way." Further room-dividers had been laid out in a line, forming a sort of artificial corridor. I followed its length until, quite abruptly, I found I had entered a huge hall, with a vast mass of people apparently congealed along its floors and walls. Unaccountably, the building's internal dimensions had expanded and it was larger on the inside than its outside promised.

That queue was an amazing thing: not a group of individuals waiting patiently in line for something but an organic entity in itself. Physically, it was merely a more heroic version of the kind that one finds at the GPO during a sale of first-day issues. It looped backwards and forwards across that vast hall with its dingy marble chip tiling and dim, low-slung light bulbs. It passed over and under and right through itself so often that no one knew where it began or ended.

No one waiting in the queue (in my section of it, at least) could recollect having seen the waiting hall empty of people, nor was there anyone present who had been amongst the first to line up; everyone there had been waiting so long that he or she had lost all track of time and had settled into that vacuum of thought and action which is our only solace in such situations. It was in this time-scale in a place where even the finest quartz watch was reduced to a useless curiosity by its sheer irrelevance, that the queue became as one animal, living, breathing and functioning as one organism and each of us in it making up its cell wall.

Nourishment in the form of regular cycles of tepid tea and stale chutney sandwiches passed through and reached every segment of the queue as efficiently and mysteriously as it appeared. We seemed to breathe in concert, each newcomer to the queue having to adjust himself/herself to the group rhythm—asthmatics had a bad time and smokers were not tolerated—until the walls seemed to move gently in and out with our respiration. The queue was constantly being depleted—as someone was finally ushered into the presence of an officer, registrar or file clerk—and constantly being replenished by newcomers to the queue and by former queue members rejoining the array in quest of yet another officer, registrar or file clerk. Since there was no distinct terminal point, each addition had to squeeze in as best he or she could; a few half-hearted grunts and tongue-clickings were raised in mild discontent, then everyone subsided once more into the vacant stupor of waiting.

For entertainment we had the endless forms, questionnaires and visiting slips to fill up, some of these transiting the length and breadth of the queue several times before being rescued by the defaulting peon and returned to the office of their origin. Sometimes we roused ourselves enough to sing *bhajans* and popular songs, sometimes there were a few listless bouts of gambling and once, someone who had brought a cassette recorder along played a taping of last year's Test matches, and everyone cheered.

There were all kinds of people in that queue—you could tell at a glance from the myriad forms filled out in triplicate the professions and personalities involved. The majority had come to check their claims for a better life the next time round: business magnates and thieves, they were each of them anxious to improve the fibre of their future lives. Others had come to look at the files of dear departed ones, to see if they could renew contact with them in the life to be; some had come to check on their antecedents, to see how well their current lives and companions matched their pasts; some had come belligerently, to demand enlightenment within the next three births or else; some had come out of idle curiosity and at least one pathetic individual I spoke to was there under the impression that he was in queue to buy tickets for *Deep Throat*. And finally, there must have been a few, like myself, who had come for dishonourable reasons but, naturally, I never actually spoke to any of the others.

Because of the irregular nature of my request, it took even more than the ordinary number of tea-and-sandwich cycles, false leads, wrong turnings along the queue and battles with insolent peons, coffee boys, receptionists and bureaucratic vagrants before I could approach my first bona fide officer—the Assistant Registrar of Files. He was a frail, desiccated, bright-eyed little man who smelt of clean old paper and wore rimless glasses. He sat behind an enormous desk generously littered with scraps of paper, forms, questionnaires and a few odd bus tickets. Holding down the papers were a dozen or so glass paperweights, the kind which look like gobs of some unspeakable mucus, quick-frozen and injected with air to produce five (sometimes four or less) bubbles inside, arranged in such a way as to keep the observer forever anxious to rearrange them more symmetrically. One of them, I noticed, a collector's item no doubt, had just one enormous tear-shaped bubble, and in it an ant had been trapped and preserved for posterity with a puzzled look on its face.

However, I had not come all the way merely to note down the details of interior decor in that musty little office. Leaning forward and putting as much earnestness as I could into my voice, I said, "Sir, let me come straight to the point: ever since I saw the signboard on the building, I have been possessed with the desire to"—I paused dramatically—"change my life." I had been looking at him directly when I said this last bit and was surprised and a little disappointed to see that the little man barely blinked. In fact he seemed on the verge of stifling a yawn, so I hurried on recklessly. "Oh, I realize this is an illegal request—even criminal you might say! But I've been waiting such a long time, and no one has so much as told me one way or another whether such a thing is possible at all." I tried to change my tack from wheedling to impatience: "I am at the end of my endurance. I must know what I need to know, even if my request is denied, but I must know. I am not going to leave this office until you tell me what . . ."

But he stopped me by raising a delicate hand. For a moment I thought he was about to fob me off, as so many minions along the course of my ordeal had done, and I had my handful of tears collected and ready to throw in his face. But he pursed his lips a moment, then asked mildly, "But, have you filled out your death certificate?"

I was a little irritated. "Sir," I countered briskly, "surely it is obvious that I have not died. How, therefore, can I have filled out the death certificate?"

He had been waiting for this. "And if you have not died, my dear madam," he said, with the sort of patient, understanding smile that might be reserved for conversations with the mildly insane, "then how is it you want to change your life?"

"Ah, but that is just the point," I said, feeling great relief. This was the moment I had been waiting for, to unburden the true nature of my quest at the desk of a sympathetic officer. "You see, I am tired of my life and want to change it. But the thing is, I want to change it now, I do not want to commit suicide or go through all the mess of catching a disease or being murdered by jealous relatives or accidentally falling down mine shafts—besides, I took the trouble of bribing someone at the first floor Department of Mortality and she assured me that my dossier had not come up for review yet. As I need hardly remind you, the dossier must reach that office three full moons before a death is scheduled, in order that suitable allocations for the next life can be made." I paused for effect. "So what I thought was this: why not change it right now, in mid-life? I want to be rich. I want to be famous. I want to be absolutely indolent. And I don't want to wait till my next life, I want it now."

He continued to be unimpressed. "Madam," he said, fidgeting daintily with his nose, "as you have stated, this is an illegal request?" He seemed to be asking for my opinion on the proposing of such requests.

"Well, yes," I said breezily, "but I don't care. I feel it can be quite simply arranged. In fact it is so simple that I'm absolutely certain other people must be doing this right now, that it must already be part of your system." I didn't want to come right out into the open and say that, since all Government concerns are corrupt, this one must be equally so. I sincerely felt that it was just a question of understanding in what dimension it was corrupt and how the cogs of reincarnation had been realigned to suit the flavour of the corruption. "All that I'm asking is that I, with my lease on life, inhabit the body of someone else, preferably someone rich and comfortable, whose number has come up. Someone whose body is intact and in working condition but whose life has run its course. Don't you see how easily it could be done?"

A blink of light played about the bare rims of the Assistant Registrar's spectacles. "And your body, madam? What will happen to that?"

"Oh come now," I said, my confidence growing. "Surely it is of little concern. The rich person dies. I discard this body like a sweaty track suit and impinge upon the other one before its mechanism shuts down forever. Perhaps it could be one of those cases of coma in which a person who has been all but pronounced dead miraculously revives. The only difference would be that instead of the original occupant returning to life there would be me! So I don't care what you do with my body . . . keep it in coma perhaps? Loan it out to some soul kicking its heels about waiting to be reborn? To visiting extra-terrestrials?" I had spent my time in the queue fruitfully, I thought, and had actually advanced my scheme to include a scope of operations wider than my petty little life. I had the notion that, if I could only discover the actual process of transferring souls from corpse to new embryo, I could set up a sort of transmigrational banking system.

After all, I reasoned, this was just another Government department: therefore there must be some sort of quota system, a waiting list of souls, a roster of lives waiting to be reborn. I imagined that there might even be a regular state-wise system of making allocations of how many lives could be legally issued per month or year or whatever—in fact I was amazed that the family planning programme had not set up permanent headquarters here. What I hoped to offer was in the way of a side attraction; a short trip to life while a soul awaited its legitimate birth. I did not feel any guilt at what I planned to do. If anything, I felt quite virtuous as I thought this might be the ideal way in which to bring home the point that it is really worthwhile to strive for release from the cycle of birth-death-rebirth. I had always felt that the system as I understood it was far too cumbersome: by the time a soul has done with being born, growing to maturity, struggling through childhood traumas and neuroses, the original purpose—that is, of leaving the cycle entirely, by attaining enlightenment—is inevitably lost sight of. It seemed to be so unfair, so undemocratic. Under my system, a soul would be able to experience life without the confusing preamble of childhood and adolescence (especially adolescence) and perhaps, thereby, understand more clearly about the sorts of lives which lead to better results in the next. Maybe these visiting souls could even be trained to be a source of inspiration to their fellows doing time on earth, like freelancing messiahs, perhaps. All in all, I thought I had a fairly wonderful scheme worked out.

And still the Assistant Registrar was unimpressed! "Madam," he said, "do you think no one has considered this subject before?" He knew nothing, of course, of my grand vision, only of the basic request. He did not wait for my response. "So many people have approached us but we have always had to turn them down." He assumed a slightly professorial tone, leaning back and attempting to bring the tips of his fingers together in the classical posture of pedantry, but not succeeding very well because the arms of his chair were too wide apart for him to rest the elbows of his meagre little forelimbs. "Firstly, this is only the Department of Files; we make records, that is all. We have no direct jurisdiction over lives. Secondly . . . have you seen the files?"

For the first time, I looked up and around me, to take in the shelves which lined the room. I saw that the shelves were filled with files, then realized with a little start that the shelves were not exactly against the walls of the room, but that they were themselves the walls of the room, that behind them lay the possibility of further such glass-fronted filing cabinets; that the chamber in which they were housed could now be of entirely arbitrary proportions. I got up and went closer to one of the cabinets and saw that the files within were alphabetically marked—they were the same tatty old box files that one sees in bureaucratic concerns around the country, with papers spilling out, edges scuffed and dust-bitten, mouldering under the excrement of generations of spiders. But the alphabets were not all in English. In fact some of them seemed barely human. "What are these files?" I asked, knowing that it was expected of me.

"All the births. All the deaths. We record everything," said that sage and prune-like man, with modest satisfaction. "Every birth, every death, every centimetre of every soul's journey along its personal path of release. Do you understand, madam, how many lives and deaths, progressions and regressions, we must be recording?"

"But . . ." I said, a vague sense of unease setting in, "I thought only people subscribing to a certain highly popular religion—only Hindus, in short—were eligible for rebirth?" I must admit that I had never really given the subject a thought until the moment of seeing the signboard. And then too, I had roughly generalized, thinking it unlikely that the government of one country would be entrusted with the reincarnation of the world's peoples. I just assumed therefore that the Bureau's operations must be restricted to those people whose religion explicitly upheld such a belief.

"According to the propaganda, that is so," said the Assistant Registrar, "but in fact it is not of the least concern to the celestial office. And of course, you realize, madam, that I am not talking of human beings alone, but all living things!" And he smiled suddenly, a frugal, neat-toothed and wrinkle-wreathed smile, because he saw that I was amazed.

"Everything?" I asked, awed in spite of myself.

". . . including plants," he said.

For a few moments, my mind reeled, processing the thought: stag-beetles; crocuses; Eskimos; pangolins; wandering albatrosses; Saint

Bernards; mindless strands of seaweed; Bengalis; hammerhead sharks and ruby-throated hummingbirds; microbes and monsters.

". . . though we stop short of single-celled organisms," he said, as if intercepting the drift of my truncated survey of life. "In fact, even now a case is being fought by an amoeba and will shortly be brought up in Parliament. Depending on that decision, we will change the rule perhaps."

"Why discriminate against amoebas?" I said, still a little dazed at the revelation he had made.

"Of course," he said, "because it is not clear that they die. How to issue a death certificate for a life form which simply subdivides?" he mused, almost to himself, sucking pensively on a scrap of food caught between his premolars. Obviously, this was the subject of feverish debate, the argument that raised factions and stoked the furnaces of human ire along the tube-lit corridors of the Bureau of Reincarnation. "It is not clear-cut with them," he said. "It will make a nuisance of the filing system. Already we are overworked. The stenotypists have threatened a protest march."

But by this time I had been recalled to the purpose of my visit and the issue at hand. "Meanwhile," I said, breaking into his argumentative reverie, "coming back to me. Consider how simple my case is, compared with that of a hydra or paramecium: here I sit, healthy and plump with life, entirely unlikely to subdivide or encystate. Isn't there any way to grant me my meagre request? Isn't it possible to slip someone a little consideration, grease a willing palm?"

The little man sighed gently and trained his eyes back on me. "Madam," he said, "that is what I have been trying to explain to you. This is only the office of files, of documented records; I could tell you which lives are eligible for enlightenment, which lives are vacant, which ripe for transfers, which doomed to a thousand rebirths. You could have the whole cosmos opened to you if you wished to know what was going to happen to which life. But the actual allocations, the actual decisions," he shrugged poetically, "that is not for us to worry about. That is done at the Transmigration Department."

I snorted at that. "The Transmigration Department! Don't speak to me of transmigration—I think that's just a convenient excuse you people have cooked up to avoid explaining what really goes on here." I was absolutely sure of my ground now because I had repeatedly been assured that my request could be dealt with at the Transmigration Department, but try as I might, I had been unable to find it.

"But yes, madam," said the Assistant Registrar, eyebrows a-twitter with the agitation of having to prove his point, "it is on the seventh floor."

"Vicious libel," I said bitterly, "because there is no seventh floor. The stairs stop short at the fifth floor and when you try to climb any further you reach the terrace. I agree, there is some cause for confusion, because there is a mezzanine floor somewhere else and no one seems quite certain just how many floors the building has, but so far I have not had any reason to believe in the existence of a floor above the sixth."

"I am telling you, madam, there is," said the man. A new expression had entered his eyes, a conspiratorial look, and of something overheard in the lavatory. "There is a seventh floor, but I will tell you a secret—it is not easy to go there. Permission restricted, secret passwords. In fact, we ourselves do not know how to go there. We only get the message and the directives. There is a rumour that some people have found a way to go there, but I cannot tell you myself, I do not know it." A note of embarrassment had crept in. "We have only a small part to play, madam. Keeping records, that is all. The rest we do not know."

A fly nattered by. I felt a tickle in my nose and the storm warnings of an imminent depression. It looked like the end of the road. There are some people who like to hammer on about what they want even when it is obvious that theirs is a hopeless case. Sometimes they even manage to get their way, merely because the other person cannot bear to hear their arguments any longer. Well, I have never been that sort. I will persevere up to a point, but as soon as pursuing my goal requires me to lose my reasonability I accept that I have been beaten and back down quietly. This point, I felt, had been reached in the Assistant Registrar's office and I resigned myself to the loss of a great expanse of time. I got up to leave and said, "I'll be going then."

In a gesture of courtesy which surprised me, the diminutive officer hopped out of his chair, escorted me to the door of his cubby-hole amidst the filing shelves and held it open for me. As I passed out through it, I heard a whisper, the merest breeze of speech: "Find the peon Gopal! He knows something." I turned in astonishment, but the door had closed irrevocably and though I knocked and hammered for ten minutes on it there was no response from within.

I will not document the course of my search for the peon. It seemed I wandered about that miserable building for hours, days or weeks, it was hard to tell. There was little or no variation whatsoever in the routines of the place from one day to the next. The lights remained on continuously and the staff worked non-stop shifts. The innards of the building were labyrinthine and it was rare to catch even so much as a glimpse of the outside world. I gave up searching for the peon at one point, only to find that it was equally impossible to relocate the entrance through which I had discovered this nightmarish place. It was therefore with considerable surprise and relief that, turning a corner at random, I discovered a lonely passageway, innocent of tube lights, with a row of windows down one wall.

The peon sat perched on a window-ledge, etched against the beams of dusty sunlight forcing their way in from between the loose slats of the shutters. He was sitting there, doing nothing at all and looked up languidly as I approached him. I recognized him at once from the descriptions and I lost no time in confronting him with my needs.

"You are Gopal the peon," I said to him. "You know something about the Transmigration Department and how to reach it. I have been looking desperately for that same department but cannot seem to find it." I had thought enough about what I would say to the peon and said it, now, almost easily. "If you can tell me this that I need to know, I will give you whatever of value I have with me now: my four gold bangles, my diamond earrings, my gold ring with the sovereign and, if they are not enough, I can . . . I can offer myself." Truly, I was desperate.

He looked up with that cynical all-seeing, all-knowing expression of peons who work in the halls of the mighty. With one glance he assayed the worth of my possessions, briefly considered the attractions of my person, weighed the true nature of my quest against his scale of values and made a spot decision. "I'll show you for nothing," he said, and got up to lead the way.

The route was, predictably, circuitous. We went down the deserted corridor, descended a flight of wooden stairs, crossed a fetid latrine crawling with unspeakable life forms, over a small wrought-iron bridge connecting two sections of the building—I had long since ceased to understand what manner of architect had been responsible for this monstrosity; it seemed to have expanded out of control. We passed by kitchens and warehouses, file clerks and laundry women, rooms full of Japanese tourists and bandicoots, rooms filled with windows, rooms empty with pigeons . . .

And along the way Gopal spoke to me about my quest. "You want to change your life," said the peon, as easily as if it were a switch in toothpaste brands. "You want to overturn the progression of reincarnation. You want to jump your place in the queue." He shrugged, worldly-wise. "It can be done."

He spoke as one who has learnt to see creation from a slightly remote and favoured position. "As for bribes, there are many ways to make them: sometimes a little incense, sometimes a few flowers, sometimes a handful of gold coins, sometimes a river of blood. They are easily bribed, on the seventh floor," he said, a little contemptuously. "Still," he continued, "they are only a different kind of clerk to the ordinary human ones. They can adjust a life here, a life there, but they cannot change the rules."

"But who can change the rules?" I asked, bewildered. I had thought that the seventh floor held all the answers, but annoyingly and like any other outsize concern, one could never seem to get to the real epicentre of things, no final resolution to one's curiosity. "What are the rules?"

The slight sense of unease that had first set in at the Assistant Registrar's cubby-hole had, by this time, settled into a compact mass of unhappiness. I knew, as I sprinted to keep up with the peon, that I was swiftly losing my grip on the situation. Running a specialized sort of travel agency for souls or changing your own life is all very well as long as it is under your own control, but I was beginning to suspect that I would never really be shown or instructed in the actual process of the transfer. I had imagined some sort of machine, something like a large, friendly computer, with the Bureau's staff acting as its maintenance team. But with every passing second, the chances of ever reaching the machine or ever understanding how to operate it were growing dimmer. I began to regret having got involved in this thing.

Also, I hated all the information that Gopal was giving me about the seventh floor. Whenever I asked him where the rules were set down and who could change them he would merely smile his dazzling smile and sweep on with his discourse, in the manner of someone who rarely gets a chance to hold forth on his favourite fixation. "Everyone knows they are terribly careless," he said. "One extra digit on the forwarding letter to the Registry of Rebirth and a pious zebra is reborn as a lusty dandelion, saints reborn as coral polyps in the Great Barrier Reef. They play terrible jokes: an incestuous couple reborn as kissing gourami, lovers reborn as Siamese twins, oysters reborn as misers."

"But," I said weakly and plaintively, as we negotiated yet another dark and slimy passage, "why are you telling me all this? I don't want to know. I don't want to hear about how corrupt they are in heaven and how meaningless it is to struggle on earth and how futile it is to live a decent life. I already know all that. It's within this futile life that I would, at the very least, like to live a rich and comfortable one, by whatever flea-bitten standards we have for such things back in the place where I live. I'm not interested in the larger issues. I just want this life, this one which I know about at this moment, to be vastly improved."

"Yes, yes," he said impatiently, running fleetly up a down-moving escalator, "that's where I am taking you, to the place where you will get a chance to improve your life." And he told me about angels and demons, ghouls and sprites, mountains of human ash, mansions of perfumed ice, pickled crab genitals and the thousand-petalled lotus.

A green door, a gust of wind and suddenly we were there at the seventh floor. I gasped and said, "It's not at all as I expected it to be." But Gopal bustled me through, talking crisply all the time. "What I am going to do is this," he said, finally approaching the specific area of my interest. "I am taking you to the . . . I call it the departure lounge. This is something I discovered for myself. I found the place where it actually happens, the exchange of life essence, from soul to flesh, and flesh back to soul."

I was amazed. "Aren't there any formalities to complete?" I asked, refusing to accept the truth about my situation, at the mercy of the peon. I wanted something reassuring to sign, something to guarantee me my own life back if I weren't satisfied, something to ensure that I wasn't being taken for a fatal ride by a power-hungry underling in an empire whose horizons now seemed to stretch from dawn to dusk. "How do I know you are not fooling me? How do I know you are not dying of cancer and are only awaiting your opportunity to grab my nice healthy body? How do I know you will not loan it out to your friends—perhaps dead friends— for free rides?" My mind had begun to fill with the various obscene and exotic horrors that this bureaucracy beyond all others seemed to offer. "How do I know you are who you say you are?"

But it was long past the time for second thoughts. The peon merely smiled lightly and ushered me into a corridor whose walls seemed to curve and melt and cease to hold their substance stable. Immediately and subtly, the atmosphere of an airport was created by a sense of current and urgency around us, by the blandness of the corridor and the impression of hosts of fellow travellers crowding alongside us in patient yet determined strides. I could see no one except Gopal and myself but all around me I could feel the pressure, though not physical, of others. I was frightened then. I could smell them, these fellow travellers: seaweed and nasturtiums, warm cubs, hot butter, the pages of a new book. It was as if each one of them carried its own personal identity in the form of a distinctive scent. I felt arctic waters douse about my stomach and my flesh begin to shimmer in an atmosphere dense with metaphysical beings. How do I smell, I wondered within me, what is my scent! Will I ever know it!

"What you have to do is very simple," Gopal was saying, matter-of-fact as ever. "I will show you where to go. You go there and then you wait, just as you might wait for the next airbus to Cochin. You won't have long to go."

"Just a moment," I said, terror flooding my inner ear. "I had very specific desires about the ways in which I wanted my life changed. What you suggest—I'm not even very sure what you suggest—sounds extremely haphazard. You've not explained anything about how the exchange is to take place, or what choices I am to get or by what means I am to make my selection. You haven't given me forms to fill or tickets to hold on to, or life jackets or airsick pills." The terror had reached my tonsils and was spilling out in little sparks and flashes, leaving a taste like ozone in my mouth. It seemed that the atmosphere around us grew increasingly thick with the passage of souls and I fancied I could feel them eddying irritatedly about me, confused at my physical presence yet fundamentally disinterested, hurrying onwards to their embarkation gates. Every so often I would feel one push straight through me, leaving behind it an aftersmell of itself and my fear would increase a hundredfold. I felt the weight of each blood cell as it fled in panic through my arteries and I felt the labour of each separate bronchiole as it processed the heavy air I breathed.

My mind began to fill, slowly, with the red and throbbing manifestation of my own life. Dimly, as if at a distance, I could feel Gopal the peon take my hand and pat it comfortingly and say, "It's so simple: you wait a short space of time and then a moment will come, when you will know you have to make your choice. At that moment all you have to do is to wish. Just wish. As you used to on falling stars and rabbits' paws." I clung dumbly to his hand, so friendly and solid in this concourse of odours and spirits, and he repeated his advice. I looked at him, or tried to—I could not focus clearly. He had receded from sight, to become a dark figure, vaguely beside me. All around us, the silent traffic of spirits, souls in transit; throbbing in my head, throbbing in my hands and feet, in my blood.

We were almost there. I could see a haze ahead of me, as if the corridor (now barely perceivable in terms of walls and floors) were widening out, then suddenly we were in a vast hall, perhaps, a vast space, blinding white. I shut my eyes and abandoned myself to my terror, now flowing out freely in glowing lines from my ears, nose, eyes and navel. I could feel my blood, red and hot with life, pounding through the lacework of my veins and arteries. I could feel it in my neck and ear lobes, across my belly and in the calves of my legs. I could feel, like distinct and terrible drumbeats, the double-clapping thunder of my heart's valves as they powered the life substance across the span of the small, warm and fragile world of my body.

It seemed as if that whole vast hall were filled with this thunder, the thunder of blood and life; the air vibrated with it. The boundaries of my body seemed to have already dissolved into the space around me so that the whole hall and all its spectral beings pulsed in rhythm to my drumbeat. I cannot say that I was truly conscious, but I could still feel Gopal pushing me firmly onwards, disengaging my hand and saying, "Don't worry, I will stay by your side. I will stay by you."

But of course he did not, or I think he did not, because after a point my mind vaulted too far out of its normal orbit to know or care much longer. I heard him say, "You need only wait a short while and then you will step out of your own accord and when the moment comes, you will wish."

I had become a live and sparking bundle of fear, so dear and pure that it defined my entire existence. I did what I had to do, without question. Stepping out, I experienced what may have been a short wait or a long one. Then, as Gopal had explained, a moment came and silence fell about me like thunderbolts. I looked around me and meteors scarred and seared my eyes, stars shot away on either side of me like hailstones and my mind reeled with radiance. I felt the mouths of a billion billion billion souls suck me in, assimilate me within their experience, renew themselves upon my life, then breathe me out with a whistling, steaming roar from their billion billion billion gorges. At that instant I knew I had to make my wish. I wished.

## A SECOND'S BLINKING

I looked up and saw the hot and shining sky. I looked down and saw . . . nothing. Nothing.

I was not there.

Perhaps, if I had had a body then I could have recorded the emotions that I felt at that moment in physical terms: the betrayal, the shock, the foolishness, the self-reproach. But instead, just like the lack of body, there was a lack of any feeling in the place where I would normally have registered emotions.

Already the Bureau, the people in it, the peon and the star-studded place were vanishing like a lazy dream and I would surely have dismissed it as one if it were not for my conspicuous loss of body. I knew then that I had been cheated and been made a spectre of; but I did not feel in the least concerned as I hung suspended in the heavy air of mid-afternoon, people bustling about and through me. I drifted gently around, not caring where I went, sometimes passing through people, sometimes through buildings, sometimes through trees and dogs. I felt like a polite visitor at the art exhibition of a friend, neither moved by nor critical of the array of minds and lives presented to me.

Towards evening I found myself approaching the place where I used to live. I remained dispassionate and allowed the current to take me there of its own accord. I entered through the walls and settled into my own room.

As I sat there, lulled into a calm and peaceful mood by all the familiar artefacts of my distant life, I gradually became aware of a sensation at my feet: I suddenly became aware of my feet, the tingle of flesh and bone against the floor. I looked down to the place where I had been used to finding them and felt an odd pleasure as I recognized them thickening slowly into substance. My feet, my hands, my head and navel, all of these and all that lay between them were, very gently and unhurriedly, rematerializing from the void. And in a short space of time I could sense all of myself, from the humblest capillary and hair root, to the muscles powering my heart, the small compact planet of my existence once more bonded together and ticking with its own familiar rhythms. I sat there in the gathering twilight of my room, with the warm thudding comfort of my life marking time within me, without me; and I felt, at that moment, a deep and savage bliss.

# Sunil Gangopadhyay  ❀ INDIA

Sunil Gangopadhyay was born in Bengal in 1934. He lost his father quite early, and the family lost its ancestral home in what is now Bangladesh in the partition of India. After settling in Kolkata, he earned his Master's degree in Bengali from Calcutta University in 1954. A year earlier he had founded the seminal Indian literary journal *Krittibas,* which sparked a renaissance among young Indian writers and ran for a remarkable 25 years. In 1962, Gangopadhyay befriended the American poet Allen Ginsberg and they enjoyed a long, productive artistic relationship. Four years later, while retaining poetry as his first love, he turned his hand to fiction, and this brought him genuine national attention. Since then, he has delivered a river of novels and short stories, establishing his place as one of the titans of modern Indian literature. Widely translated, two of his novels were made into films by the beloved, late Kolkata director Satyajit Ray.

# VIRTUE AND SIN

*Translated from Bengali by Sheila Sengupta*

IT HAD BEEN RAINING SINCE THE MORNING, A DRIZZLE that had stopped intermittently, but the sky had still not cleared up. After continuing this way throughout the day, it started raining cats and dogs towards the evening.

On such days, one did not feel like going out. It was an ideal occasion for relaxing at home. However, on such days, incidents of thefts and dacoity were found to be rampant. There was no end to people streaming in and out of local police stations.

This locality had no electricity as yet. Two hurricane lamps burnt dimly on the table nearby. At times, a strong gust of wind from outside almost extinguished the light.

Rehman Sahib looked around once, and ordered, "Shut all doors and windows."

Then, keeping his diary aside, he put his feet up on the table. Loosening the belt around his waist, he muttered, "Enough! I have done enough work for the day." Then he raised his voice a little and called out again, "Ali, Ali go get me some *muri*—"

Ali was a thin, squeaky man. One could not tell his age from his face. He could be thirty or even fifty years old. At the slightest hint of a command he would start scampering around hastily.

Ali came and stood by the inspector's table. Rehman Sahib was a large man, very fair, with a well-trimmed moustache. He spoke in a thunderous voice, but at heart he was nice. Even the common man could speak his mind out in Rehman's presence.

Flashing out a rupee note from his pocket, Rehman Sahib said, "Go get me some *muri* for eight *annas* and fried cutlets with the rest. Make sure the cutlets are piping hot. If they are not, then get them fried fresh, alright?"

Folding his hands together in respect, Ali said, "Yes, Sir."

"But remember, if you take more than ten minutes, I'll chop off your head," Rehman Sahib said with a smile on his face. "Now, run, and don't forget to take the umbrella."

As soon as Ali left, Rehman Sahib started moving his knees to and fro, absent-mindedly. Sub-inspector Dhiren Saha had been down with fever for the last three days. Ever since the only literate constable Jagdish Saha had been transferred from this *thana*, no one had come in his place. For the last few days, Rehman Sahib had been handling everything himself.

On the other side of the table, some people sat quietly on a bench. They were all thugs, thieves and smugglers, about five of them—arrested, during the day. All of them knew that the inspector was now hungry. It would not be wise to disturb him at such a moment.

Constables Haranath and Siddiqui were standing outside the door exchanging news and munching *khaini*. Haranath was on night duty today. Siddiqui was going to leave any moment now. But having heard the Inspector Sahib send for cutlets and *muri*, he decided to stay back for a while.

Ali returned quite quickly. Spreading a newspaper on Rehman's table, he poured the *muri* over it. The potato cutlets were sizzling. Popping a handful into his mouth, Rehman Sahib said, "What about green chillies? Didn't you get some chillies?"

"No, Sir," Ali said.

"When will you ever learn? Tell me, can anyone have *muri* without green chillies? Run. Get me some chillies—quick."

Ali almost ran out of the room. Raising his voice again Rehman Sahib said, "Come on Haranath, Siddiqui, where are the two of you? Come, have some *muri*."

The group of thugs, thieves and smugglers sat quietly on the bench facing him. Rehman glanced in their direction. After all, he was a gentleman. He couldn't possibly eat alone in public without offering some to others.

"Haranath, give those people a handful each. They have been waiting for long," he called out.

This idea of offering the motley group *muri* bought with Rehman Sahib's own money was something that Haranath disliked immensely. Taking just a handful he looked despondently at the convicts and said, "Here, take this. The Inspector Sahib has given this to you."

By the time Ali returned again, the *muri* was almost finished.

Rehman laughed and said, "*Arre,* what shall we do now? Will you get me some more *muri*? After all there's nothing like crisp *muri* on a rainy day."

Another man had come with Ali this time. He was standing alone in the dark.

"Who is that?" Rehman Sahib asked.

"*Huzoor,* its me—Pratap Singh . . ." the man answered, stepping forward.

Rehman looked at the man standing before him. A lean frame clad in a *dhoti*—it seemed he had not eaten for a long time. He knew no language other than Bangla. It was a little difficult to believe that his name was Pratap Singh. But over the years a lot of people from different parts of the country had settled down in Murshidabad. During the era of the Nawabs, so many Rajputs, Pathans, and Punjabis had come here in search of work; many of their descendents had by now changed and joined the feeble clan of Bengalis and become part of the local crowd.

Pratap Singh had earlier been a petty thief. Now he was a police informer. He had recently opened a shop in Jiyaganj selling *bidis*.

Rehman Sahib didn't like Singh's presence at this moment. This man often brought stray information from various sources.

"What do you want?" he asked.

Pratap Singh took a step forward and said, "Sir, I have confirmed news."

"What is it? Tell me."

Coming closer, Pratap Singh began to whisper something in Rehman Sahib's ears. Rehman Sahib listened attentively as he kept nibbling at the bits of *muri* spread on his table.

At one point, he looked excited and said, "Really?"

"Sir, I have seen with my own eyes."

"But you had seen him many times earlier too, isn't it."

"There is no mistaking this time, *Huzoor*."

Rehman Sahib stood up and started tightening his belt. There was a certain urgency and excitement in his movement as he called out—"Darwaza!"

Ali came running. "*Ji Huzoor!*"

"Come with me! Who else will come? Haranath!"

"*Huzoor*, who will stay back at the *thana* then!" Haranath said.

Correct! Someone had to stay back at the *thana*. That was Haranath's duty. On the other hand, they needed an armed constable to accompany them. Ali was of no use. Then they might as well take Siddiqui with them.

Siddiqui's duty was over for the day. Still, he did not refuse to accompany Rehman Sahib.

The next moment, three cycles wheeled out on the road. In spite of having made several requests to the Zilla S. P., this *thana* was yet to receive a jeep. Even the inspector had to move around on a cycle! Today, Siddiqui offered to carry Pratap Singh on the pillion of his cycle.

Pratap Singh had brought news of Shivmangal. Even after many desperate attempts, the police had failed to arrest him all these years.

Had Shivmangal been just an ordinary criminal, Rehman Sahib would not have set out on such a stormy night. An arrest warrant in his name had come from a place no less than Delhi. Shivmangal was wanted on grounds of stealing and transporting valuables to countries abroad. He had even stolen treasures from the museum in Hazar Duari!

It was not raining hard, but a strong wind still blew from time to time. The road ahead lay in pitch darkness. Rehman Sahib turned around and asked, "Which way do we go now?"

Pratap said, "*Huzoor,* it's just behind Hatkhola, near the bank of the Ganga. He's right there—in Chapala's room."

Rehman was surprised. He knew Chapala. She was one of the three or four prostitutes who lived in the colony behind Hatkhola. Only the very poor visited such places. What was Shivmangal doing there?

Even though Shivmangal was a dreaded thief, he was quite old now, certainly not less than sixty. He had been evading the police for many years. Why would he be visiting prostitutes still?

Pratap said, "*Huzoor,* Chapala is his daughter!"

Rehman was amazed. Whatever the man was today, a thief or a scoundrel, he had heard that Shivmangal actually hailed from an aristocratic family. One of his uncles was a prospering businessman in Calcutta. Another had even gone abroad during the days of the Freedom Movement. Had he been alive till after Independence, he would certainly have become a minister. Could a person from such a family be a common thief?

Shivmangal's surname was Singh, but now some members of his family had started writing "Sinha" instead, and assumed a Bengali identity.

Rehman looked around. Most of the rooms in the locality were in darkness. Probably, the women inside had not got any clients on such a stormy night. They must have shut their doors and fallen asleep with the cool breeze wafting into their rooms. The doors and windows in Chapala's room were also shut, but a streak of light could be seen coming from under the door.

Getting off from the cycle, Rehman Sahib started walking towards the door.

Turning to Pratap, he said, "How did you get the news?"

Without feeling the least bit embarrassed Pratap said, "*Huzoor*, I have been visiting Chapala from time to time."

"Did you come here today also?"

"Yes, *Huzoor*."

"And then?"

"I saw someone in Chapala's room. I got curious and peeped over the fence at the back. I saw . . ."

He broke off in the middle of his speech and said, "Sir, please go ahead and knock. I will not go any further."

Saying this he turned around swiftly and vanished in the dark.

Rehman watched him for a while and laughed silently to himself. Could someone ever get another man like this Pratap Singh? Once a thief himself, now he helped the police in tracking down others like him. He visited Chapala frequently but not other girls like her. If he had been a regular here, he could easily have gone into another room. He must have had a soft spot for Chapala. Yet, he had gone to inform the police about her father, possibly in the hope of a reward.

After all this would be over, he would possibly visit Chapala some day and express sympathy for her father's arrest.

"Go and guard the back of the house," Rehman Sahib ordered Ali and Siddiqui. "In case the old man tries to escape, just shoot him down."

Saying this, he went and knocked on Chapala's door. Hushed voices audible from the room till now suddenly stopped. When he knocked once again, Rehman heard Chapala say, "No, it will not be possible today. I have an all-night customer with me right now."

Rehman Sahib knocked on the door with a greater force this time. As soon as the door opened a bit, he pushed himself in.

Shivmangal was sitting in the centre of the room. He had just started eating. On seeing the Inspector, he stood up immediately. A meal of rice, *dal* and boiled potatoes was laid out on a bone china plate on the floor in front of him. Shivmangal had just taken a mouthful or two. By his side were two large silver bowls containing *paneer* and curd. He stood with his hands still unwashed. Chapala's face looked pale and frightened.

"Siddiqui, Siddiqui," Rehman called out.

Siddiqui entered the room with a pointed rifle. "Go and stand next to him," Rehman Sahib ordered.

Siddiqui walked over to where Shivmangal stood and clutched him by his shoulders.

Chapala, almost in tears now, pleaded, "*Babu*, please let him finish his meal . . ."

Rehman Sahib said, "But, a *Mussalman* has touched him now. Can he still eat that food?"

"*Huzoor*, I am very hungry today," Shivmangal cried. "I will not be able to walk if I don't eat properly."

"Siddiqui, let him go," Rehman Sahib ordered again.

Shivmangal sat down immediately. Taking two or three mouthfuls of food he said, "Chapala, ask the Inspector Sahib to sit down. Offer him a chair."

There was no place to sit in Chapala's room—other than her bed. Rehman Sahib would not sit on it. Chapala laid out another soft rug on the floor. It was rather funny for Rehman Sahib to sit facing an offender on the same floor; but he accepted the offer and sat down.

"*Huzoor*, would you like to have some water, or maybe a cup of tea?" Chapala asked.

"No."

Shivmangal was now concentrating on his food. Chapala went inside and brought him some rice in a bowl. "Have some more rice," she said.

"Alright. Do you have some more *dal?*"

"Yes."

Rehman kept staring at the scene in front of him. Here was a daughter serving food to her father with such caring hands. Chapala now looked like any other girl from a middle-class family. She didn't have any rouge on her cheeks, nor was she wearing a cheap nylon sari. She was dressed in a simple white sari with a red border—the sort one wears every day. All this—even though she had referred to her father as an all-night client!

Rehman Sahib looked at Shivmangal and smiled to himself. How many residents of this locality could afford even a set of cheap crockery let alone such good quality porcelain! There were two silver bowls also. Not surprising, after all they were from an aristocratic family! Of course, Chapala had served water in an ordinary glass. Shivmangal must have made a great fortune. Who knows how he spent it? Why else would his daughter have to hire a room in this locality—Hatkhola!

Shivmangal finished his meal. Scraping out the last crumb of food from his plate he said, "*Huzoor,* may I please go and wash my hands now?"

Rehman Sahib gestured to Siddiqui with his eyes, asking him to accompany the man. Then he turned to Ali and said, "Go and wash that plate and bowl yourself. We have to take them to the *thana.*"

At the very thought of having to wash a Hindu's plate, Ali scowled. Seeing him hesitate Rehman Sahib lashed out, "Do as I say."

Chapala intervened, "*Huzoor,* I'll wash them myself. The tap is just outside the door."

"Where are the rest of his belongings?" Rehman asked her.

"I have no idea *Huzoor.*"

Rehman looked at Chapala with eyes full of anger. He was certain that all kinds of people including thieves and dacoits visited her room regularly. She wouldn't have survived if she had felt intimidated by such people. It was as if she had accepted everything as part of her life!

"Is Shivmangal your father?" he asked.

"Yes."

"Where's your mother?"

"She has been gone for a long time now."

"Does Shivmangal live here? Doesn't he have a place of his own somewhere else?"

"He had, once upon a time. Now he doesn't."

As soon as Shivmangal returned, Rehman Sahib stood up. Without another word he swung around and slapped him hard. This sudden spurt of anger that he felt towards Shivmangal was not because the man was a thief. He had seen many such scoundrels in his profession. But he just couldn't bear the sight of this man sitting and enjoying a meal at his daughter's place even after driving her to prostitution. On top of that he didn't seem to have any resentment or sympathy for her!

Having received such a sudden blow, Shivmangal lost his balance and sat down on the floor, resting his head in his hands. Even though most of his hair had turned white, his body was still quite strong. No one could make out that he was a thief just by looking at him. Had he dressed well and mingled with other gentlemen, he would have easily commanded respect from one and all. That was in fact the strategy he used for stealing valuables from people's houses. Using some pretext or disguise he would make his way into old aristocratic homes and start removing priceless treasures one by one.

"Where are the stolen goods?" Rehman thundered.

"Please don't hit me *Huzoor.* I'll take them out for you."

Crouching low, Shivmangal pulled out a bag from under the bed. As soon as the bag was opened, a number of things rolled out: bright and shining silver knives and forks, an ivory snuff-box, two jade dolls, and a fashionable knife with a beautifully designed cover.

"Is this all?" Rehman asked.

"Yes, *Huzoor.*"

Well, if this was indeed the entire booty, he could be jailed for a maximum period of six months only, but Shivmangal was a fish of much deeper waters. Apprehending an arrest any moment, he was always prepared with only a few stolen articles at hand.

Seeing Rehman Sahib lift his hand again, Shivmangal bent low and said, "Believe me *Huzoor,* I have nothing else. Only a few more wooden dolls, but they are not very expensive."

The dolls were taken out of the wooden cupboard. Shivmangal took them out himself. They were all terracotta figurines probably removed from some ancient temple, the kind that was of immense value to foreigners.

Rehman Sahib could make out that this was only the secondary list of stolen goods. This too was an act. The most valuable things had not been brought out yet. Shivmangal's eyes moved restlessly.

Rehman Sahib ordered Siddiqui and Ali to search the room thoroughly. Chapala didn't have many belongings; a tin suitcase, a clothes rack, and a wooden almirah were all that she had. It didn't take long to search those. In the end, nothing except a silver spoon was found. Chapala had probably hidden this without her father's knowledge, one could easily make that out from the look in Shivmangal's eyes.

Rehman lit a torch and started searching the corners. It wouldn't be surprising if he found a hole somewhere on the floor. He looked at every nook and corner to see if he could find one.

In an alcove a little above the door, he noticed a stone idol covered with some flowers and *bel* leaves. Each time the light fell in that direction, something glittered. Possibly something was hidden there.

Flashing the torch in that direction and holding the beam of light still, Rehman thought for a while. Then he told Chapala, "There's an idol there. Move it. I want to see what is behind it."

"How can I touch the deity, Sir?" Chapala asked.

Indeed, how could a prostitute dare to touch a deity? There were too many restrictions in their religion.

"Then, who kept that idol there?"

"I had requested the Brahmin priest to keep it."

Rehman Sahib began to repent now. He wished he had brought Haranath instead of Siddiqui. Haranath was a Brahmin, even though he was a policeman. It wouldn't have mattered if he had touched the idol. As for himself, Siddiqui, or Ali, touching a Hindu deity was sacrilegious.

Shivmangal said, *"Huzoor,* I'll clear that place so that you can see for yourself and feel assured. Why should you let any doubt creep into your mind?"

Yes, Shivmangal could touch a deity in spite of being a thief. Possibly, that would not be a blasphemy. But his daughter could not! Holding the idol tightly in his hand, he quickly moved aside the flowers and leaves. There was nothing at the back.

"I told you *Huzoor.* See, there is nothing else."

Rehman Sahib looked absent-mindedly at Shivmangal's hands. Suddenly he felt a shock of surprise. Turning the torch light carefully in that direction he let out a cry of alarm.

It was a small idol of the goddess Kali, an exquisitely beautiful idol with its eyes and tongue made of pure gold. But it was not only because of this; it had a greater value for some other reason. Two weeks ago an idol of Kali had gone missing from the prayer room of the Zamindar of Akandapur, and the news had been flashed in bold letters in all the important newspapers. A circular had been sent out to all the *thanas* and a prize of two and a half thousand rupees would be awarded to the person who recovered it.

Even before anybody could say anything, Shivmangal said, *"Huzoor,* I had bought this for my daughter from a fair at Natore. It is designed in bronze."

Rehman frowned angrily. He had never imagined that he would have found such a prized thing here. "You son of a—, give it to me. Give it to me right now," he roared.

Shivmangal held on to the idol tightly—"*Huzoor,* don't touch, a Hindu God."

"What? A God? Or, the stolen booty?"

"*Huzoor,* we worship this daily."

Rehman Sahib withdrew his outstretched hand. This was a very puzzling affair indeed. Who could tell whether by touching the Kali idol he would be sparking off a communal problem? It was true that the idol had been worshipped with flowers and *bel* leaves. But Shivmangal was also an extremely shrewd man.

Rehman's hands were now getting impatient to beat the hell out of this man. But he could not hit him. Shivmangal was still holding the deity in his hand. Who knew whether it was a sin to touch him now?

"Sir, don't touch that," Ali cautioned Rehman Sahib.

"Examine it carefully," Rehman ordered Siddiqui. "See if it matches with the description of the Goddess Kali that was stolen from the Zamindar's house in Akandapur."

"Sir, it matches perfectly. There's no doubt about that," Siddiqui said.

In the meantime, having heard about the arrival of the police, some locals had begun to collect around the house. Stepping outside the room, Rehman addressed them.

"Is there any Brahmin among you?" he asked.

Without a word, all of them ran away. Even Rehman Sahib knew that this was a predominantly Muslim area, and that there were not too many Brahmins here.

Maybe that man who fried cutlets by the roadside was a Brahmin. But where could he be found at this time of the night?

Turning around, Rehman Sahib asked Chapala, "Has this idol been worshipped daily?"

"Sir, it's a living god. If we don't worship it daily, will we not die horrible deaths?"

How strange indeed was all this! It didn't hurt their consciences to steal a living god, and yet it had to be worshipped every day. Had

Shivmangal brought the idol for the purpose of mere worship, or had he wanted to sell it?

"Who performs the *puja?*" he asked.

"The Brahmin priest, *Huzoor*. He lives on the other side of the river."

So, there was a Brahmin priest somewhere across the river who even visited a prostitutes' quarter to perform a *puja!* A great man indeed! Where could one contact him now?

Rehman looked at Shivmangal and said, "Let it remain in your hand. Come on, let us go outside."

"*Huzoor,* will you take it away by force?" Shivmangal asked, raising his voice.

Had this happened during the day, this man would probably have tried to spark off a communal riot. But, now there were very few people around.

Rehman Sahib said, "You know, I have orders to shoot you down, if needed. Come on."

Siddiqui was about to hit Shivmangal but Rehman stopped him. He didn't want to engage in any kind of physical contact. But it wouldn't be forbidden to touch him with a rifle, after all, it was made of just wood and iron. "Push him from the back with the rifle butt," he ordered.

"Inspector Sir, if you remove this idol from my room, what will happen to me?" Chapala asked, with tears in her eyes.

"Listen, this belongs to someone else. Now move, get out of my way," Rehman replied.

Shivmangal refused to go on a cycle. How could he ride a cycle with a Muslim while holding a Hindu deity in his hand?

Rehman Sahib ordered, "Walk—all of you."

The rain had by now changed to a heavy downpour. Dark clouds had gathered in the sky. They were to walk about seven miles in this weather. What else could be done! Had Haranath been here, Rehman Sahib would not have faced such a problem.

Then again, how was he going to keep that Hindu deity, a living god, in the *thana!* Who knew what was forbidden in the Hindu religion—and what actually amounted to committing a sin!

On reaching the *thana*, Rehman Sahib decided that he would

immediately wake up the Sub Inspector, Dhiren Saha, explain the situation to him, and then hand over charge to his Sub Inspector and Haranath. God knows, he had never been in such a difficult situation before!

The roads were by now mushy with rain water. Nothing could be seen clearly. Only the howls of wolves in the distance pierced the silence of the night.

Suddenly, Shivmangal stopped and said, "Inspector Sahib, take the silver with you. Just let me go."

"Come on you scoundrel," Rehman roared back.

"What will you all do with this statue?" Shivmangal asked again.

"Move on, move on."

"I promise you I will not sell it. *Huzoor*, it's a living god. May I be struck with leprosy if I sell it. Let me go, please."

"I said—move," Rehman ordered again.

Shivmangal suddenly lifted his hand in the air and muttered, "Then let it go to hell." He flung the idol onto the ground and heard it fall with a thud. Obviously, he did not want to keep any evidence with him.

All this while, the three men could not touch him. But there was nothing to stop them now. Their pent-up anger burst out.

"Beat him hard. Beat up the rascal," said Siddiqui, hitting Shivmangal on his back with the butt of his rifle. Ali too kept punching him, laying his hands wherever he could. Whether it was for real or whether he feigned it nobody knew, but Shivmangal immediately lost consciousness.

Holding the torch in his hands, Rehman ran to where the statue lay on the ground. After some searching, he discovered it. The idol lay on the mud, its jewelled eyes glittering in the torchlight.

Rehman Sahib bent down to pick it up, but controlled himself at the last moment. There was no one here—but even then, why touch it?

After all, it was a different religion, a different god—what if all this lost its sanctity at his touch?

Rehman turned around and ordered his men, "Here, put that man on your cycle and take him to the *thana* with you. Tie up his arms and legs first. But be very careful, Shivmangal is a very crafty man. Put him in the lock-up. Then go and see if you can find that Brahmin *meshir* who fries cutlets in that roadside shop. If you can't get him, just bring Haranath along. Inform the Sub Inspector Sahib."

After they left, Rehman Sahib kept standing alone in pitch darkness, surrounded by swarms of stinging mosquitoes. His cycle lay by the roadside. Had that stolen item been anything else, he would have easily picked it up and carried it to the *thana* on his own cycle. After all, it was only a statue.

Hordes of men and women prostrated and wept before this idol—some even made vows to be fulfilled in case God granted their wish. Some said it was a living god.

But, right now that god was lying in the mud. Would it be a sin to wash it and keep it in a cleaner place? Shivmangal had flung it onto the ground—hadn't his heart trembled even once? And to think that it would have got sold off to a foreigner just as an antique?

Rehman Sahib flicked the torch once again, pointing the light on the idol's eyes. The eyes and tongue of the stone idol were made of gold and harmonised so beautifully with the rest of the body!

Was it a new moon tonight? Suddenly, Rehman Sahib started feeling somewhat scared.

Ashamed at his own weakness, he tried to brush off his nervousness. Right from his childhood he had studied the ways and rituals of the Hindus. His own religion was far from all this. Even so, he felt a slight tremor under his skin. He could not leave this place—he would have to wait even in this darkness and suffer the stinging mosquito bites until Haranath arrived.

Suddenly, a thought flashed in Rehman's mind. He realised that within the separate circles that existed in the life of every individual—Shivmangal, Chapala, Siddiqui, Ali, Haranath or even his own—there was enough place for virtue and vice to coexist side by side.

It was as if at that moment he had stepped outside the circle of his own life. As if he was standing completely alone in this large universe. The fact that he could stand on this new moon night guarding the deity belonging to a different religion made him feel somewhat proud.

Nobody was watching him now, but that really didn't matter!

# Niaz Zaman ❧ BANGLADESH

Niaz Zaman is one of South Asia's, and the Islamic world's, most esteemed writers. A professor of English at the University of Dhaka, she has also taught at The George Washington University, and from 1982 to 1983 served as Educational Attaché at the Bangladesh Embassy in Washington, D.C., where she later completed her doctoral studies. Among her major publications are *The Art of Kantha Embroidery*—the first book-length study of the *kantha*—and *Strong Backs Magic Fingers,* about indigenous backstrap weaving in Bangladesh. As a creative writer, she has published the autobiographical novel *The Crooked Neem Tree, The Dance and Other Stories,* the titular story of which won an Asiaweek Short Story Award, and *Didima's Necklace and Other Stories.* Her other books include *The Confessional Art of Tennessee Williams* and *A Divided Legacy: The Partition in Selected Novels of India, Pakistan and Bangladesh,* which won a National Archives Award. She has edited *Contemporary Short Stories from Bangladesh,* and co-edited *Fault Lines: Stories of 1971* and *Caged in Paradise.*

# THE DAILY WOMAN

THE THOUGHT OF THE OTHER CHILD WOULD COME at odd times. Like when she was picking the rice, or sweeping the floor, or grinding the red chillies that made her hands smart. At the beginning she had thought of it—her, really, but the child had been taken so early from her that she rarely thought of it as her—when the little one who remained strained at her thin breasts. There had been so little milk for even this one that she had none to spare for the other. This one was a boy. Everyone said boys were better. They would look after you in your old age, they said. That is, if the daughters-in-law let them. Also this one had been bigger. More chance of surviving.

Every year for the last five years—she had been married one year before the first one was born—she had given birth. Not one had lived beyond a day or two. And she had thought that she too, like Fatema, was cursed. And then, she had the two together. Together, they were only a little bigger than the little ones who had died. How long would these two live? she had wondered. Would they too die after two days as the other little ones had? But three days passed, and they were still there. Only one had seemed smaller and weaker than the other. More like a wrinkled old woman. Then the two white men had come to see her with Abdul. And almost before she realized it, there was only one child left.

She did not pause as she ground the chillies. *Ghater ghat, ghater ghat.* The heavy stone roller smoothed the dry, red pods into paste. One did not have to think when one ground chillies, so one could think about the other things one had no time for. A few dabs of water, and then off again, *ghater ghat ghater ghat,* as the soft, red, paper-thin skins melted into the flat, yellow seeds and merged to form red paste. A pause to stretch her back, and then another dab of water, and the roller started going back and forth on the smooth grindstone. She must tell them to have the stone pricked once more. The pockmarks all over had disappeared. The auspicious fish design on top had also completely faded. It was really too smooth to grind the chillies. Most people had started buying powdered chillies, but there were some who liked their spices ground fresh every day, so there was still some work for daily women like her who could not work *bandha.*

She washed the grindstone. Put it back in its place under the sink. What was it like to work *bandha?* she wondered. To leave husband and children and remain in other people's houses. At least for people who worked *bandha* there was a dry place to sleep in at night. In the hut, during the rainy months of Asharh and Sraban, everything got wet. One's clothes, one's floors—everything. The smooth, hard floor, which she smeared with a mixture of cow dung and mud so that it was almost as nice as Khalamma's floor, turned to muddy paste. But people who worked *bandha* slept inside. There were some even luckier. Like Ali, who got a room all to himself, next to the kitchen. It was small, just big enough for a narrow *chowki,* and when there were guests, the drivers would be

given food in his room, so he was expected to keep it clean and just as
Khalamma wanted it. But Ali could stretch out there after his fourteen or
sixteen-hour duty—not like some others who could not go to sleep until
everyone else had gone to sleep, because one never knew when the guests
would leave or who would want to come into the kitchen for a glass of
water or a cup of tea.

The bundle on the ground stirred. Even before the tiny eyes opened
and the mouth started its fine wail, she had scooped it up and put it to
her breast, covering it modestly with her sari *anchal*, so that the head of
the baby was inside the *anchal*, and only the ragged *kantha* with which
she covered its frail limbs was visible. She had promised Khalamma that
the baby would not disturb anyone. Khalamma would never hear it cry.
The nursing soothed the baby, and it was hardly a moment or two before
it went back to sleep, its hunger satisfied for the time being. She waited a
moment longer to make sure it would not wake up and fuss as soon she
put it back on the ground. Satisfied that it was asleep, she put it back,
tucking the soft *kantha* round the little body so that it would think it
was still being held to her breast. She was fortunate that she could bring
the child to work with her. Not like Fatema who had to leave her baby
at home. Fatema had not been able to give up her job because she had a
paralysed husband who couldn't work. And she hadn't been able to bring
the baby with her to work. The baby had to be given a bottle because
Fatema could not always come back to feed it. And when the baby died,
the health worker said the milk had killed the baby. And now Fatema's
husband too was dead. It was true that in a way Fatema was better off
without a paralysed husband, but what woman would rather work than
have a family? And who would marry Fatema now? A woman who had
killed her husband and child? A black-foreheaded woman? But weren't
all women black-foreheaded? Well, not all. Not her Khalamma. Every day
a fresh sari and shoes the same colour as her sari. And she smelled nice all
the time. Sometimes like roses. Was this what Paradise must smell like?

Ali handed her the fish and explained that it had only to be scaled and
its insides cleaned out. Not cut. Khalamma wanted it to be made into a
*bideshi* dish, so she must be careful with it. And leave the tail whole. Be
sure not to nick the tail the slightest bit. After it was cooked it would look

like a fish—only its scales would be golden because of the carrots. Occasionally, when she had cleaned the fish, she had slipped one or two pieces of fish into her waist knot, but she wouldn't be able to today, she thought. The insides she could keep. They never had any use for them. Even Ali scoffed at her for eating what she was sure he ate with relish back home. The oil was particularly good to cook with *sag,* made it special. Perhaps Ali would let her have some of the cauliflower leaves that they threw away. These rich people did not know how to cook. They threw away chicken skins as well. One hardly needed anything more than a pinch of salt, a dab of oil and two pinches of *haldi* and chillies to make a tasty meal out of chicken skins. They never ate the feet either. The first day she had come to work, she had cleaned the feet and put them in with the cut and cleaned chicken. Ali had scolded her. Since that day she had kept the feet aside to take home with her. After removing the feathers carefully, she had enough skin to make into a dish for two meals.

Fridays were bad days, because that was when the weekly bazaar came and everything had to be cut and cleaned and put away in the cold box. Khalamma would be rushing in and out of the kitchen because that was the day Khalu would have lunch, and no matter how late the bazaar came he had to have it by one o'clock. In most houses the men went to the mosque for Friday prayers, but Khalu didn't. On Fridays her back hurt with all the cutting and cleaning, and she could rarely make it home before *asr* prayers. But Friday was also a good day for her. Because she could carry home all the *bashi* stuff, like the old vegetables that had been kept in the fridge and gone a little stale and dry. Fridays were also the days after their parties, and there would be *polao* to be scraped up from the *hari,* in addition to the *khabar* that Khalamma always kept for her. Nice things like chicken *korma* or beef *kupta.* Once or twice there had been *biryani* and pieces of chicken *musallam* with *badam* and *kishmish.* And of course there were always sweets. Especially *roshgulla* and *shandesh* and *laddoo.* And *halwa.*

The clothes were already soaking in a pail of warm, soapy water. She had learned this new way of washing from Khalamma. When Khalamma had first poured the soap powder into the pail and told her to wash, she had been perplexed. How was she to wash the clothes without

rubbing them with soap and then beating them on the *pukka* floor? Then
Khalamma had shown her how the water was full of soap and all she had
to do was to rub the clothes against themselves or each other. There was
no need to beat the clothes, just go rub, rub, rub, dip once more in the
soapy water and keep aside. After the white clothes were all out of the
soapy water there were a few more clothes—red, yellow, blue—that had
to be kept dry and then dipped one by one quickly into the water so the
colours did not run into other clothes. Then she could throw away the
discoloured water and fill the bucket with clean water to rinse the clothes.
Once, twice, thrice, so that there was no more soap left in the water and
the water seemed as clean as fresh water. Then squeeze all dry, all of
them, except the nylon ones. Those had to be hung until the water had all
dripped out and then hung out smoothly so that there were no wrinkles
in them. And then she could have her *chapatti* and hot tea. It was always
a pleasure to have sweet, hot tea. Two spoons of sugar in the tea—though
Khalamma herself always had tea without any sugar. How did they drink
tea without sugar? She grimaced at the thought of the sugarless tea that
Khalamma drank.

Ali explained to her that Khalamma was afraid of getting fat. All
*barolok* were afraid of getting fat. That's why she did not have sugar
with her tea. Nor rice nor potatoes. Sometimes she would go on what
Ali called a diet. Then she would have nothing but tea and toast in the
morning and cucumber in the afternoon. At night, however, she would
eat with Khalu—a spoon of rice only, or one *chapatti*, the small *chapatti*
she had Ali make for the table, not the big, fat ones that Ali made for the
kitchen help and himself. They were allowed three of the *chapattis* with
their tea. One she ate sitting in the kitchen, but the other two she took
home with the leftover *bhaji* or *jhol*. In that way she only needed to cook
a pot of rice for him.

Sometimes she wondered whether, if she had this job when the babies
were born, she would have given the little one away. But she could not
have brought both with her to work. Of that she was sure. And then it was
only after the babies were born that she had met Abdul when he came
with the *bideshis* and afterwards got her the job at Khalamma's place. Ali
was from the same village as Abdul. That is how Abdul had known that

Khalamma was looking for a daily woman to help in the kitchen. He had come with her and told Khalamma that he knew her—though he really didn't. But he had to say it, otherwise Khalamma would not have given her the job. And after that day she had never seen him again. Rahima had told her that Abdul must have got a lot of money from the *bideshis*. But she could not believe it. Why would they give the money to him and not to her?

She didn't know whether Abdul had got money, all she remembered was that those had been bad days. The days that they had first come to Dhaka from the village because the river had taken away the last bit of their land. She shivered, remembering those days. Everyone had told them how easy it was to get work in the *shahar*, and they had believed what they heard. There were always roads to be broken or built, and houses high as the sky, sprouting like frog umbrellas after the rains. And if one didn't get work as a day labourer, there were always rickshaws to pull in the city. Sometimes people said there were as many rickshaws in Dhaka city as there were people. One could keep all the money one earned after deducting what one had to pay to the *mahajan*. People in town didn't walk. So there was a lot of money in pulling rickshaws. But rickshaw pulling hadn't been easy. His legs and arms had ached and she had to heat mustard oil and rub him down. And then he had fever for three days, and she had to buy medicine for him. And during the rains no one wanted rickshaws, because everyone stayed home and there was no building either and they starved. Then they had to pay for the *chhaptra*— something they had not reckoned on. Two hundred for a place hardly big enough for the two of them to sleep in at night. And always the rain coming down, making everything wet, making the floor into mud. Then the fever had come back, and he had coughed until she thought his eyes would jump out of his head. His body had felt like fire, and she had prayed that he wouldn't die. She had promised that if he lived, she would fast for seven days, so she had fasted and the babies had popped out before the ten months and ten days that babies took to be ready were over.

How hungry she had been, and the two babies crying together were enough to make her go mad. No one she knew had ever had two babies together. No one in the *para* had seen two babies together, and everyone had come to see her and the babies. The white men had also come with Abdul to see her. The man with the red beard had explained to her— sometimes himself—but when she could not understand the way he spoke, Abdul had explained that the other white man wanted to take her child, if she would give it up, seeing she had two. The man wanted to take a Bangladeshi child because he had stayed many years in Bangladesh as a child. Now that he was grown up, and his wife and he could not have children, they wanted to adopt a Bangladeshi child. Abdul explained to her that the white man would look after the child well. Then too she must realize that she had nothing to eat herself. How could she feed one child, let alone two? So she had said yes. God who gave her two children who lived would give again some other day. The white man who wanted the child said he would bring his wife the next day. He wanted the child to be a surprise to her. That is why he had not brought her. He wanted to see the child first himself. They had been disappointed earlier.

She had looked at the girl child for a long time the next morning. But she had felt nothing in her heart for the child. She did not even feel a sense of relief that the child would have a future. *Amrika* was too far away for her to know anything about it. All that she knew about it was that these tall, pinkish-white people came from there. She didn't believe it when Rahima told her that black people also came from there. She had seen no black *Amrikun*. Only these pinkish-white people in their big cars, driven by smart drivers like Abdul. Rahima told her that she was doing a bad thing and God would be angry with her. In *Amrika* they would make her child pray to *Jishu*. She would surely go to hell because she let her child go with *Kristans*. But *Amrika* and *kristan* did not make much sense to her. All she could remember was how hungry she had been all the time, and if it had not been for the scraps of food that Rahima gave her, surely she herself would have starved and the babies too.

The two men had come the next day, and the white woman with them. She looked old enough to be the man's mother. White hair and wrinkles near her eyes. And thin. No breasts. Or behind. Flat as a dried fish. Her arms were like jute stalks and the big round bangles made them look even thinner. Everyone gathered round their *chhapra* to look at the *bideshini* who had come to take her little one away. The man with the red beard explained that there were some papers to be signed—a *tip shoi* would also be all right, if she couldn't sign her name. Just to show that the baby had been voluntarily given up by the parents, not stolen or kidnapped. Some papers were in English, some in Bengali. The same thing in both. One for the authorities in Bangladesh, one for the *Amrikuns*.

The *bideshini* held out her arms for the child. As she put the thin, wrinkled infant into the white woman's arms, she had thought how dark her little one looked next to the white woman's skin. The woman saw her looking at her arms and muttered something to her husband. The man took the child from his wife and stared at it as if he was seeing a baby for the first time. The wife took off her shiny, golden bangles and slipped them onto her wrists. She had not wanted to take the bangles. She was not selling her child for gold, but because she could not feed it. The woman bared her grey teeth in a smile and patted her arms.

After the car drove away, the people continued to crowd around them. She went back inside her *chhapra* where there was only one little figure now, sleeping peacefully, undisturbed by the departure of the sister he would never know. The child stirred, and she picked it up, just to feel it was there. One at least. Proof that she was a mother, not like the *bideshini*, who, despite all her gold, could not be a mother. The golden bangles glistened against her dark skin. And, despite herself, she wondered how much they were worth. Enough to feed them for ten years, surely. How was she to keep the bangles safe so that no one stole them? After all, the whole *para* had seen the *bideshini* giving her the bangles. She would take the bangles off at night and tie them into her waist knot so that no one could steal them without her waking up.

When Rahima came in late that night after her work, she showed her the bangles, somewhat embarrassed, lest Rahima think she had sold her baby. But Rahima had laughed. "Those are not gold," she said. "They're brass." She drew her arms back from Rahima. No, she had not sold her baby. But she could not believe that a *bideshini* would wear brass, much less give brass to a poor woman whose child she had taken. "I have seen gold," said Rahima, "if you haven't, and I know what is gold and what isn't. Go with me to the goldsmith tomorrow if you don't believe me."

So the next day she went with Rahima to the goldsmith and tried to sell the bangles to him. But the goldsmith had laughed, yes, laughed. Not asked her where she had stolen the bangles from. He didn't buy brass, he told her. She could get maybe twenty *takas* from the *bikriwala* for the bangles, maybe even twenty-five depending on their weight. But not from him.

She sighed and drank the last of her tea. So that was what a Bangladeshi girl child was worth. Two brass bangles. She picked up the boy. Would he have been worth four brass bangles?

# Keshav Meshram  🌼 INDIA

Keshav Meshram was born in 1937. A prolific author, he was a member of India's Dalit community, which comprises 15% of the population and has suffered historically as a result of India's deep caste restrictions regarding untouchability. Arjun Dangle, from whose anthology *Poisoned Bread* this story is drawn, notes that Dalit "traditionally connotes wretchedness, poverty and humiliation . . . Dalit literature portrays the hopes and aspirations of the exploited masses." Meshram spent his early life as a manual laborer, but was eventually able to secure a teaching position in the Mumbai area. *Utkhanan* (Excavation), a collection of poetry, brought him to critical attention, and his authority as an important Dalit voice was secured with publication of his acclaimed novel *Jatayu,* which reflects the plight of a talented but economically marginalized young Dalit man. The author of more than 40 books, Meshram had colleagues in the radical Dalit Panther movement, and the influence shows in the shocking conclusion of "Barriers." Generally, however, he was respected in India for holding to more moderate critical practices. He died in 2007.

*Note:* the reference to neo-Buddhism harks to the conversion of millions of Dalits to Buddhism in the 1940s and '50s under the leadership of their hero Dr. Ambedkar as a way of renouncing Hindu caste discrimination against them.

# BARRIERS

*Translated from Marathi by Priya Adarkar*

ZINGU CROSSED THE RAILWAY GATE AND WALKED on, his eyes wandering here and there. If he met a well-dressed man, he bowed to him, addressing him as "Dadasaheb," and proceeded briskly on his way.

His manner of walking seemed out of tune with his scrawny build. Perspiration welled up on his face. As he walked he kept lifting the hem of his dust-stained *dhoti* held together by knots. His shirt, too, was full of holes. He carried a roll of bedding under his arm and a thick stick in his hand. His *dhoti* had turned almost black from wiping away sweat and dust. Dirt from the road and the layer of fine dust thrown on him by passing cars and trucks had turned his naturally dark skin an unsightly colour.

Narayan followed after his father, carrying a thick gunny bag in his hand. He was as dark as his father but he was quite tall and well-built. He had visited Murtijapur twice—once when he was in the fifth standard and again when he was in the seventh. So he wasn't as awestruck as his father at the sight of the district town.

The school in his village had classes only up to the seventh standard. There were just about seven or eight households of neo-Buddhists in Dadhi village, but their enthusiasm for educating their children was great. Everyone in the village insisted that Narayan be sent to Murtijapur for his further education. They said that he could stay comfortably at the Gadge Baba hostel.

Since the decision, his mother Sitalabai had been crying for days because her dear son was going to live all alone, away from her. "Is my one and only son too much for you to feed?" she reproached her husband, driving him mad with her incessant wailing.

"Be quiet. Are your wits better than mine?" Zingu, already half sick with worry, growled even louder at his wife.

"But won't you listen to your betters at least? Deshmukh's wife said that ..." Again and again Sitalabai urged her husband not to send Narayan out of the village.

The mention of Deshmukh's wife softened up Zingu a little. "Well what does she have to say?"

"The poor thing was thinking ... her sister's at Nagpur. They've got a big bungalow and motor car. The boy could make himself useful about the house. He could study too." Sitalabai was carried away, pleased that her husband was listening to her.

"Now what's this new thing you've come up with?" said Zingu, confused. "Just the other day you were saying there's work right here in the Deshmukh field and farm house."

"But you wouldn't agree to it," said Sitalabai, gesticulating at him. "What's the use of learning so much? If the boy has to be sent away he might as well be sent according to the wishes of those who have fed us for generations." And Sitalabai stopped, heaving a great sigh.

Deshmukh had also tried advising Zingu. From Zingu's father's time they had served in the house of the Deshmukhs, who had helped their family in times of need. On festival days they were given new clothes by the Deshmukhs. Every other day, they were given buttermilk, and sometimes curd. They had standing permission from the Deshmukhs to take away cakes of cowdung fuel. Zingu was not prepared to accept that such a generous patron would not think about his interests.

But for the last two or three years there had been huge gatherings here and there. The speakers had told the neo-Buddhists to throw their idols into the river. A crowd too huge for the gaze, large enough to tire your eyes, had assembled in the village of Dadhi-Pedhi. Zingu had not seen such a large number of people since his childhood.

"People who worship animals but treat human beings like beasts— they do not belong to us and we do not belong to them." Resolutions and speeches on such themes were made. The rich and the high caste people did not stir out of their houses for three or four days. It was a new discovery for the seven or eight *Mahar* households of Dadhi village, that those whom they had feared since their childhood were equally afraid of them and of those who spoke on their behalf. Although three days before, Devake Saheb had described the gods as monkeys and pot-bellies, he was neither struck down with fever nor was his body pierced by divine wrath. He went on giving speeches everywhere, sometimes on foot, sometimes by bullock cart, bicycle or even a snub-nosed jeep. Seeing all this, they felt as if they were living in a new village. They had a chance to experience something novel.

For a month the atmosphere of the village seemed fresh and new. Then habit, need and poverty brought them back to where they were before. Rituals began again, though without the idols. Fasts, *Mariai*-worship, incense-burning, festivals, fairs, the *Govind Maharaj* feast day, the birthdays of Dr. Ambedkar and Hanuman were once again celebrated. The Deshmukhs and the Kulkarnis breathed a sigh of relief. They were happy that the people remained the same in spite of changing their caste names.

Zingu, however, was determined to educate his son. However much Deshmukh reasoned with him, he wouldn't listen. "Saheb, the two of us are here to serve you till we die. Let the boy go out. Let him see this new type of raj, this democracy, the one you mark with a cross." Zingu was firm in his decision.

Finally it was discovered that the headmaster at Murtijapur was really a relation of the Deshmukhs and Deshmukh gave a sealed letter to this relation, Dongre Saheb. Deshmukh's wife too gave a letter addressed to her brother. Guarding those two letters as if they were a hundred-rupee note, Zingu had reached the *taluka* town at noon.

As they walked they came to a well where the two of them stopped to slake their thirst. There was quite a traffic of women to and from this well. Whenever a woman came there, Zingu approached her with cupped palms in the hope of water to drink, but the woman would draw water for herself and go away. After about fifteen minutes Zingu was given some water.

"Narayan, my child, have some water," said Zingu, glancing fondly at his son, who sat apart looking glum. But Narayan shook his head. "Don't you want some water? You've been asking for it for quite some time," said Zingu, surprised. He wiped his face and hands with the end of his *dhoti* and started walking ahead.

"You go on. I'll follow you," said Narayan to his father. Zingu thought that Narayan wanted to ease himself, so he went forward slowly. The sun was declining in the sky. The shadows of the trees had lengthened and twisted. A dog ran up panting, raised its leg and pissed an oblation on the edge of the well. It thrust its head into a half-filled bucket of water and happily took a drink. Then it bit at its own tail, screamed at itself and scampered away. Narayan enjoyed the sight.

Narayan put aside his bag and got up. He threw out the rest of the water from the bucket. He propped his left foot on the parapet and lowered the bucket into the well. Slowly he drew it out, then washed his hands right up to the elbows, washed his face and his feet, wiped his feet with the cloth round his neck and tied it around his neck again.

Just then a shadow fell across him. "Who're you?" a fair old man with a Brahmin's top knot and bare to the waist asked him. Narayan went and put the bucket near the well. Then he looked at the old man and smiled. Pressing the muscles of his arm, he said, *"Baba,* I'm Narayan Zende from Janata High School."

"Good, good," said the old man, contentedly nodding, and twisting his sacred thread. Narayan smiled again.

Zingu was watching all this from a distance, his eyes popping and his heart palpitating. Narayan hastened his steps to catch up with his father.

"Narayan, my dear boy, you shouldn't do things like this. Suppose someone had seen you and caught you? It isn't good to be bold and forget our station in life. It's a sin—you can go to hell for it." The words broke out of Zingu as if he were suffocating. Narayan said nothing.

At last they reached Headmaster Dongre's house. A message went in that someone had come from Nanasaheb Deshmukh of Dadhi village. Dongre came out and enquired, "Who're you? Are you Zingu who's come from Bapu?"

"Yes sir, that's who I am," said Zingu, bowing low from the waist, with folded hands. He gently put down the two letters on the step. "Vatsalabai, bring the silver bowl," Headmaster Dongre called out. "Sit down, Zingu, you must be tired. You've been sent all the way by my sister and brother-in-law." At these words Zingu bowed again from the waist. Narayan, who was standing some distance away, was astonished at the welcoming note in the words. He came a few steps closer.

Headmaster Dongre had now noticed him. A question rose in his mind about who this boy could be, his height equal to Dongre's own. The question broke out onto his lips. "Has my brother-in-law employed a new farm-hand?" he said to Zingu, pointing towards Narayan.

Zingu hurriedly stood up again. "No sir, he's mine. He's my son Narayan."

"Really?" said the headmaster.

A middle-aged woman hurried out. There was a silver bowl in her hand.

"I've brought the cow's urine," she said. The headmaster dipped his fingers in it. He flicked a few drops here and there and scattered a few on the letters lying on the veranda. Then he returned the bowl to the lady, who quickly went inside.

The headmaster read both the letters again and again, his expression continually changing. He had the habit of winking with his left eye. From time to time he kept looking at Zingu, and then glancing at Narayan.

"Well done, Zingu. You've really got guts. That's a clever piece of thinking. We'll take good care of your young master Narayan," he said, nodding.

Zingu had conveyed something to Narayan while the letter was being read. Narayan nodded. At the headmaster's words Zingu got up again. He smiled, contorting his body in a queer fashion, and repeatedly bent down to salute the headmaster. Narayan came forward and joining his hands, said, "*Namaskar, Guruji.*"

"Why, the boy's accent is really pure. He's smart," said Headmaster Dongre, looking pleased.

By now the darkness had thickened about them. Vatsalabai had brought out food served on leaf platters. Dazzling white rice. Hot millet *bhakris.* Pounded chutney. Hot *zunka* with linseed oil poured on it. Zingu and Narayan gratefully ate their fill.

There were two aluminum pots filled with water. Zingu put the pot to his lips and drained it. Vatsalabai refilled it with water from the earthen water pot. Narayan raised the pot but poured the water into his mouth from above, gulping it down in a steady stream, his throat bobbing up and down as he drank. Vatsalabai stared at his throat and bare chest. They washed their hands, cleared away the leaf platters and went to throw them away at a distance. Two or three dogs dashed up hopefully. But the leaf platters, wiped clean of food, must have blown away with the wind, for hardly had they turned their backs, than the dogs ran barking in a different direction.

Telling the headmaster again and again to look after Narayan and reminding his son that a *guru* was next only to God, Zingu had turned back to go home. For a long time the noise of the barking dogs came through the darkness. Then that too quietened.

With his father's departure Narayan felt a great emptiness. For a while he was numbed. He could see or hear nothing. The light outside the house had been turned off. Inside, the headmaster had sat down to his evening meal. Narayan was to stay there in the night and set out for school next morning for which the headmaster was to make the arrangements for him. For a long time Narayan sat clutching his roll of bedding. It made him feel as if he were lying asleep in the crook of his father's arm.

Good arrangements had been made for Narayan at the hostel. The school too was good. Narayan had been admitted to standard VIII C. He was the tallest and best-built of all the boys in classes eight and nine. On the first day many boys asked him who he was and asked him his date of birth. "Narayan Zingroji Zende, 4 July, 1945." There was an expression of wonder on the boys' faces as they realised that this strapping champion of a boy was only twelve or thirteen years old like themselves. But apart from his size, he seemed just like one of them. One or two of them struck up a friendship with him.

"It's a good thing you are built like this. These wretched boys may look small but they're little thugs. If anyone gives me trouble, you'll hammer the fellow, won't you?" said Sampat Karhade, putting a friendly hand on his shoulder. "Let's be friends too," said Ashok Savji, introducing himself.

A few days went by. There was to be a speech by Raghba Kamble at the hostel. Raghba Kamble was a smiling man who had lost the use of a leg in battle at the height of his youth. He was head of the Backward Castes Association of Akola District. His chief occupation was to tell students about the new ways of thinking, and to explain Buddhism and humanitarianism to them in simple language. He used to make the boys laugh so much at the anecdotes he told that not just the backward caste boys but the others too were mad about him. His name commanded respect in schools and colleges. The inspector of police used to snap out a salute on seeing him and the *tehsildar* would stop his car for him.

Textbooks and notebooks were distributed to the boys in the hostel. Raghba Kamble's address had been written up on the hostel notice board. He looked after matters in Akola and Amravati districts. His train, the Bhusaval Passenger, arrived late at the station, and so Narayan, who had gone along with a few boys to send him off at Murtijapur station, reached school late.

As Narayan hurried towards his class, the headmaster appeared in front of him. Narayan tried to hide but was unable to. "Stop!" called the headmaster and Narayan halted, his head lowered. "Is this the time to come to school? Is the free food you're getting making you oversleep? You people are the government's sons-in-law, aren't you? Freeloaders, one and all!"

Headmaster Dongre was tearing a strip off Narayan, who tried once or twice to offer an explanation but the headmaster's voice was too loud. His Marathi teacher, Agashebai, came out of the class for a minute but went in again.

During the next period, Narayan went and sat quietly on a bench at the back of the class. Karhade and Savji tried very hard to get out of him what the headmaster had said but he wouldn't tell them. "I'll tell you later," was all he would say.

When the geography lesson was over, the peon brought a note. His teacher, Kakade, told him that the headmaster had summoned him after school ended and he signed in acknowledgement and returned the note with the peon.

With lowered head, Narayan explained the reason for his lateness that morning and asked for forgiveness. Some thought appeared to be going through the headmaster's mind as he listened.

"Look here, this is your punishment. You're to come to class fifteen minutes before school begins. You're to sit on the bench at the back. In the lunch break you're to go to the station to drink water. Ten minutes after school closes, you're to see me before leaving."

Narayan nodded. At first Narayan was happy that the headmaster had given thought to his studies. But he could not hear too well from the bench at the back. It was a strain to walk ten minutes to the station in the noontime sun. But he was determined to earn the headmaster's approval by working out his punishment to the letter.

One day, he had come early as usual when the school peon came and told him that the headmaster had called him. He went. "Narayan," said Headmaster Dongre, "there's a lot of work I want done." Narayan nodded.

"Our cook at home has called you. Go and see what the matter is. Take your books along with you."

"Sir, I can come this evening, straight from the hostel," said Narayan.

"No. It must be something important. Go right away."

Narayan went, but reluctantly. As he got out, Ashok Savji was coming to school. Ashok gave him an enquiring look, which Narayan answered only with a finger pointed at the headmaster's room.

Narayan trudged his way to the headmaster's house but when he reached there, there was no one at home. Just as he was deciding to go back, Vatsalabai appeared, carrying a water pot.

"Oh, you've come. I just went to relieve myself. Planning to go away, were you?" She put the water pot outside, took up some ash and went inside to wash her hands.

"What's happened is that a cart full of firewood arrived yesterday. There aren't too many logs. It was I who told Dadaji, 'Narayan's a sweet-natured boy. I'll look after everything.'" She spoke as if she were talking to herself. As she spoke she gestured to him to follow. In a large court-yard behind the house, a heap of firewood lay under the shed. She gave Narayan a *laddoo* on a castor leaf and fetched an axe for him.

Narayan looked at the heap of wood and then at the lady. She was leaning back against the door, one foot propped on a high log of wood. Narayan took off his shirt. He took out his pencil from the pocket of his shorts and put the pencil and his books away to one side. He ate the *laddoo*. "Just wait, I'll bring you some water." The lady brought some water in a bowl. "Take that water pot," she said, pointing towards a dented aluminum pot.

With a great deal of force, Narayan hit a log of wood with his axe. That aluminum water pot was the one the lady had just used for her ablutions after relieving herself. What's more, it was the same water pot from which he had drunk at his meal on the first day. Narayan declined the water with a gesture of his hand. Chips of wood flew fast and furious. By three o'clock he had split the entire heap and made a neat pile of them. He was soaked in perspiration. In the past few hours, the lady had come out several times, stood watching for a while and gone in again. The school peon had come and taken away the headmaster's lunch box.

Narayan did not put his shirt back on, but wet with perspiration as if he had just had a bath, had wrapped his books in his shirt and was walking back to his hostel, bare to the waist.

Anasuya Chabukswar, a tenth standard student in his school, was looking at him with a strange expression in her eyes. She was the daughter of Raghbadada Kamble's sister. She too had been to the station the other day.

Narayan had won all the events at the school sports—long jump, high jump, running and wrestling. The name "Narayan Zende" was well-known to the five hundred or so students in the school. This new boy from a small village had smashed all previous records. The students were all talking about how the school would shine in the district sports. That whole week Narayan was drunk with excitement.

After much entreaty Narayan went to Sampat Karhade's house. Sampat's mother listened to the news of all his exploits with interest and affection. Sampat told his mother that since his friendship with Narayan had begun, no one had picked on him. His mother brought some bananas on a plate and gave them both milk to drink. As Sampat bent to pick up the plate and glasses, his mother said, "Let it be, I'll do it myself. Just give Narayan company till the end of the street."

Though Narayan said, "I can manage on my own," he liked this courteous custom of giving a guest a send-off.

As they turned to leave, they heard someone saying in a harsh voice, "Where do you think you're going?"

Narayan said, "See what it is, I'll be off." And saying his goodbye, he briskly walked away.

"Useless brat, you've defiled our entire clan! You smuggled in this arrogant, lying, thieving outcaste. He's a *Mahar* and he had the nerve to draw water from the well and drink it. I just learnt about it." Sampat Karhade's father had him by the scruff of the neck and was dragging him along. The dismayed and bewildered Sampat was allowing himself to be dragged, yelping like a reluctant puppy at the end of a string.

Headmaster Dongre saw to it that Narayan was kept too busy to stay in class. Once he gave him the job of cleaning out the sludge from the well in his courtyard. Narayan was hard at work in the well from morning to night. Food was thrown to him from above. He ate his food right there and drank the brackish water of the well to quench his thirst.

The various teams of the district sports meet had left for Amravati. The headmaster stated that the dates for the individual events had not yet been received. The sports festival came to an end. All the boys were surprised that this year, for the first time, the post office should not have delivered the letter giving details of the individual events.

Raghbadada had come to Murtijapur. He was to visit the school along with the deputy education inspector. Narayan had told him about everything that had been happening. As he told how he had not been allowed to participate in the sports meet, his eyes had filled with tears. Narayan, who usually did not allow his emotions to show, shed tears in Raghbadada's presence.

Anasuya Chabukswar too had some complaints. Headmaster Dongre used to teach her class too, and used to make fun of her spelling and punctuation in front of the whole class.

"So what's this lady to do if she matriculates? Become a scholar like Pandita Ramabai? Or marry another Baba Ambedkar?" And he would wink in emphasis at the words "bai" and "baba."

Raghbadada listened quietly to all this and then said, "Children, our day will come. If a mouse never leaves his home for the mountains how will he ever see the sky?" With quips like this he made the children laugh while he smouldered inside. He gave Narayan a fountain pen as a present, without there being any specific occasion for it.

Raghbadada Kamble slipped into Headmaster Dongre's office. The peon politely told him that the headmaster was busy, as the deputy inspector was to visit the school that day.

But Raghbadada said, "What's this, Headmaster? You seem to be very hostile to our children. It doesn't injure just them, but the school, the district, and the country too!"

At Kamble's abrupt plunge into the subject, the headmaster was flustered. "Which children?" he said.

"Chabukswar, Zende, Zinzade, Gaikwad, Kathane, Khobragade—how many names do I have to tell you?" Kamble knew exactly what he was talking about. "And Headmaster, remember, Deputy Inspector Gavai is my brother-in-law. If you go on showing hostility to our children, make jokes about Babasaheb Ambedkar and his wife, prevent prize-winning athletes from entering sports competitions—it'll not just be a transfer for you, but the law of the jungle. It may be a democracy, but the next example of wrong-doing will mean a big stick. And if it's serious wrong-doing, the house at Dadhi will be ashes!" Kamble's threat had the finality of an ultimatum, sharp as the blow of the sacrificial axe on a buffalo's neck at Dassera. And he walked out with measured steps.

For a couple of weeks after this there was no summons from the headmaster for Narayan. All the other children were envious of Narayan. They had imagined that it was out of special affection that the headmaster called him so frequently. Narayan just smiled at this.

One day while he was having a drink from the school tank, Headmaster Dongre was making his rounds. He did no more than look at Narayan. Flustered, Narayan had greeted him but his gesture drew no response.

Narayan entered the classroom. He was sitting in the front row next to Savji. Agashebai was teaching them the lesson entitled "Indian Culture" by Sane Guruji. Narayan was writing something in his notebook. It was hard to concentrate on Agashebai's teaching that day. He had been feeling quite upset since meeting the headmaster's gaze.

On his way back to the office, Headmaster Dongre passed Narayan's classroom. The squeaky noise of his shoes filled the corridor. Then he halted and turned back. His steps came towards Class VIII C. He came into the classroom. The entire class rose and greeted him. "*Namaste Guruji.*"

At a gesture from him the class sat down. He often made a casual visit to a class in this manner. Agashebai went on teaching.

"We have inherited a great legacy worth teaching the entire world," Agashebai was saying in a high-pitched voice. As Headmaster Dongre was leaving the classroom he stopped for a moment at Narayan's bench. He had a good look at the pen in Narayan's hand and peeped into his notebook. "What's this you've drawn?" his voice boomed out, sudden as a drum-beat. Agashebai stopped abruptly. And all the students started staring at Narayan. "Nothing, Sir, nothing," said Narayan, rising, his notebook covered with his hand.

"See me in my office before you go home," ordered the headmaster, his former grim expression restored to his face, and he went out.

"What've you been up to?" asked Agashebai. "Nothing, nothing," said Narayan, shaking his head violently. "Who knows what you've done to annoy him?" said Agashebai, pulling the notebook away from him.

Her face fell. She returned the notebook to Narayan and said to the children, "I'd like you to read now, I've got a headache," and she sat down on the chair. In his notebook, Narayan had written "Indian Culture" and then "Sane Guruji." There were no further words on the rest of the page. He had not taken down a thing Agashebai had said. He had just used his pen to draw a picture of a donkey.

In the evening Headmaster Dongre said to him, "Don't draw such stupid things. And don't use a pen. You'll spoil your handwriting." As he spoke he was briskly signing, one after another, the papers on his desk, reflections of light gleaming from the cover of his pen.

Narayan nodded. "Don't draw anything like that again . . . so, will you come to my house tomorrow morning?" Narayan nodded again and left the office.

When he went to the headmaster's house the next morning Dongre was about to leave for school. Narayan sat down on a block of stone on the veranda. Vatsalabai had brought him some tea in a thick broken cup without a handle. Narayan said, "Sir, I just had some tea. If I have any more it'll kill my appetite."

"Why don't you have it since it's offered with such love?" Vatsalabai had taken the cup from Dongre's hand and gone inside. Narayan gazed at the retreating cup, so delicate and milky white, and drank down his tea in one angry gulp and banged down the cup. "Just see to things in the house," said Dongre, "I'm off." He put on his coat and went off to school, his shoes crunching the ground.

Narayan spent that day at Headmaster Dongre's house, reweaving tapes onto the cots. Vatsalabai moved around him, addressing him caressingly. Narayan did not eat any lunch. Although Vatsalabai asked him many times, "Shall I serve you lunch?" Narayan said each time, "No, I'm fasting today." Finally she stopped importuning him.

There was a bustle of dusting and tidying at the school as preparations for Gandhi Jayanti got under way. The classrooms gleamed with cleanliness. Speeches were learnt by rote. The political leaders of the village dressed themselves in dazzling white and moved cautiously through the different neighbourhoods. A special programme had been arranged at the hostel too. The teachers and the villagers were to visit the hostel along with the chief guest.

Raghbadada Kamble too had arrived. Anasuya, looking very grown-up in a white sari, handed out flowers to the guests as they arrived. Some guests took the flowers from her smiling; others avoided touching them. There were speeches by the leaders. Raghbadada too gave a speech of gratitude. He declared emphatically that men everywhere were the same. There was a rattle of applause. But some of his listeners sat with stony faces.

Headmaster Dongre was cracking jokes as he accepted a *jalebi* from Narayan's hand and ate it. He was chatting with the others present. The *jalebis* had been sent by the local Gujarati Samaj and it was Kamble who had asked Narayan to distribute them.

Two days later a summons came for Narayan in the evening. Headmaster Dongre ordered some medicines for Vatsalabai's stomach-ache from the tribal settlement about a mile away.

It was not Narayan's practice to say no when asked to do something. He kept in mind his father's words that a *guru* was next only to God. He felt dejected.

That evening—it was a Saturday—he met Savji as he left the city limits. Savji stopped him, exclaiming, "You're going all alone where the tribals live! They'll kill you!" But leaving Savji behind he went ahead, pushing through the darkness.

The darkness had deepened considerably by the time Narayan returned to the headmaster's house. It was after nine. The "medicine" given by the Bhil, Desa, was *Mahua* liquor. A policeman by the railway crossing tried to stop Narayan, who fled for his life.

Headmaster Dongre seemed surprised to see him. "Didn't anyone stop you on the way?" He sounded disappointed. Narayan shook his head.

As mealtime at the hostel would by then be over, Narayan agreed without a fuss when asked to stay on and dine.

He was very conscious of the reek of *Mahua* liquor from the house. Narayan was sitting on the veranda eating his dinner off a leaf plate. The headmaster's voice grew louder. He was rambling. As he ate Narayan remembered the gossip he had heard about the headmaster in the hostel. What was Vatsalabai to him? Why hadn't they married? He had heard all about the headmaster's love of religious rites, his observance of the rules of ritual purity, his habit of drinking on Saturdays—both heard and experienced them.

"Gave me a *jalebi* with your own hand, you mongrel dog!" the headmaster was muttering. "How did you dare?" Vatsalabai was trying to lead him inside by the hand. "Desa Bhil spared you. Constable Arjuna also spared you. The cheats!"

Narayan had returned to the hostel. For a few days Narayan was not to be seen in class. Headmaster Dongre enquired where he was.

"Sir, he has gone to Akola with Raghbadada for Anasuya Chabukswar's engagement," Ashok Savji and Sampat Karhade informed him.

The night was heavy with darkness. Cicadas chirped. It was a Saturday, Headmaster Dongre's day of rest. The whole of the past week Narayan had been absent from school. Dongre had written to his sister and brother-in-law at Dadhi that if Narayan had returned to the village, they should keep him there or send him to Nagpur to work.

In the middle of the night Narayan swiftly made his way to the headmaster's house. He was dressed in a *dhoti* and turban. The whole house was silent. The smell of liquor still lingered. Narayan sprinkled kerosene all around from the bottle that he had. He struck a match and threw it on a pile of wood. There was a burst of flame. Narayan quickly turned away.

Narayan, now dressed in shorts, was going to Akola in the Nagpur-Bhusaval Passenger. From the train he could see that the house corner was a roaring mass of flames.

## Jharna Rahman ❦ BANGLADESH

Jharna Rahman was born in 1959. She received her M.A. in Bangla from the University of Dhaka and has been writing for the last thirty years. As a poet, author of fiction, and playwright, she deals with the various crises, obstacles, hardships and potentialities of Bangladeshi society with all its multidimensional joys and sorrows. Her 19 published works include the short story collections *Swarna Tarbari*, *Agnita*, *Krishnapakhsher Usha*, and *Perek*, the poetry collection *Noshto Jotsna Nosto Roudro*, and the play *Briddha o Rajkumari*. An Assistant Professor of Bangla at Bir Shreshtha Noor Mohammad Rifles Public College, she is also a regular singer on national radio and television.

# ARSHINAGAR

*Translated from Bangla by Shabnam Nadiya*

ARAFAT AWOKE. HE SAT UP IN BED.

A zero-watt bulb dimly illuminated the room. Five children scattered here and there on the enormous bed, under the mosquito net. The pungent odour of piss. All three of the younger children peed in bed. Halima was sitting up. Her long untidy hair flowed downwards, covering both sides of her face. But Halima was not busy changing the pee-soaked sheets. She sat as if she was stricken by some bedevilment of the night. She gazed with dazed eyes. Which way was she staring? Was Halima in a waking dream?

Arafat felt as if Halima was watching him.

Halima's face had been bent over the sleeping face of Arafat.

Her hair was tickling his cheek.

It was Arafat that Halima had been watching.

Had the astounding event that happened two months ago created a different response within Halima? Arafat examined Halima intently.

Arafat could tell whenever Halima got up and left his side.

Halima had to get up at least two to four times each night anyway. There was always one baby or another around. They were usually not that far apart in age. Changing the nappies. Preparing the milk. Stopping them from crying. Breastfeeding them—these were the things she had to do. She would lie down again. Arafat could tell what she was doing even as he lay in bed. He would be irritated at having been woken up. Suppressing his sleepiness, he would say in an irritated voice—Why can't you get rid of the girl's habit of nursing at night? She eats rice now as well. What does she need a bottle at night for? The two of them disturb my sleep. One is wailing all night long, the other is nursing. All kinds of botheration.

Halima understood quite well what this "all kinds of botheration" meant.

One by one she had become the mother of five children. The children were afraid to sleep in a separate room. In any case, although Aklima and Tahrima were eight and six, the third, Sobhan, was still much too young. Four years old. The next two were right on top of each other. Jannat was two and the youngest girl barely six months old. Halima slept in a huge bed with all of them. There was a separate bed for Arafat in the next room. He could easily go and sleep there without having to endure all this botheration. Arafat read for quite some time after the *esha* prayers. The *Neyamul Qur'an,* the *Sayyedul Mursalin,* the *Qasasul Ambia,* the *Tazqeratul Ambia,* the *Fazayale Amal* or the *Fikah Sharif.* The alarm clock was set. He would get up at the right time for *tahajjud* prayers. The prayers were said with absolute absorption in the isolated room. He could place himself at his Lord's feet with a deep sense of sacrifice. Still this multi-dimensioned bed—the nagging of the children, childhood illnesses, the stench of pee and shit, milk, medicine, sleep, rocking—attracted Arafat. Unless the intoxicating aroma of Halima reached his nose, the night did not seem like night at all.

While Halima busied herself with getting the children to sleep, Arafat had a lot to do as well. He was the owner-cum-manager of the Sonali Printing Press up in town. The accounts, orders, deliveries for the press, the different jobs for the different clients—most of the workers were prone to slacking. Arafat could barely handle it. A lot of times it was Arafat himself who had to check the proofs to ensure timely delivery. Then alongside the toil for this life there was the toil necessary for the afterlife. Devoted, untiring Arafat. When he came to bed after finishing everything, Arafat's weary body would yearn for conjugal bliss.

Most of the times Arafat would call Halima to his bed.

But that was more awkward. Perhaps the baby would start wailing just as he was about to climax. Halima would flinch and turn herself off. Of course, that did not make a difference to Arafat's sexual enjoyment. But the sweetly pleasurable numbness of letting his sex-weary body rest on his wife's—that he did not get. The moment he ejaculated, Halima would disengage herself from her husband. Embarrassed, awkward, apologetic, she would bunch her petticoat between her legs and shuffle off to the next room. As she left she would present him with some excuse in a guilty tone—Khuki's got a bit of a temperature. She won't go to sleep if she hasn't got my nipple to suckle on. I'll come back at dawn.

It was to avoid all these botherations that Arafat would come to the big bed. Even if the youngest one awoke while he was at it, Halima would cling to her husband riding her with one arm while patting the awakening child with the other with a peculiar expertise. Placing herself in this simultaneous role of wife and mother, Halima felt bewildered at times.

Why was this happening? Was sin entering Halima through these acts? A child. An innocent angel. This thing in front of them . . . but this also was a duty. Husband. Her shelter in both this life and the next. Whose place was right after Allah's—it was her sacred duty to provide him with pleasure as well. Halima couldn't think beyond that.

So while her child suckled on one of her breasts, Halima would offer the other one to Arafat to fondle and kiss. She pondered the mysterious ways of the Creator as she satisfied both husband and child.

Arafat was very happy.

Halima was such a good little wife. Just what he had wanted. Salt of the earth. Their family was large, a joint family. Like a phalanx of unending mouths. Six brothers, two sisters, father, mother, bedridden elderly grandmother, widowed childless aunt, maid, cattle-tender, servant, other labourers, all in all a veritable marketplace of twenty-two people. Although his sisters Salema and Fatema were married, they spent most of their days at their father's home with their three or four brats.

Halima was the eldest daughter-in-law of this household. For the first six years of her marriage she had been the only one. In the last four years the number of daughters-in-law had increased to three: Johora and Ambia were the two wives of the brothers Shahjalal and Badruddin. They were looking for a wife for the fourth brother, Nawshad.

Arafat's father, Mowlana Mohammad Zulfigar Ali, was a very religious man. An elder of the village. Secretary of the village's Mosque Committee. He was an honoured arbiter in the various disputes, judgments, problems of the Dashra village. By the good grace of Allah, he directed the happenings of his home within the confines of this huge house, Ali Manzil, in accordance with the regulations of Islam, the strict discipline of the *Shari'ah*. All six sons were very obedient. Religious. Of good character. Both Shahjalal and Badruddin were *madrassah* teachers. The fourth son, Nawshad, was a reporter at the *Daily Sunrise* in Dhaka. The younger two were still students. His daughters were as pretty as fairies. So he had handed them over to eligible grooms of reputable families at a tender age. Both his sons-in-law lived in Saudi Arabia. So the daughters spent most of their days in the loving care of their parents. On top of all this, he had this huge house covering five or six *bighas* of land with fruit trees, cattle, poultry, fish. Where was the joy in all this if it could not be enjoyed with grandchildren?

Fifteen-year-old Halima had been bewildered when she first arrived in this enormous, jam-packed household. Most bewildering were the dark narrow rooms of the female quarters—the *andarmahal*. So many rooms! Like rows of shops! A dining room for the men, a dining room for the women, kitchen, pantry, the grandmother-in-law's room, the parents-in-law's room, one for the cousin, for her sister-in-law, for the grown-up girls, for prayer—rooms for so many different things. Halima had no idea how many rooms there actually were in the outer quarters, not even after ten years of married life in this house. The sitting room, for the *maulvis*, for her brothers-in-law, the *maktab*, for the servants . . .

It was rare that Halima needed to set foot in the outer yard beyond the *andarmahal*. Occasionally when she was on a rare visit to her parents, or was suffering from some severe illness or pregnancy-related problems—when she needed to visit the maternal and child healthcare hospital uptown—only then. Other than that, the women of this house, especially the daughters-in-law, were inhabitants of the *andarmahal*. Their mysterious world existed behind the strict veil. The men of the household could at least hear the voices or the sounds of laughter of the daughters of the house; the daughters-in-law never spoke above whispers.

Halima had become so accustomed to this that even when she whispered with her children, she would gesture with her hands, fingers, eyes and head rather than use her voice.

Her eldest daughter, Aklima, would say sometimes—Mother, are you mute? You always speak in gestures! Halima would smile. She would caress her daughter's head and reply—It's not good for women to talk so loudly. It's a sin if other men get to hear the voices of women.

Aklima would argue—Mother, are my uncles, my grandfather, Uncle Dayal "other men"? They are of our own household!

Still, can we tell from inside here when people who are not of our household come or go? Anyway, if you get a bad habit once, it's no good trying to get rid of it. So you have to practise these things from when you're young. You should speak in a soft voice, gently and politely. You should read the Qur'an in a low voice. So that only you can hear your own voice. You should read your books silently. That way what you study enters your heart. But it is best to read the Qur'an aloud. Always keep your head covered.

Aklima would cover her head more precisely while listening to her mother's words with intense concentration. As if Halima was not talking, as if she was droning the Qur'an . . .

Never be without the veil. Do you know, even after death one must continue practising *purdah*. When a woman dies, no one other than her own brothers, father and husband can see her face. Similarly, the face of a dead man cannot be seen by women other than his mother, aunts, wives, daughters. Women will bathe the dead bodies of women; men will do it for men.

Tahrima would also listen to her mother's preaching with great interest. Because Halima would tell them so many stories in between the preaching. Saddam's paradise, the tale of the angels Harut and Marut, the ark of the Prophet Noah, the serpent staff of the Prophet Moses, the drowning of the Badshah Feraun in the Nile, the magical throne of the Prophet Suleiman, Khare Dazzal and Imam Mahdi—so many different sagas rested in Halima's treasury! Tahrima loved hearing about the *hurs* and the *gelmans* of paradise, and about the fruit of the *Bancchataru*. And she hated hearing about the Gacchak Well, the Gislin Falls and the Zaqqum Tree of Hell. Whenever Halima began to talk, the children would gather around her one by one, hungering after a tale.

Tahrima shuddered when she heard the rules for bathing the dead—Mother, then how come father has bathed me so many times? He wiped my privates clean when I was naked. Was it a sin, Mother? Father is a man, and I'm a woman, isn't it so, Mother?

Halima smiled—Silly girl. He's your father. He gave you life. To a father a daughter is a gift from paradise. Pray to Allah—Allah, give us another sister. If it were Aklima, you, little Jannat and another little girl, it would be lovely, wouldn't it, dear?

Halima strokes her swollen, seven-month-pregnant belly. Yes, it would be lovely.

Tahrima opens her palm like a flower. The thumb is Sobhan and the other four—paradise. Four sisters. She says to Halima—What is the thumb, Mother? The one brother? Is he Hell?

*Nauzubillah.* Halima is confounded.

She would often face these little stumbling blocks while trying to teach the children about this world and the next, fate, virtue and sin. Quickly she said—No, silly. Why should your fingers be Heaven or Hell? You were just counting your brothers and sisters on your fingers. You gave your thumb to your brother, and the remaining four you took for yourselves. One is still inside my tummy, you don't even know whether it's a brother or a sister!

The next moment the solution occurs to Halima.

The thumb is the guardian of the four other fingers. It looks small. But it has more knowledge. Can you hold anything with only your four fingers? Can you pick up a fistful of rice? A pen? A spade? A plough? Why, you can't even pick up a flea! Those four taller fingers—they're totally worthless without that smaller thumb. In the same way women are worthless without men. Hence, your younger brother is also your guardian. Even if he is younger.

Tahrima found it funny. From then on she began calling Sobhan "Ole Thumb." The grownups started calling him that too. Pretty soon, the "thumb" dropped off, becoming Ole Man.

Ole Man was full of life. Running around here and there all the time. Halima would always be very worried about this only son of hers. But it was just that—a bit of worry. At times her heart would begin pounding. The boy had been out of sight for quite some time. Had he gone down to the pond? Climbed the gate onto the outer wall? Or perhaps walked to the high road? Rickshaws, autos, trucks were rushing by constantly.

But the next moment Halima's worries would lose themselves in the hundred things she needed to do in the house. The cooking fire was constantly alight in the kitchen. Huge pots were bubbling with curry like the food for a funeral. Lentils. Vegetables. Rice in an enormous pot.

Halima's raw gold complexion was turning coppery from her constant exposure to the intense heat of the kitchen fires. During the summer days, her whole body would be covered in a reddish-white heat rash like *kaun* grains. Locks of her hair would tumble down onto her face drenched with sweat. The heat rash on her face would grow red and inflamed from constant itching.

Sometimes a few drops of sweat would drip into the lentils or the vegetables. So Halima always kept her head covered with a bonnet with a sponge border. It made her head very hot. But what else could be done?

During the daytime Arafat came home once, at noon. He finished bathing, said his afternoon prayers and had lunch before leaving for the press again. Her mother-in-law sat in front and tended to the sons' meals. She confessed her bias in favour of her sons quite frankly. She took good care that none of her sons became too attached to his wife's skirts.

Most days Halima never got to see her husband before bedtime.

Work, work and work.

At times it felt as if this vast world of Allah's had only been created to feed humans. From dawn to dusk, all this running around, just for food!

Arafat was without any worries.

No one in the house had any complaints against his hard-working, devout, subservient, simple wife. It made Arafat proud to think that this house could not run without his Halima. He had another secret pride as well.

Halima was very beautiful. A round, fair face. Large, soulful eyes under deep blue brows—intense and calm like a river. When she smiled, her teeth emerged like rows of pearls. Whenever Halima heard praise from her husband about her teeth she would start smiling and then feel embarrassed, covering her mouth with the border of her sari. By now it had become her habit.

When he first saw Halima's face during the *shahnazar* at the wedding, Arafat had flinched in amazement and fear. Such beauty! She wasn't the daughter of a *jinn*, was she? Could a human being possess such beauty? Beauty was destruction. A venomous serpent. As soon as he had brought his bride home, Arafat declared that the men in the immediate family would get to see the face of the bride only once during the *bou bhat*. That would be it—forever. This ruling would be in force even for his brothers. They were "other men" to their sisters-in-law. Even if sisters-in-law were supposed to be like their mothers, they were *mahrum*.

Halima knew only the names of her brothers-in-law. She sometimes saw their shadowy silhouettes. When there was need to talk to them, speech was conducted from behind a door or a curtain in a low voice.

At times Halima felt that even her husband Arafat was unknown to her.

The man was not to be seen throughout the day. The little time they were together—it was as if Halima could not raise her eyes to Arafat's virtuous, bearded face. It was Arafat who would gaze at Halima's face like a man intoxicated. Her whole body would shiver. As if under the gaze of another man.

Halima would grow anxious and say—Why do you stare like that? What are you looking at?

Arafat would kiss his wife's face and reply—At a *houri* from paradise. Allah has given me a *houri* from paradise right in this world.

Arafat's praise would make Halima more embarrassed: resting on Arafat's chest she would scrunch herself up into a ball and say—Allah has given me paradise on this earth as well. You are my paradise.

Now it felt to Halima as if a *zaqqum* tree had taken root within this heavenly garden of happiness. That tree was extending its branches, entwining her head to feet. Engulfing her.

Halima couldn't sleep. She stared at the sleeping Arafat in the dim light of the zero-watt bulb. Who was he? A strange shiver ran through her body. Was this Arafat? Father of her five children? An ache began in her heart. She felt all muddled inside her head. As if someone was grinding her brains.

Halima could not forget that unbearable memory of two months ago. Would she be able to forget it in the rest of her life? Not just Halima, every single member of this household, even the people of the village— would they ever be able to forget it? Had anything as incredible as this ever happened before? Only the Divine Being knew what game He was playing with Halima.

Arafat was now a legend of Dashra village. The hero of the story of how God's chosen follower had been resurrected after death. It was still a fascinating story for the villagers—an unbelievable tale.

Two months ago a terrible accident happened on the Dhaka-Aricha Highway. A bus carrying passengers lost control and overturned into a deep ditch about three or four kilometres after crossing Savar Bazaar. Seventeen people were killed on the spot. The rest were critically injured. The villagers nearby recovered the dead bodies and laid them in rows beside the road. The police, journalists, villagers, passersby gathered at the scene of the accident. It was chaotic. Amid all this a journalist suddenly began screaming—Brother, my brother. A moving, heart-rending affair.

It appeared as a boxed news item in the next day's papers. Reporter Nawshad went to cover the massive accident on the Dhaka-Aricha Highway and discovered the dead body of his elder brother. Nawshad had gone to Jahangirnagar University to cover a terrorism-related incident. He rushed to the scene of the accident as soon as he heard of it. There he identified the body of his brother Arafat, who had been staying at the Kakrail Mosque in Dhaka for the past few days to attend a *Tableeg*. He was killed on his way back home. Pictures of the dead Arafat and the journalist Nawshad appeared in the papers.

Everything happened very quickly. The news of Arafat's death reached his home before his corpse did. Arafat was popular because of his honesty, his piety and his courteous behaviour. And he was important because he was the eldest son of Mowlana Zulfiqar Ali. When Nawshad brought his brother's dead body home after finishing with all the hassle of the police, the post-mortem, the death certificate, etc., it was close to midnight. After eleven.

Still, almost the entire village gathered around. Arafat's daughters hid their faces in their grandmother's lap, crying, scared at seeing their father's disfigured, crushed face. Halima took one look at the face and fell to the ground like a cut vine. She lost consciousness. Nawshad babbled on about how good-looking his brother had been and wept. He turned aside the part of the face that was mutilated. Zulfiqar Ali took to bed mourning his son. The sisters stroked his face and beard like madwomen and wailed—*Bhaijan*, where have you gone, leaving us behind? Open your eyes. Look, your Ole Man is sitting by your head. *Bhaijan*, please, look.

Ole Man only gazed in incomprehension.

Death he understood only slightly.

He said—Why did Abba come by bus? If he had come by plane he wouldn't have died. There are planes in Dhaka!

Arafat was to be buried the next day after *zohr*. A piece of land on the eastern side of the pond, bordering the mango-jackfruit grove, was selected as the family graveyard.

Arafat's face was shown for the last time to the women of the house before his *janaza*. Her face on Arafat's face, Arafat's mother began gasping. Aklima and Tahrima were scared of their father's mutilated face. They covered their eyes with their fists, screaming, "Abba, Abba."

Salema, Fatema, Zohra and Ambia looked upon the face of their brother and brother-in-law amid silent prayers.

As she looked at her husband's face for the last time, Halima thought—They had spent so many years together, yet it was as if she had never really looked at her husband properly. As if she had never had the strength to raise her eyes to his face without shame. A feeling of needless yet powerful embarrassment, a secret shame had always kept her husband a distant person. Today he had truly gone far away. She would never see him again. Not in this lifetime.

At the last moment, an emotion racked her body, twisting it violently. She clasped at her dead husband, rubbing his *surma* and *loban*-dust-bedecked face with her own. She washed away the preparations for his final journey with her tears. Today no shame restrained her emotion.

A *gandharaj* tree had been planted at the head of the newly dug grave.

The women were reciting the *khatam-shafa* in the *andarmahal*. Halima herself had taken on the responsibility of reciting the *Kalema Tayyeba* twenty-five thousand times.

The Qur'an was being recited in the outer quarters. It was to continue for four days. A discussion meeting was to be held in the presence of the important and respected people of the area. Nawshad became busy with all these arrangements.

The neighbours had brought over food. The cooking fires would not be lit for four days in this household. The elderly women of the neighbourhood were trying to coax the mourning women into eating something.

Around ten in the evening, the news arrived like a sudden bolt of thunder.

Islam, the elder son of the Talukdar household next door, came to deliver the news—they had just received a phone call saying that Arafat hadn't died. He was alive. It was Arafat himself who had spoken on the phone. He would reach home the next morning.

Everyone was dumbstruck for some time at the suddenness of this news. Then the extreme shock made every single person in the household restless. They had buried Arafat with their own hands. His body had been identified by his own younger brother. Shahjalal and Badruddin had gone to bring the body home. The whole village had looked at him for one whole night and half a day. His father, mother, brother, sister, wife, daughters, relatives, everyone was mourning his death. They had turned to stone on seeing his dead body. How could Arafat still be alive? Wasn't there some kind of mystery here? Was Islam sure that he had recognized the voice? The people of the house twisted within a spiral of belief and disbelief, sorrow and joy, confusion and amazement.

Arafat arrived and stood in the front yard at eight in the morning. He called, "Where's Mother?" in an eerie, broken voice and ran to the *andarmahal*.

Amazement! Wonder without limit. It was Arafat who had returned. Yesterday's newspaper in his hand.

The news spread before the wind. First as a rumour—the man they had buried the day before—that same man had risen from the grave the next day. He had walked to the front of his home. Gradually the dramatic colours of the incident began to fade. And the essence emerged.

The next day, again, there was a boxed news item.

Two people with exactly the same appearance. The parents, siblings, even the wife of the living Arafat had believed the anonymous dead man to be Arafat. The true identity of the dead man was yet to be discovered.

On the evening of the accident, another follower of Arafat's *pir* had suddenly died of a heart attack at Kakrail Mosque. Arafat had to leave for a remote village in Netrokona with the dead body. When Arafat's own household was occupied with mourning and arranging for his funeral, the same preparatory rituals were going on in that other household. Arafat had been busy all through that day with these arrangements. When the burial was over, he heard about the accident at Savar from people. Then he heard about the identification of a dead body by a reporter. The name of the reporter, the name of the village also reached his ears. Worried, Arafat got hold of a newspaper from a local teacher and was astonished. Arafat couldn't find any similarity between himself and the dead man. Except a general similarity due to the beard and the hair. But he became alarmed thinking of what might be going on at his home. At the suggestion of the local people, he went to the police station and informed them of the whole incident and then called the Talukda house.

After Arafat returned, a different kind of celebration went on in the village for a few days. The whole village poured in to see Arafat. And along came the reporters. Listening to Arafat's life story, exhuming the dead body, re-photographing the dead man, collecting his clothing, attempting to identify him—it all went on. Finally, after six days, the dead man's wife and father arrived from Tangail. The dead man was Abdul Hanna, *muezzin* of the Tangail Jame Mosque. He had been on his way to his sister-in-law's, to visit his sister who was ill.

*Muezzin* Hanna of Tangail received the honour of a first-class citizen in the family graveyard of Zulfigar Ali of Manikganj. It was the earth of this place that Allah had destined for him.

In time the furor raised by this incident died down. The story spread its branches, becoming a great tree. A tree of divine miracle. The story was this—whatever one wished to say, it was through Allah's will that Arafat had been resurrected. He was truly a man who had arisen from the grave. Not a man. A *jinn*.

The joy, excitement, amazement of the inhabitants of the Ali house also died down gradually. But silently another tumult was aroused within Arafat. At first Halima didn't notice. In her joy in regaining her husband, she was engrossed day and night in grateful prayers and counting the rosary.

Amid all this, one day she noticed that Arafat was looking at her with an intent gaze. Halima no longer hid herself behind the veil of embarrassment she had used for so long. She looked at her husband's face with love. Certainly Arafat was also afloat on this tidal surge of new and deep understanding. As if they had been reborn.

One day Halima shivered all over.

Why did Arafat watch her like that? Was Arafat truly Arafat? Or was he a *jinn*?

Trembling furiously, somehow she managed to ask Arafat in a wavering voice—What do you look at like that?

Arafat said in a strange voice—At you.

Why? Haven't you seen me before? Don't you know me?

Yes, I know you. But Halima, don't you know me? After seeing me for such a long time . . .

Oh dear, why wouldn't I know you? You're the person closest to me. Without you . . . As she spoke of her simple emotions, Halima lifted her candid gaze towards Arafat.

Arafat's voice changed even more—Then how could you mistake that *maulvi* from Tangail for me?

Halima shivered. What did Arafat want to say! She managed to say—But everyone thought the same. Father, mother, your siblings, daughters, I swear by Allah, I've never seen so similar a . . .

A wave of fire emerged in Arafat's voice—Forget about father and mother. They're old. They can't see properly. Anyway, they were distraught on hearing that their son had died. Forget about my siblings or other relatives. No one can sit around waiting to look at the face of someone who had just died. They have to mourn. They have to weep. They have to arrange for the burial. But you? You're my wife! Shouldn't you have been able to recognize me at a single glance?

Halima felt helpless. She could search through the whole world for an answer to Arafat's question but not find one.

Halima truly could not understand how blind the news of her husband's death had made her. Why hadn't she recognized him once she had regained consciousness? Why hadn't she been able to tell that this was not her husband, even after rubbing her face all over the face of a stranger?

Harsh guilt, a deep sense of sin, a terrible fear like a darkness covering the horizon pervaded her senses.

Within her stupor, Halima quickly turned over the pages of the ten years of her married life. There she could not find a single private moment, where she had seen, known, possessed Arafat as her very own, within herself. As if, with all the responsibilities, activities, the day-to-day being busy with the household, shyness, hesitation, fear, respect, Halima was a dweller in a different land.

Arafat placed a tender hand on Halima's back.

What's wrong, Halima? Why are you sitting up? Do you want to go outside? Are you feeling ill?

Halima didn't answer. She gazed at Arafat with unfamiliar eyes. As if she was within a trance. Arafat pushed his wife gently—Halima, what's wrong with you? Have you had a dream? Do you want a drink of water? What are you looking at like that?

Suddenly Halima woke up from her trance. She looked at Arafat with an intense gaze. There was fear in her eyes. Arafat was scared. He took her by the shoulders and shook her again—Halima, hey, Halima?

Inside, he was afraid. His taciturn wife wasn't going mad, was she?

Halima hissed at him—Who are you? Are you really Aklima's father?

Arafat got down from the bed quickly and turned on the lights. He brought her water.

Drink some water, go on, drink it. You've become weak. Neurotic. No more fasting for you.

Halima drank the water. She continued to look at Arafat with the same fixed gaze as he stood with the glass in hand under the bright light.

Arafat stroked her head and her shoulders.

Are you scared, Halima? What's there to be afraid of? I'm here! I'm right here!

Halima asked again—Who are you?

Arafat laughed—You've been dreaming. You've gone off your head. Don't you know me?

Halima's thoughts roamed through the sky and the earth as she slowly shook her head from right to left.

## Pradeep Jeganathan 🌸 SRI LANKA

Pradeep Jeganathan was born in Colombo in 1965. Educated at Royal College, MIT, and Harvard, he went on to earn his Ph.D. in cultural anthropology at the University of Chicago. He has written extensively on the anthropology of violence, and has taught the subject at Chicago, the New School's Graduate Faculty, and the University of Minnesota, where he was McKnight-Land Grant Professor from 2000 to 2002. He is now a Senior Fellow at the International Centre for Ethnic Studies in Colombo and edits the Centre's scholarly journal, *Domains*. In 2004 he was short-listed for the Gratiaen Prize for his story collection *At The Water's Edge*, from which "The Street," with its all-too-familiar portrait of Developing World exploitation and trafficking, is drawn.

# THE STREET

THE MEN RAN TOWARDS THE CARS AS THEY SLOWED down at the traffic light. The *mahatturu* in the cars lowered their windows to look at the bunches of *rambuttans* the men held up. If they liked the look of them they would taste one, breaking the furry red outer cover with a quick bite, spitting it out quickly and then sucking, nipping and licking on the white meat on the nut, lips wet with the clear sour-sweet juice.

Then came the bargaining. You had to be quick, the traffic lights changed fast. The cars moved on and you readied yourself for the next red light. It wasn't always *rambuttans*—other kinds of fruit if they were cheap or in season—grapes, sometimes. Or packets of cashew nuts. Once they had tried large prawns, holding them high in bunches. Karuna remembered the rhythm, and the cracks and edges of the pavement on her feet, as she had run up and down, helping Piyasena when business was good. But he had stopped selling things after the car had hit him five years ago.

155

He had only been in hospital for a few days, it hadn't been such a big thing, but he had stopped.

Today Karuna stood alone at the junction trying to hear the woman over the noise of the traffic. "So put the children in a *madama*," the woman selling earrings had said, the loose flesh on her arms moving with a life of its own, "I'll find a place for them like this." She snapped her fingers to show how easy it was going to be. "I know a *mahattaya* who knows about things like this." She pursed her lips and nodded wisely.

Karuna who had told her story in little spurts between deep breaths looked skeptical. "Then I won't see them again," she said.

"No, no," Kaluamma pacified her, "in this *madama* they will be looked after very well, and you can see them any time. Just what you need. Leave your man," she went on, "the beater of women, I bet he can't even stand up to a Tamil. With weaklings like him around, it's no wonder the Tamils are beating the Sinhala up."

She eyed Karuna speculatively. "He can't do it anymore, can he?" Karuna nodded, biting her lip shyly.

"Don't worry about the children," Kaluamma said. "I got my cousin's friend's children into the Thavutissa *madama* last week. That one is a very good *madama,* run by the famous Balasuriya *mahattaya.* He is so noble and generous—a perfect *mahattaya.* My *mahattaya* knows him well; your children will come out really posh; like proper *mahatturu* and *nonala* from that one. Just a little money and I will arrange the rest," she said fingering the small wad of notes tucked into the waistline of her cloth. "But come on, why should you be drying yourself out in the sun?" She patted the worn yellow mat beside her—"Come sit in the shade with me. Now what about a pair of earrings for you?"

"No, no, I don't have any money for things like that."

"Tell me which one you want—I don't want any money," said Kalu-amma, expanding her chest generously.

Karuna looked at the little cart that housed Kaluamma's collection. In it were hundreds of earrings, small gold studs, big red rings, earrings set with blue and green stones—they were as good as anything she had seen in Dubai. Karuna hadn't bought a pair when she was working there because she wanted to save all the money she could. But now she could have a pair for free. Slowly, her eyes went from earring to earring, savoring the pleasure of choice. Now and then she bent to caress an especially lovely pair. "These are nice," she said finally, cradling a pair in her hot palm. "Are they too expensive?" she asked diffidently.

"Oh, these are very fine. I can see you have a good eye. It is almost real gold—did you know that? And see how delicate these hanging gold chains are."

Kaluamma held the earrings to Karuna's ears. Her hands felt rough against Karuna's soft lobes. She could feel the little chains brush the side of her neck.

"Delicate but strong," Kaluamma went on, "you couldn't break them if you wanted to; you will have them for a long time." She released Karuna from her grasp then, weighing the earrings in her hands, added, "But you can have them free." And she snapped her knuckles as she did when she made a good sale. "You are going to look very nice in them," she went on smiling, "a little lipstick and you will be perfect. My *mahattaya* might even have a job for you."

❈ ❈ ❈

Karuna was combing Sudu's hair as she hissed urgently to wake her other daughter. She wanted them up and off to school before Piyasena woke up and rose from the cardboard bed. Her back blocked the faint morning light from touching his face. There were no other openings in the cardboard walls of the shack; but even so the water found its way in when it rained hard. Piyasena was sleeping on his back, his chest exposed. She could see the old tattoo on his chest that she had liked so much when she had first known him. "My only treasure is my mother," it said, the black letters now blending into his brown skin.

His arms had felt like iron rods as they smashed into her flesh the day before. She screamed she didn't have the money he wanted. But he didn't believe her. He said he wanted to sell *rambuttans* at the junction again. But she knew he would spend it on drink as he had all the other money she had saved. "I don't have any money," she wailed over and over again, keeping her eyes averted from Kota's big school textbook, where she had hidden the last of the Dubai money.

Then he picked up the *manna*. And he raised it to bring it crashing down on her. She ran straight into him—clutching the big knife—pushing down. The knife cut him. Blood spurted from his chest. She had never done that before. Afraid he might kill her for it, she ran out onto the road and all the way to the traffic lights. Out of breath, looking back over her shoulder every few minutes, she had stopped near the earring-woman.

This was the first time he had done something like this after she had come back from Dubai. In the first few months after her return he had been so gentle, just like he had been when they had first been together, that she really thought he had changed back to his old self.

Before she went away he had broken her nose. He would be waiting for her, seething, when she came back from working at the Wickramasinghe bungalow, the slightest little thing setting him off. She didn't know what he knew or didn't, but she could sense he had heard something on the street. It was then that she had decided to stop working there and try the Dubai job. But he had disliked that idea even more.

Too ashamed to tell the doctor who stitched her up what had really happened, she made up a story about falling into the canal. But this time she had blurted out her story to Kaluamma.

❦ ❦ ❦

"So you are back, huh?" Wickramasinghe *nona* examined her like a picture. "Looking quite different too. Not like when you used to work in my kitchen." She laughed, as if remembering. "You might almost be a *nona* yourself now."

Karuna smiled submissively, and stared at her feet hoping she looked contrite enough. It had been a long walk to Mountbatten Crescent, from the *watte*. She didn't want the *nona* irritated with her today.

"So when did you come back?"

"It is a few months, *nona*."

"And you didn't come to see us?"

"I have been looking to come, *nona*."

"And how long were you there?"

"About a year, *nona*." Karuna counted the months on her fingers, saying each out aloud, softly. "I went in January '85."

"So you must know foreign cooking now, aah? When are you going back to work for Dubai *nonala?*"

"Anay, I don't know, *nona*—I can't do anything because of the children. Their father didn't send them to school when I was away; he put them to work at the Goonesekere family's house down the road. There is no one to look after them in the *watte.*" She paused, shifting her weight from one foot to the other. "I came to ask you if you could get the girls into a *madama* for me."

The *mahattaya* walked slowly onto the verandah. He walked with his heavy upper body bent slightly forward, taking steps that seemed full and lumbering, but still kept him from moving forward. His body swayed very slightly, as he stood and his upper arms flexed, as if they were happy to do nothing. He looked at her lazily with the familiar glance she remembered so well and Karuna felt her earlobes burn, the heat running down into the gold chains fixed on her ears. She lowered her eyes, and tried to turn her head in a futile attempt to hide the earrings; she wished she had worn the old, plain studs instead.

"She wants to put her children in a *madama*," the *nona* told Mr. Wickramasinghe.

He looked her up and down again. "A woman should look after her children. What is the world coming to? She has got all these ideas from her foreign jaunts, no?"

"It is a magic word for these people—*madama*. You get rid of the children and live happily ever after," Mrs. Wickramasinghe went on.

"Why do you want to do this?" the *mahattaya* barked at Karuna.

"If the children are safe, I can leave the *watte*. I can work in a house and live there. I can't live with my man anymore; I have taken enough." She paused. Her right arm pressed across her body, clutching her left arm at the elbow. She spoke in a rush, stumbling over the words. "He beats me, and when he is angry I'm afraid he will kill me."

She looked up at them for a moment, but their eyes were cold. "And he hit and cut me with the *manna* yesterday."

"Really?" said the *nona*. "Where?"

"Here," she said vaguely, her hand going to her chest. She could see that the *nona* didn't believe her.

"Well the wound won't heal if you wear such a tight dress, will it?" the *nona* said.

It was the *mahattaya's* turn. "You must try to live in peace and harmony with your man; without making him angry. Remember, the family is one of the building blocks of our society; if you break up your family it will be bad for our society. And what is more, no good will come to you." He inhaled as if he had been emptied of everything he knew and needed replenishing. "So give up this idea of a *madama*. Anyway they are over-flowing with orphans; there is no room for children who have parents." He looked her up and down again. "You can come and work here," he added.

"No, no, I'll send for you if I need you," said the *nona*, looking at him sharply.

They turned to leave. "I will go then." Karuna bowed her head, and got a nod in return. She could hear them talk as they were walking indoors. "Did you see how she was all tarted up, with her fingernails painted and all that. She probably has another man she wants to shack up with—that is why she wants to give the children away."

"And another thing," said the *mahattaya*. "She must be acting big with her Dubai stories and irritating her man."

❧ ❧ ❧

"And this was my room in the house where I worked." Karuna was showing her daughters Sudu and Kota the photographs from Dubai. Their eyes moved slowly across the picture, from the long mirror on the wall to the white sheets on the bed. "You had this room all to yourself?" asked Kota with disbelief. This was not the first time they had looked at the photographs. Every so often the girls would want to see them again, and after they had asked many times Karuna would give in. She would take out her suitcase, which served as a prop for the cardboard bed, and find the album among her other mementos. "Did they let you sleep on that bed every . . ." Sudu stopped and looked up, frightened.

Piyasena was standing at the door. Karuna knew he was drunk. "Put that good-for-nothing book away, you whore," he screamed. Karuna dropped the album, and slowly backed into a corner.

That's right *putha*, you tell her." It was Piyasena's mother who lived in the adjoining shanty. Rosalin had raised five children and never tired of telling the world about it. "She has been bad luck ever since you brought her. I told you at the very beginning but you wouldn't listen." Rosalin was shouting again. "That she-devil must have cast a vicious charm on all of us. That is why you had that accident. And now you can't even work as a laborer. And look at me—struck down in the prime of life." She had a stroke and was crippled, but could shout as loud as ever.

"Don't worry about anything," he slurred, "I can handle my woman." He lurched towards her but fell on his face as he lunged. Karuna hurried out with Sudu and Kota, a stream of abuse from Rosalin hitting them as they left.

🌸 🌸 🌸

Karuna stood very straight on the narrow walk between the hut and the canal. She had just finished washing the clothes and they were in a basket balanced on her head. Piyasena sat on his haunches out in front of the shack. The cut on his chest where the *manna* had hit him was red and raw. "You should get the wound dressed, or it will become infected," Karuna said softly.

"Don't tell me what to do, you bitch," he snapped. "Save it for that motherfucker *mahattaya* you give your arse to." He chewed slowly on his wad of *bulath*, pushing it from one jaw to the other with his tongue. "Remember that suitcase of yours?" he said, his nostrils flaring.

"Yes?" Karuna was startled.

He spat out a long stream of *bulath* juice onto her feet. She could feel his hot, thick saliva dripping down between her toes and into the earth below.

"I sold it."

🌸 🌸 🌸

Karuna stood at the traffic light junction, looking carefully at every car that passed her. Kaluamma had told her to stand there. "The car will come from the *madama*," she had said. But it was late at night and

Karuna didn't feel safe. She stood carefully on the pavement, feeling the breaks and spaces on the surfaces her feet knew well. It was harder today, because she was wearing the very tall shoes with the thin straps that Kaluamma had given her—and she could feel her calves pinching and twitching, as Kota and Sudu tugged at her hands from either side. They each had brown paper bags, with all their belongings.

The traffic lights kept changing, cars pulling up, and then purring off.

A car drove up quietly. "Get in," said the driver. He drove fast and soon she didn't know what road they were on. "Will you come and visit us at the *madama*, Ammi?" asked Kota. Karuna put her hand on the girl's head. "Now don't you keep whining for me all the time, *duva*," she said. "Be obedient and do as you are told." The car skidded to a halt. "I'll come whenever I can." She held Sudu's hand.

"Get out," said the driver. "No, just you, not the brats."

The car had stopped at another traffic light junction Karuna didn't know. There was a streetlight flickering above, and two pretty girls were standing in the half-dark, white light it gave off. "No, no, Kaluamma promised me I would be able to see the *madama*."

"What are you jabbering about? Do you want to work or not?"

"But Kaluamma said . . ."

"Look, I don't know this Kaluamma, and I don't care what she said. The *mahattaya* said I was to pick you up for work."

"But the *madama* for the children?"

"Ah! The *madama* . . .! That will be all taken care of—don't worry about anything—the children will be well looked after. But if you don't work—no *madama*—that is what the *mahattaya* said. If you don't work how will you be able to pay for the *madama?* Don't worry about anything." Karuna was silent, trying not to move. Her earrings felt heavy and the chains scraped her neck.

"Don't try to show me how modest you are—show that to the *mahatturu*, some of them like that," said the driver. "Looks like you're ready for work, huh?" He turned around and looked at her. His lips curled back, exposing his black teeth. "This is the right job for you," he said.

# Mridula Koshy ✿ INDIA

Mridula Koshy was born in 1969 and lives in New Delhi with her poet-schoolteacher partner and three children. Previously, she worked in the United States as a union and community organizer, although her varied background also includes stints as a cashier at a Kentucky Fried Chicken, backstage dresser at fashion shows, house painter, legal receptionist, collator of tax forms, and reading fairy at the library. *If It Is Sweet,* a collection of her short stories, won the 2009 Shakti Batt First Book Prize, and presents a range of characters from different social and economic backgrounds who inhabit an increasingly unsettled world. Her work has appeared in *Wasafiri, Prairie Fire, The Dalhousie Review, Existere,* and in anthologies in India, the UK and Italy.

# A LARGE GIRL

SHE WATCHES *DEVDAS,* REMOTE IN HAND, SO THE magic of instant access to any moment in its 184 minutes of sequinned shimmer is hers. She is a large girl. I knew her in school. She was there in school as early as Standard II, she tells me. But I didn't see her till maybe VII or VIII. Overnight, she came to our attention because she grew boobs and kept popping her buttons. Then she did the long jump on Sports Day and her skirt did that thing cheap umbrellas do, spine buckling and bowl upturning to heaven. There she landed, and she was so pink, I thought: tulip.

Everyone else was laughing. But there were some things I knew even then, maybe about the world, maybe about me. In any case, the last thing I wanted to do was laugh. What I wanted was to slip my hands down those trunk-like legs. My own were so inadequate. What must it be like, I thought, to have so much?

In Class VIII, she brought in a biography of Marilyn Monroe. Held between desk and knee it circulated down the row, across the aisle, down row two, and so on through the class: girls in one half, boys in the other. We flipped to the marked "hot" pages, to the forty or so pictures in black and white, there to give some meat to the printed word, which in any case we ignored. Unlike the blackmarket-quality pages with their bleed-through words elsewhere in the book, these thicker glossy pages in the middle were adequate for the task of delineating each angled thigh's unsubtle and tight press to hide—what? Nipples pulled oblong by raised arms floated free in what was already let loose—levitating fruit—front and centre of head thrown back and wide, arched smile inviting—what?

Pushpa, the idiot-mouse of our class, burst into tears. She was necessary comic relief; the sacrificial victim of our collective misgivings. What had we seen and how would this act now mark us? There was a sense of Class VIII's free period having been turned, in Sridevi Nair the teacher's absence and with the aid of Janet's wicked pinkness, into a communal orgy. "Quick, let's forget."

She was there till Class XII, and I knew her as the nuns' charity-case, the unclothed girl to steer clear of. The nuns would punish girls whose hems rode above their knees. How they allowed hers to creep up and up and stay there so that we were, I was, forced to obviate her—well, that's a question between the nuns and their gods. Obviate her, I did. There are no other incidents to recount till we reached Class XII—just the buttons, the jump that tuliped her, and Marilyn Monroe.

Our last day in school, the girls wore saris, the boys wore suits, and we prepared to dance—girls with girls and boys with boys. The school's Annual Day that year had revolved around a historical play, set in the colonial period, written by a team of nuns and credited to the Head Boy and Girl. For the play we had rehearsed a waltz fifty times in a day: boys in suits were paired with girls whose mothers cut saris into some understanding of ball gowns. On the strength of this earlier experience, the nuns urged us the evening we danced our goodbyes to pair up, boys with girls. The Head Boy and Girl to their, and everyone else's, discomfort led the line-up and the rest of us, in one of those stray acts of shame-faced rebellion, refused to follow suit. And so it was I found myself in Janet's embrace and, for the five minutes our feet described a dip-rise-dip square on the floor, I examined anew the corkscrew self, the twisting slumbering worm of me that had longed for this. Her hands on my shoulders and mine at her waist, and before or during that last dip, hers travelled as did mine from there to here, and then very quickly there were samosas and autographs and true and false expressions of sorrow across the throng of 120-odd crying-smiling-unfeeling-anxious-about-to-die youngsters.

In school she was presented, whether by herself or by the nuns or somehow, as an orphan. But here's the story she tells me now: her father arranged her mother's death—murdered her. He was an electrician—stripped the insulation off the wire and lined it up so her mother would be the one to turn on the washing machine. He basically, as Janet puts it, "fried her." I read a short story, Hitchcock's, once: same plot. Maybe her father read it too. But in his case the ending was different. Where Hitchcock's man kept his mouth shut and got away with it, Janet's father told his brother who turned him in. I have a brother and cannot imagine doing that—turning him in—no matter what the crime. Her father has been out of jail for some time. He's written to her, and she wants me to go with her to meet him. What kind of man would write to his daughter thirty years after murdering her mother and expect that she would want to meet him?

Her favourite story—she reads it out loud to me, in her favourite reading position, lying full length on top of me, her belly smashed into mine, book propped on pillow above my head—is *Kabulliwallah*. She is addicted to my stomach. She likes that I am the one who has given birth and worked my way back to flat, whereas she . . .well, I like her large and soft. She weeps in the reading. Every time. But how am I to weep when this is the fifteenth reading, and with every turn of the page, she must shift her weight and belly must renew acquaintance with belly with that sweaty, burp-cheer sound I find so funny? She weeps some more. Then she gets angry and says: "You don't understand me." And even on those occasions when I accept this as truth—and there are more of these occasions than not—she still must push on to the inevitable: "How can you understand me? You are the little Miss Richie Rich who ignored me all through school."

Here's what I tell her. Here's what I say that mollifies her: "God, give me another life so that I can do it right next time. Another life, so I can appreciate you and love you as you deserve to be." I deliver this without rolling my eyes. I don't shrug my shoulders or in any other way temper the fact that I mean this with all my heart. This life has not been enough and will continue to not be enough to love Janet. And it's not because her hunger is so beyond the pale. It just is the case that the love she wants is not in my means to give.

Here's another story from the past that Janet's father's recent resurrection has laid to rest. For the longest time there was a rumour in school that she was not a complete orphan; that her father was alive, even if her mother was dead; that he was alive and—get this—sailing the seas, an Australian sea captain. Why Australian? Don't ask me. She likes her stories sequinned. She likes them to shimmer. So she embroiders. Some of us embroider, and others of us will briefly hold in our hands a particularly fine piece of embroidery, so we can admire the journey the needle has taken.

We did not believe this story in school, although it would have accounted for Janet's name, her fairness, the breadth of her shoulders, her large bones. But she was not the first Anglo-Indian the rest of us had encountered, and her Australian-captain father only made the class titter. I know now where she got the story from. My daughter is eight and addicted to a character in a book series—*Pippi Longstocking*—an enormously self-sufficient orphan girl whose missing sea captain father she claims is still alive: a Cannibal King marooned on an island.

My own father, mother, brother, daughter and husband are alive and well. My marriage has been a good one for nearly fourteen years. It was an early marriage. I agreed to marriage because I lacked the imagination then to see how else a girl might make a life. My imagination, Janet believes, has continued to be lacklustre, and so she attempts obligingly to fill in where she senses inadequacy.

When I loan her money for the one-plus-one in the Shahpur Jat area, she immediately has us moving in, not just my bed and dresser set, which she admires, and the cut crystal in the dining room display, which is a wedding present from Mohan's parents, but also my daughter Rohini, and even Mohan's newest pup, Chetan. The thing about Janet's claim to gifts of imagination is that this imagination of hers too conveniently, it seems to me, skirts the truth.

We go through a phase where she questions me endlessly about Mohan—his likes, dislikes. Yes, the likes and dislikes of our lovemaking are uppermost in her thinking. I never feel it necessary to answer these questions. But I have told her what I thought of him when I first saw him. We met at my house with the parents around, his and mine. I don't count that as a first meeting. I never really saw him that day. No, the first time it was just the two of us was at the club near his parents' home in Anand Niketan. He had more or less grown up in that area, and he met me at the club entrance with this certain assurance, and we went inside this room and talked. We passed through the topic of exes quickly, and I teased him some and asked him what qualities in him had attracted these other girls. He looked so terribly pleased as he said, "You'll have to ask them."

Then there was some fumbling when the waiter came, and he ordered club sandwiches for both of us. He apologized to me for not doing better with the waiter and told me then that this was his first time in The Room. The Room being the room we were in, a room in which children were not permitted, a room meant For Adults Only. He had celebrated Diwali in childhood at this club and spent summers swimming in the pool and I suppose had become an adult and moved away before he could take advantage of adult privilege. He was feeling grown up that day and so was I. So in the end I married, I think, because it was the grown-up thing to do and right that I should do it with this grown-up that I was becoming fond of.

Janet refuses to understand this story. "Yeah, so you are fond of him. But tell me you have the hots for him and I promise I will believe you." She doesn't really want my answer. "You can't say it, can you? Yes to hots? No? No hots." She thinks she is taunting me.

Or lying next to me, when I turn inviting her to spoon me, she will peel back instead and run her hand from my shoulder to my butt and slap me there and ask, "What's his favorite part?" If I remain silent she will pinch or poke at me. "Is it here, your butt? Men always like a woman's ass.

They never think to like her elbows or her toes. Or maybe he has a foot fetish? Does he? Maybe he sucks your toes, heh princess?" It's no good keeping my back turned. She will move on from favourite body parts to favourite positions. I turn to her and busy myself nibbling her front.

She keeps a picture of Rohini, and one of Chetan with Rohini, along with the many others of me in her room. She would no doubt have a perfectly imaginative tale with which to dress up the addition of Mohan's picture to this tableau. I can't imagine what this would be. In any case, I tell her, "No, it will make me uncomfortable," and refuse her the picture when she asks. With Janet, the truth, if inconvenient, is something to be ignored. I can't live that way.

Janet and I first run into each other in the parking lot outside my gym. She is coming out of a shop in the same complex. It turns out to be a beauty parlour, and she turns out to be working there. We light up, standing between the cars; breaking my big rule about public smoking. It would take any busybody in that gym, to whom Mohan is known, seeing me smoking, for me to get into a lot of trouble. For all that Mohan is a chain smoker, I am not permitted to smoke. On the rare occasion, say if we are good and soused, on an anniversary, at Buzz, or better still at The Imperial, and if I beg and nag, then, maybe then, he'll light me one and hand it over.

But my girlfriends and I always smoke when we get together. We do it on the roof. I keep a mat rolled up on the stairs. We take it up with us when we go. Ours is a rented place, and I have done nothing by way of plants and things to beautify the roof. The mat serves to soften the crumbling concrete on which we have to crouch to prevent nearby tenants from invading our privacy. The mat is where Janet and I first kiss.

The first time we kiss, she lights a cigarette and passes it to me, and then she lights another one. We are talking, but not easily. After the cigarette in the parking lot, and the exchange of phone numbers, a month passes before I realize she will not be the one to call. I call. She comes over. There is all the awkwardness of her taking in the toys scattered throughout the house—most of them Mohan's, I explain to her. I am not the gadget freak, and the endless updating is his way of flexing his muscles.

She is subdued downstairs, but loud enough on the roof, so I am relieved when finally we sit quietly, leaning back on the short wall. I wish for time to get the clothes cleared from the line before they get infected with our smoke. But it is also strangely peaceful as they stir, combing their shade-fingers of coolness over us with each breeze. My shoulder is touching hers and she slides down and rests her head on my lap and from there squints up at me. She is still as she was in school—large hands and long legs. I am still as I was—content to keep within myself; my inner curve, in its own circular fashion, yearning itself. So then why am I unfurling as she reaches for my face, her one hand doing the bidding and the other still locked onto the cigarette? A second passes, her hand is on my cheek, and I follow her example, my free hand cradling her cheek, so we are both leading and following together into that first kiss.

It is not a kiss to get lost in—we are each of us balancing, one half engaged in not accidentally burning the other. She flicks her cigarette away and with both hands pulls my head to hers. But I don't have her sophistication or just plain old ease. I am still balancing as she searches my mouth—her tongue acrid, like Mohan's.

I take to leaving her. After the first, second, third, fourth time, she stops mourning and starts instead to throw me out. I leave and the leaving is unbearable to me. For a day or two I remain gone from her. My last memory of her is of a graceless shrug of dismissal; the slam of her eyes shutting me out.

I leave her for many reasons. The first time—when Rohini comes up the stairs to the roof one afternoon, and the metal stairs, instead of clattering as I had expected, absorb her Keds tread silently, and suddenly she is there—looking at us. "Mummy," she says. She is wearing a stricken smile. She is saying with her eyes, "I don't see you with a cigarette in your hand." She is saying, "I don't see the pack placed square between you and aunty."

"Mummy," she says, breathless from the run up the stairs, shame-faced from the discovery she has made. "Nina threw the Frisbee hard at Indrani, and now Indrani's nose is cut, and, and," she says riveted by the competing drama of the story she has come to share and the story she has just discovered, "Indrani's nose has sooo much blood coming out of it. It's everywhere."

For the next two days, I try to tell Janet we shouldn't smoke together. I even tell Mohan the truth: "Janet and I were on the roof, and you know she smokes. Well, she lit me one, and the next thing Rohini was up there, and I think she saw us." Mohan does not get angry. "Let's see if Ro says something. There is no need to bring it up if she doesn't." After two days he and I agree Rohini had forgotten. But I remain frantic that Janet should understand why we can't smoke up on the roof. The more she turns her ears off, the more determined I become that I will not only stop our little smoking ritual, but also that I will never smoke anywhere, for any reason, ever again.

I am supposed to go to her place some days later. I don't. A week passes, and she texts me: "talk?" I can't help myself. She greets me at the door, pulls me to her and kisses me on her side of the length of fabric she has hung in the doorway. My one hand automatically searches behind me for the wood beyond this cloth, till she imprisons my hand in hers, pulls it between us and slips something into it. Our foreheads are touching and we both look down to what our hands are doing—transferring fruit—light green and translucent, from hers to mine. Then, she looks straight into my eyes and hers are smiling. *"Amla,"* she says. "It will be the oral fix you need to quit cigarettes." My mouth is already puckering. The fruit is sour and tense in taste, but leaves the mouth sweet and wet as if washed with rain. We kiss, and I forget about the door. She shuts it in the end, pushes me ahead of her into bed. But the *amla* is really only for me, and afterwards she lights up as always, ashing her sheets, pillows, my hair.

The fighting continues. It becomes about her father. She insists she needs me with her when she goes to see him for the first time. I tell her, "Faridabad is too far away. How will I account for a whole morning, afternoon and evening?" She is stiff in anger: "You spend the whole afternoon here. No problem."

"But," I say, "I am always there to pick Rohini up at 3:30."

"Tell your husband to get her this once."

"No, I can't. He doesn't like to interrupt his work like that."

"This is important to me," she says.

I don't believe her. Her neighbour has told me that her father has already been by to see Janet. I wonder if perhaps they have met more often than this once.

I don't say to Janet: "You're a liar." I wonder why she wants me to see him. She has not repaid me the loan, which I wheedled out of Mohan. I wonder if she is going to ask for more money; if, perhaps, her father needs money. I don't say: "You're a liar." Instead I say: "No." Then, "The truth is I am a married woman. And a mother."

She says, "That's never been a problem. What's there in that?"

We are silent. I think about her father in her room. I wonder if he wondered what we—Rohini, I, and not to forget Chetan are doing on Janet's walls. I wonder what story Janet concocted to explain us to him.

"Why do I have to meet your father?"

She regards me seriously. "I just want him to know that I have a good life. And you are part of what makes my life good."

But I feel stubborn. "No," I say. Mostly I am thinking, "Why do I like her? She is so vulgar."

I cautiously tell friends from school that I have run into Janet, and their reactions are uniformly similar. I think it is Shilpa who says, "She must have had a hard life," and I concur.

The last time we are together at her place, she meets me first at the bottom of the stairs leading up to her flat. She is four floors up, and the walls all along the climb are repulsive, stained with the spit-splat of *paan*. On the second floor landing someone has lined up some potted plants on either side of their front door, and above on the wall is a pencilled-and-taped-to-the-wall sign in Hindi: "Spitting on Plants is Not Permitted." On the flight up from the third floor landing she turns to me and says, "You're having your period." I nod, and she adds, "I can hear your pad rustling."

The very last time we are together, she kisses me under my stairs. She has thrown me out the week before when once again I refuse to accompany her to her father's. She says that he is asking to meet me. I am adamant in my refusal. At the end of a week's silence, she shows up and gestures to me from the service lane that fronts my place. I wave back to her from the upstairs balcony, more to reassure the flower-seller who is studying the proceedings, than to indicate any sort of welcome. But then she crosses the lane, comes in the gate to the front door, and I pull her in from there. She takes her hand out of her pocket and, glistening in her cupped palm, are two *amlas*. I rest a fingertip on one and gently rock it in her palm where it bumps repeatedly its sister-self. And again Janet and I are facing each other. She is my height, I realize: her largeness is all in her breadth. There is a way we line up—eye to eye—that feels like pleasure.

"Take it," she indicates the *amla* with her chin. I take one, and she folds her hand shut over the other. "You don't want us to continue?" she asks.

"No." I am wooden. "Janet, I don't want to be destructive in any way. In my life or yours. You have to understand that."

"Tomorrow," she asks, "You won't change your mind?"

"No, Janet. Tomorrow, I won't change my mind."

She kisses me before she leaves. This, our last kiss, is quick. It is a kiss of dismissal, but also sweet. In the lean of her face, I feel her eyelashes brushing mine, and her tongue has no anger to it; nor any persuasion.

A time will come—a time that is starting now—when I will no longer know her. I will attend the Jahan-e-Khushrau festival and, sitting in the last rows, I will be surprised to see Anju seated two seats away from me. We will press hands across people's laps, and I will be embarrassed as I tell her that I will come soon to pick up the tailoring I have left at her boutique some months before. She will laugh and say, "I have kept it all together for you. It is ready." Rohini will place her head in my lap and ease the mobile from my purse and proceed to play a game on silent mode. I will be irritated and will want to scold her to enjoy the music. Mohan will put a hand on my knee and will still me. We will together whisper and wonder who it is that owns the splendid house with lit banks of windows overlooking Humayun's tomb and the festival. "They are so lucky, dining there on the rooftop," we will think. The next day, I will meet at a party one of the diners from the night before. And I will exclaim: "This is such a small city. I never thought . . ."

At Café Turtle, I will overhear a man talking about Jhumpa Lahiri's *Interpreter of Maladies,* and the next day the same man will be at Confluence, with another woman this time. He will turn out to be an authority on steel sculpture. I will meet him, and he will talk shyly about his expertise. It will be on the tip of my tongue to say to him, "What a small world we live in. Just yesterday . . ." But he will break in and say much the same words to me.

I will stand one evening, in line, at the PVR in Saket and Mohan's attentiveness will leave me feeling cherished. He will agree to watch *Memoirs of a Geisha* not because it is the only movie showing at 5:15, but because he will know how much I will enjoy this movie. In the next line, we will see our old neighbours quarrelling and we will happily embrace them. It will have been years since they vacated from above us.

I will begin soon to live all the days ahead of me. In the afternoons, I will think: Do you miss me? Do you miss me? A thousand and one chances will come and go in this small city, in this small world. I will never see you again.

## Ela Arab Mehta ❀ INDIA

Ela Arab Mehta was born in 1940 near Jamnagar, Gujarat. She was educated
in Bombay and received a postgraduate degree in Gujarati literature from
the University of Bombay. The author of numerous collections of stories and
novels, she is known as a reflective author with a concern for life's shifting
existential situations. Mehta is also one of two literary sisters—her sibling,
Varsha Adalja, is also a well-known Gujarati novelist. Mehta has stated that
Gujarati women writers are still expected to toe the line by writing on harmless
domestic themes or for children. To write on subjects that challenge traditional
views, she argues, particularly on matters of sexuality, is still a taboo for women
authors and invites censorship from within one's own family and from society.
She has taught at the college level and lives in Mumbai.

# BABLU'S CHOICE

*Translated from the Gujarati story "Bhaiylo" by the author*
*with Devina Dutt and Pratik Kanjilal*

"HEY, YOU! COWARD! WHY ARE YOU CRYING LIKE
a girl? Come on, come on. Get up!" Papaji's voice reached Milan's ears,
rising up from the compound of the building and coming in the window
of the second floor. He wanted to go hide in a corner. After some time,
he slowly drifted over to the window and looked down.

Down in the compound, little Ankur and some girls had quarrelled.
Ankur was crying. Papaji, Milan's father, was angrily shouting at Ankur:
"Are you a girl? Come on, get up, don't be a sissy."

Frightened and ashamed, Ankur picked himself up and ran away.
Watching this little drama, Milan shivered. He knew what would happen
when he handed over the circular into Papaji's hands. The circular which
offered a choice of subjects for the students of the ninth standard at

school. He knew his father well—he'd had fifteen years to get to know him. He was Papaji's youngest child, born several years after his older brother Vipul and sister Sujata. He was darling little Bablu. Papaji came into the house. Milan waited till he had had a bath and some tea before silently going up to him and handing him the circular. Without waiting for his reaction, he turned away and hurriedly flopped down on a sofa.

Papaji stood reading the circular. He saw the subject which Bablu had ticked. He stared at it, refusing to believe his eyes. Then he bellowed: "Bablu!"

There was no answer. He shouted again.

Silence engulfed the house. Suddenly, everybody in the house seemed to get very busy with some chore or the other. Mummy went into the kitchen and silently busied herself with the cooking. Grandma sat down before her small temple and started singing *bhajans*. His older brother started reading his medical journal and Sujata-didi turned on her computer.

Nobody responded to Papaji's shouting. Nobody dared to face him when he was annoyed.

Papaji was also quiet for a while. Then he started pacing up and down the room, trying unsuccessfully to control his temper. Suddenly, he erupted: "Change it! Change it, I say!"

Milan did not answer. He sat on the very corner of the sofa, staring down at the floor. He would have liked to run into his room and close the door behind him, but lacked the nerve.

Of course, Papaji had never struck his darling boy. He had only raised his hand once or twice, as if to strike.

"Where has everyone gone? Am I supposed to handle this alone?" Papaji said loudly. Mummy could tell that he was exasperated, perhaps even angry.

Reluctantly, she emerged from the kitchen and stood in the corner. She looked at Milan, imploring him to accept whatever Papaji said.

Milan averted his face as if rejecting her plea and saying instead, "No, I won't. Please let me do what I want to do."

Papaji coughed briefly and tried to collect himself. "Look, son, you are a nice, intelligent boy. Give up this stupid idea. If you do such idiotic girlie things, people will laugh at you—and at me, too."

He paused and then continued. "I work so hard for all of you. I make good money, and for whom? Isn't it all for you? So that when you—all three of you—grow up, you become somebody, somebody much better than me."

He put the circular in Mummy's hands.

"Read this."

Though she had read it before, she read it again, just to please Papaji. Nodding in agreement with her husband, she said, "Bablu, your father is right. Come tell us which subjects you have trouble with in school. Maths? Science? Don't worry. We'll engage a tutor for accountancy."

"I have already asked Ramnikbhai to send his tutor Deepak Sir to us. I'll remind him today," Papaji told Milan. His tone of voice implied that he was talking to a mentally challenged boy.

"Bablu, don't worry. You will score good marks in all subjects. Look at Unmesh. His mother was telling me how they all helped him with his SSC exams, how he got 80 per cent. So don't worry, Bablu," Mummy said soothingly, as if she were singing a lullaby.

"Why talk about Unmesh? Look at our own daughter Sujata!" said Papaji. "Your elder sister. Who would say that she is a girl? She is far ahead of all the boys and always gets a first class. She is no daughter—she is my son."

Sujata's eyes darted from the computer screen and rested on Milan for a while. Then she went back to her work. "Speak up, you idiot, Bablu!" Papaji exploded.

"Sujata-didi is clever and is comfortable with all subjects. She likes to study them," Milan answered in a low voice.

"Oh, God! That's what I have been trying to explain to you for the last hour. Don't you understand? You must study hard. Where is your attention? On the television? All the children in this country went crazy the day 24-hour television started!"

Papaji's anger had crossed the danger level and Mummy was now worried. She was thinking of his blood pressure. "Please calm down. Everything will be all right," she said.

All at once, everyone was relieved. Now, it was Mummy's responsibility to get Bablu to toe the line. Papaji, Vipul, Sujata-didi, Grandma and Mummy went out in quick succession. Milan was alone in the house.

He switched on the TV. Today there was a programme of Bharat-natyam dance by Karthikeyan, a young dancer from Chennai. Milan was keen to see his recital. Thank God, he was alone now. The small screen before him was no mere TV—it was transformed into a land of divine beauty and Karthikeyan was its undisputed king. The matchless grace of his movements, his *mudras*, his *bhavas* mesmerised him. Unawares, he started to sway to the rhythm of Karthikeyan's dance.

His eyes filled with tears. This is what he wanted to learn—to dance. His school had offered two optional subjects to all ninth standard students: accountancy and dance. Milan had chosen the latter and all hell had broken loose. Papaji's shouting, Mummy's tears, his older siblings smiling indulgently, when all along he knew they were really saying, "Bablu, you girlie baby!"

Papaji went to his school to meet the principal. "We send our children to your school to get an education, not to learn dancing," he said sternly.

"Mr. Kapadia, please be patient, let me explain," the principal said. "Our time was different. It was the age of stereotypes. Girls had to learn to sew and cook, and boys had to study engineering and medicine. But today, our society no longer has any use for this stereotyping. If a girl can become an engineer, a boy can become a dancer."

"What rubbish!" Papaji got up and almost raised his hand before he could control himself. "Is this freedom or foolishness? My son wants to become a dancer—he wants to learn to dance."

"Mr. Kapadia, please talk to your son," the principal said. "He can take another subject, you know."

However, the question of talking to his son did not arise. It was discovered that in a class of a hundred students, only two people had opted for dance. Milan was one; the other was a girl. Everyone else had opted for accountancy. The school had had to hire an extra teacher for accountancy.

Right from the ninth standard, the school was preparing students for the final examination the following year. When the school was driving the students so hard, could the parents lag behind? Tuition, coaching classes, special notes from a Deepak Sir and a Bhatt Sir—they arranged for everything. Papaji hired special teachers for his son for maths and science.

Once, in the midst of all this, Milan was caught watching a classical dance program on Doordarshan. Right when he was imitating the *mudras* of the dancer on the TV screen, his brother Vipul had walked into the room. When everyone got to know, they laughed at Bablu's passion for *mudras*. "Oh, Bablu, you are still a girl-child!" they said.

And so Milan stopped dancing. He passed his final examinations with more than seventy-five per cent. Sujata-didi stood first in the Intermediate Chartered Accountancy examination. There were phone calls and flowers from friends and relatives. Papaji's joy knew no bounds. "Yes, yes, she is my son, like Vipul." He repeated this several times.

A function was held at the City Hall to felicitate top students. Sujata and Papaji were invited up on the *dais* while other family members sat with the audience. The president of the community, a very old man, was speaking into the mike.

"Dear friends, this is a very proud day for an old man like me. There was a time, not long ago, when our daughters were married off at an early age. They were beaten and burned alive by cruel in-laws and we were silent onlookers. Not anymore. Now they are like our sons. We have given them the freedom to be who they are."

The audience gave the old man a standing ovation. Bablu looked at Papaji, who was clapping the loudest, and thought, "Father, you have set your daughters free. Why do you keep your sons in chains?"

## Firdous Haider ❧ PAKISTAN

Firdous Haider is an important Pakistani writer best known for her short stories. She studied at Lahore College for Women before receiving her M.A. at Peshawar University. Her writing career began while she was a teacher of Urdu. Following a painful divorce, she published a third collection of stories that brought her significant critical attention for the emotional content of her work. As Haider's writing developed under the influence of the Progressive Writers Movement, it became more socially engaged and did not flinch at addressing women's issues, rebuking Pakistan's patriarchal culture for its treatment of women—a fact that led to her being criticized for her outspoken style. Since then, she has also published travel journals and emerged as one of Pakistan's major television scriptwriters. Haider lives in Karachi, where she maintains her interests in art, painting and inner cultivation.

# THE UNBURDENED HEART

*Translated from the Urdu story "Khali Hua Yeh Dil"*
*by Jai Ratan and Pratik Kanjilal*

NANAJI HELD MY FINGER AND WALKED ALONG THE village path, surveying fields that stretched before us. This land, once so fertile, was now barren. It was the salt in the soil. "Forgive me, my precious land," moaned Nanaji over and over again, wiping salt-laden tears on his sleeve. "I could not save you. I'm so sorry." His voice was heavy with remorse.

He looked wistfully at the villagers who passed us on their way to work. He wanted to stop them and unburden his heart. He believed that he could still save the land and, with the government's help, find a cure for it.

He wrote petitions on his ancient portable typewriter on weekends and holidays, and delivered them to various government offices. Nothing worked. No one took any notice of him.

Finally, sorely disappointed, he would plant himself outside the iron gates of the multi-storied building that housed the government offices. "Don't you know that canal irrigation has raised the level of groundwater?" he would plead with the people who gathered around him. "It mixes the minerals the crops need with chemicals. With the minerals made useless, saline water comes to the surface, and you know that salinity is poison for the crops."

The onlookers who formed his willing audience would shake their heads dolefully. Encouraged, the old man would continue, "One-fifth of the world's land mass has become barren because of salinity. To save our arable land, we must launch a campaign against the construction of dams."

"Who has the time for this sort of thing?"

"You'll have to make time for it! Or your land will meet the same fate as mine. My land is a victim of salinity."

The crowd would start to disperse but the old man would block their way, trying to convince them of the truth of his assertion.

"We live in Karachi," someone would sneer. "The land is not ours, neither is the sky. We are cooped up in flats. Come, join us there and have a good time."

The people in these offices started avoiding him. If they saw him coming, they quickly left the room. Nanaji watched them flee. Having failed in his campaign to save the land from the curse of salinity, he returned to his village.

I had felt bad about leaving the village with Nanaji. Not because I had happy memories of the village folk, but because Nanaji's woes had become a part of me. I wanted to share his troubles. He would have certainly stayed on in the village indefinitely, keeping himself busy writing letters to the newspapers. But then Uncle, Nanaji's son, came from Islamabad to fetch him.

For the first time ever, I heard Nanaji raise his voice in anger. "What cheek! It is preposterous that people sitting in air-conditioned rooms should take decisions on matters they have no clue about," he fumed. "Let them come here and taste the blasts of hot wind that we fill our lungs with. What do they know of the terrible hardships we bear, raising crops under the burning sun? Why are the poor forced to make such sacrifices for the so-called 'common good'?"

Uncle listened to him calmly. When Nanaji had finished, he started packing Nanaji's books into cartons without casting a glance at me. Then he said, "You should thank God that I, your son, am an officer of the highest cadre. I have ample room in my house to make you comfortable. I can give you whatever you might need. In place of that barren land of yours I'll get a nice city plot allotted to you in Islamabad. Stop worrying. Why are you so bothered about this village and its people? It's not your business."

As I rose to help Uncle pack the books, his eyes fell on me. They flashed the same contempt that I had seen in the eyes of my classmates. I was appalled.

A boy who sat next to me in school had once told me that Maulvi Saheb, who taught Islamic religion, loathed me. Of course, I didn't believe the boy. But one day, Maulvi Saheb said that those who sinned were made to eat thorns by Allah. He also made them burn in Hell.

This was too much for me. I got up and said angrily, "Allah loves his people. He forgives their errors."

Maulvi Saheb stood up and strode towards me, furious. With two hard lashes on my hand with his cane, he said, "There are some sins that Allah never forgives. For instance, your mother's sin of marrying a Christian."

"Y-e-e-e-s!" the boys chorused, in a strange mix of venom and surprise.

I dashed out of the classroom, leaving my schoolbag and books behind, and ran home to take refuge in Nanaji's lap. "Child, Christians too believe in God," Nanaji said. "And for the sake of your mother, your father had converted to Islam."

I believed Nanaji. But I refused to go to school. So to help me face my classmates on their own ground, Nanaji took my mother's *nikahnama*, the marriage certificate, to show around in the school. When we reached the school, Maulvi Saheb was holding forth on Islam.

"Here, take a look at my daughter's *nikahnama*," Nanaji said. "Yes, see for yourself. And don't ever trouble my child with your wrong ideas. Religion doesn't approve of hurting people's feelings."

Nanaji spoke softly. Maulvi Saheb apologised at once, and Nanaji accepted it with grace. But then Maulvi Saheb said, his voice wreathed in a smile, "I hear he converted to Islam in order to marry your daughter. It was just a trick to get what he wanted. I learnt later that as soon as he reached America, he converted back to Christianity." Without a word, Nanaji grabbed my hand and took me home. From that day, I never had to go to school. Nanaji would teach me himself. I was pleased. I wandered the countryside with him and spent a good deal of my time in his home library. It was he who told me that not long ago Bangladesh, Pakistan and India were a single, united entity stretching across the subcontinent. Then came discord and dissension, and the gulf kept widening, leading to their final separation. I was sorry to learn about this. Nanaji also told me that an individual has the right to lead his life his own way. It is all part of the game. Even brothers can fight over a piece of land. Such differences over material gain lead to murder and bloodbaths. Women are dishonoured. Rivers of blood flow. But, as Nanaji said, this is all wrong and should never happen.

Nanaji could talk on any subject. He had all the facts at his fingertips. He got magazines and books from all corners of the world. He added new dimensions to my learning. He once told me that the rift between him and Maulvi Saheb had benefited me. Now he was teaching me things that were beyond the comprehension of all the other teachers put together. These teachers did not go beyond prescribed textbooks. He said the times in which he had grown up and lived were different from the present. In those days, students were encouraged to read beyond their textbooks, which added vastly to their knowledge. Since I was studying under his guidance, he once remarked that my mental age was much higher than that of my classmates. Such encouragement made me turn to my lessons with even greater zeal.

We were busy packing. Uncle watched me intently, his eyes fixed on my face. I stole a nervous glance at him, expecting some nasty comment about me. "Why don't you send him to his father in America?" Uncle asked Nanaji suddenly. I looked up.

"Why should I? He'll stay with me."

"You tried to liberate your daughter, and look what happened."

"Don't forget that she was your sister too."

"I know; but unlike her I did not marry a social activist. I married the daughter of a rich industrialist and I'm having the time of my life."

"That's the problem. You've distanced yourself from the common man."

"Your social activist son-in-law could not take your daughter to America with him."

"He most certainly would have. It was just held up by immigration rules. He had taken pains to complete all the paperwork."

"But why marry an alien, of all people? You gave her too much liberty. You even allowed her to work with an NGO, for no apparent reason."

"I have given you a long rope too—to live your life your own way."

"But I did not take undue advantage of it."

"Nor did she, if you ask me. How do you decide what's right and wrong? What's right for you could be wrong for me."

"Even so, there are norms that you can judge by."

"I just know one thing: her love endured. As long as she lived, she lived for the common good. And she died a natural death."

"Oh no, you know very well she died in childbirth. And what is to happen to him—he who brought about her death?"

"What will happen to him?" Nanaji almost shrieked. "He is perfectly happy with me."

Both lapsed into silence.

Such quarrels were quite frequent and continued even in their letters. Then their correspondence would stop abruptly, sometimes on a bitter note. It would be a while before they got back to writing to each other.

This time, Uncle had taken the initiative. "I've been promoted to a higher grade," he had written. Nana wrote him a congratulatory letter. Thus the correspondence was resumed.

The upshot was that we came to Islamabad. Uncle lived in a big bungalow, had several cars and a retinue of servants. He had a daughter whom we called Shahzadi—the princess—at home, though she went by another name at school. I never saw Auntie at the dinner table. I only saw her from a distance, coming home or going out. She would give me a contemptuous look as if I were her servant's son. Shahzadi, in her expensive dresses, would plant herself before me. When I raised my eyes from my book she would give me a scornful look and sail out of the room in tailor-made glory.

Presently, I realised that I had to complete my education as soon as possible. I buried myself in my lessons, day and night, preparing for the senior graduation 'O' level exam. When the results were announced, Nanaji was thrilled: I had passed with credit in all subjects while Shahzadi had failed in several. But she showed no sign of distress at her failure, nor did she seek consolation. To her, education was not important for girls, as long as they learnt the social graces and decked themselves in finery. She focused on her future as the decorative daughter-in-law of a rich family and prepared for it.

That evening we sat down to dinner and listened to the nine o'clock news. India had tested its nuclear bomb. Nanaji and Uncle froze. They couldn't believe it.

For days afterwards, newspapers and magazines were full of this underground explosion.
- Pokhran in shocked silence!
- The whole desert quakes!
- Sand and earth hurled high in the air as explosion sends shockwaves through the region!
- More than 1,000,000 degrees Centigrade! Heat of atomic explosion equals heat of sun!

Day after day, Nanaji and I would read the news and exchange glances in stunned silence. Nanaji believed that man is his own oppressor. I could read his mind from his expression. I could feel his agony. But I did not know how to comfort him, for I was in agony myself.

At the dinner table, the conversation was about the havoc that the bomb would unleash. We gathered news and comments from all sources and discussed them over dinner.

The grain-laden paddy fields that sway gently in the countryside will burn down. The rivers will be poisoned. When everything is incinerated, the world will plunge into darkness. Tonnes of smoke will blot out the sun. The temperature will drop below freezing point. The water will turn into poisoned ice. Life on earth and in the sea will become extinct. Apparently, iodine pills were an antidote for atomic damage. But who would survive to take iodine pills?

We read such horrendous news and exchanged notes.

In spite of the panic of the holocaust, there was a demand that rose like a surging wave—that Pakistan should also detonate an atom bomb. As if it was a cricket match between India and Pakistan, in which Pakistan must beat India. Now it was Pakistan's turn.

Nanaji started writing articles for various newspapers. Lahore is barely thirty miles from Amritsar, he explained. If Lahore is bombed, all of the Punjab will be destroyed. If Karachi is bombed, Rajasthan, Gujarat and Bombay will not escape ruin either.

We must have faith in Allah, he said. This universe is His divine gift. We must use all our energy to wipe out poverty and illiteracy from this earth. We must start a campaign, that although we have the best nuclear technology, we shall not use it for the bomb.

Once again, Nanaji went around the city and, planting himself outside government offices, lectured passers-by, explaining the utter futility of detonating atom bombs. We must not forget Hiroshima and Nagasaki, he warned. He detailed the horrors of radioactive material. People would stop, hear him and move on, as if wholesale devastation was such a remote possibility that it didn't matter.

Then one day Uncle confronted Nanaji and said sharply, "It has to stop. You will not write to the newspapers nor harangue people near government offices anymore. I forbid you. It's sacrilege! Why can't you understand that I hold a responsible position in the bureaucracy? That's why I enjoy such handsome perks—stylish living, posh cars and all the rest. If the higher-ups hear a word against me, I'll have to face their wrath."

"Then I must leave your house and go away," Nanaji said angrily.

"It makes no difference whether you live with me or go away. You'll always be my father. You're identified as so-and-so's father. You must not forget that." He pointed to me. "This grandson of yours follows you around like a dog. And the way he glows with pleasure at what you say, he can easily be taken for an enemy agent. It's because of you that I have given him shelter under my roof."

"You too . . ." Nanaji's voice choked. He took my hand and led me to his room.

So Satan had his way at last. This was the day he was waiting for, the day for which he had begged Allah. The world, which was a thousand billion and sixty million years old, was doomed. Satan had triumphed. Man was vanquished.

I felt sorry for Nanaji. He suddenly looked feeble, old beyond his years. All his strength seemed to have drained from him. I helped him to bed. He asked me to fetch a bundle from his suitcase.

"I have corresponded regularly with your father," he said, taking the bundle of papers from me. "He works for the Red Cross, in several countries. These days, he is on an assignment in Bosnia. I didn't tell him about you because I feared he might not be in a position to shoulder the responsibility of a father. This bundle also contains documents relating to your parents' *nikahnama* and your birth certificate. Today, I set you free—go wherever you want and make your own life. From now on, you're on your own."

I looked at Nanaji, flabbergasted. According to the impression that he had conveyed to me, my father was very happy with his American wife and children and had evinced no interest in me.

"I'll write to your father and make a confession of my moral aberration. I also ask your forgiveness. Pardon me, if you can."

"Nanaji, what are you saying?" I started crying. I was utterly confused.

"I had lost my daughter," he said. "With you, I felt she was restored to me by Allah. Just think of it: without you, how would I have coped with my long, dreary life, as formidable as a mountain peak? Your father got himself a new wife, and children too. This bundle also contains their photographs."

Nanaji stopped going to the dining room. After dinner, I would take up a tray for him. I forced him to eat, for he seemed to have lost interest in food and, for that matter, in life. Sitting alone, I would read my father's letters. There was not much difference in Nanaji's and Daddy's ways of thinking; they held similar views on most things. Daddy's goal in life was to help the needy and the oppressed.

Nanaji grew very silent. As he ate, he would repeat in a constant refrain, "You're the extension of my life. You must carry on my mission. Your Daddy has started a campaign against nuclear fission. You must join this movement."

He stopped watching television. He would just lie in bed and stare at the ceiling.

The day they carried out the atomic tests at Chagai, the driver put the day's paper in Nanaji's hand. Before I could snatch it away, Nanaji had read the headlines. "The mountain has turned white," he mumbled. His face was very pale. As I rushed to support him, he collapsed in my arms. Just as I used to fall into his lap as a child, to seek comfort as I sobbed my heart out. But Nanaji did not cry. He did not even open his eyes to look at me. He fell asleep forever, as if he had finished his life's work.

## Usha Yadav ❧ INDIA

Usha Yadav is Professor of Hindi at Dr. Bhim Rao Ambedkar University, Agra. She was born in Kanpur, Uttar Pradesh in 1946. She has published six novels, *Neelkanth* (1998) being the most recent. A new novel, *Amaavas Ki Raat,* is forthcoming. Her three short story collections include *Jaane Kitne Cactus,* and she has also published poetry, drama, and children's literature. Her novel *Paras Patthar* was a prizewinner with the Children's Book Trust, Delhi, in 1987. Her stories for children and adults have also been published in numerous journals, including *Samkaleen Bharatiya Sahitya, Sarita, Kadambini, Parag, Nandan* and *Suman-Saurabh.*

# LIBATIONS

*Translated from Hindi by Ira Raja*

WHO WOULD THINK OF DYING IN THE HEADY MONTH of Phalgun, in the midst of all the excitement of Holi in Krishna's own playground, Vrindavan? But Saptadal, of the Amarbari ashram, chose to embrace death on that very day.

Well, if she's dead, she's dead. It's not as though she has left behind a family to mourn her loss. As for the well-meaning relative who had abandoned the ten-year-old widow in Vrindavan to earn *moksha*—she could not even remember his face clearly. A lifetime had gone by since then, singing *bhajans* in various ashrams. Even today she had had a good lunch as usual, and retired to her little room to rest. A short while later she complained of uneasiness to Ananda Dasi who was nearby, there was a slight convulsion and it was all over.

The day she decided to die also turned out to be the exact day that the caretaker of the ashram, in keeping with old Braj tradition, was visiting his in-laws for Holi. Among the sixty-five widows aged between sixty and one-hundred-and-five there was not a single man present.

"Saptadal is gone." Within minutes the news had spread like fire through the ashram. Incredulous, the old women of various ages rushed with unsteady steps towards her little room. Eighty-year-old Ananda Dasi worked her toothless mouth rapidly—the gist being that Saptadal, even at her advanced age, had not abandoned her teasing ways. She is enjoying the fun—eyes shut, body stretched out, pretending she's dead: tickle her feet a little and she'll sit up laughing.

"It's not a prank this time; it's true." One-hundred-and-five-year-old Lakhi Dasi somberly confirmed the matter of death, leaving Ananda Dasi speechless.

Suddenly, some women started to sob, unnerving Ananda Dasi even more. She looked about her anxiously, struck her forehead and whispered, "You can't forsake me, Saptadal! You came to fetch me each time you saw an open kitchen or a free distribution of blankets somewhere! Who will look after me now?"

Another old woman turned tearful. "I can't even see properly! My eyes are so weak . . . with your support I found my way to the *bhajans* in the temples. Without you who will bring me strength, Sister?"

A wet pool of drool, phlegm and tears; some toothless mouths agape; a few wrinkled hands holding the damp wall for support; a few decrepit bodies falling to the floor in a heap, full of tears; a deeply moving spectacle of sorrow.

Old Lakhi Dasi, the first to emerge from this welter of grief, suddenly spoke, her voice anxious. "Stop this crying and sobbing. We need to think instead of the difficulty facing us now."

Some women stopped crying, and puzzled, murmured: "What kind of difficulty?"

"The caretaker is away. He won't be back until tomorrow. It may even be the day after! We can't keep Saptadal here that long."

To some, Lakhi Dasi's attitude towards their recently departed companion seemed out of place, even heartless. Sensing this, Lakhi Dasi began in a choked voice, "I can hardly bear to bring up the matter of her last rites. But what can we do, there's no help. We have to be practical."

No one spoke.

Rubbing the tip of her nose with the edge of her sari, Lakhi Dasi tried to make the silly old women understand—"Look, it's the month of March. Summer is already upon us. If we don't immediately seek our neighbours' help in cremating Saptadal we won't find any men for another two days because of Holi."

And sure enough it was *Holika dahan* that evening and the play of color the day after. The festival of Braj, the rustic Holi, the play of colors, the Holi of *gulal,* the Holi of mud and mire. The numerous faces of Holi danced before their eyes. Who would leave the vivid and colorful festival to help cremate a corpse?

Leaving Saptadal's lifeless body in the care of their even more feeble companions, the old women of Amarbari stepped out of the ashram and soon scattered like beads from a broken necklace in the numerous bye-lanes of Vrindavan. They walked from house to house, pleading. Some people opened their doors while others chided from within—"Seek another house, brother. Everyone's busy; it's festival time. Who can step out now to give you alms!"

Alms?

The one rupee a day which they received for singing *bhajans* in big and small temples had seemed like earnings more than alms to the old women. They had always accepted those one-rupee coins with their heads held high. But today, the last rites of their dead companion had virtually made them beggars. It didn't take them long to realize that amongst this crowd of false angels, who dropped a fistful of flour in their brass bowl or pressed a rupee or fifty paise in their hands, there was not one like that Great Giver Karna. No, not one who would give even four grains of pity.

Turned away from one door after another, old Lakhi Dasi was so disheartened by people's callousness that she collapsed outside the next house even before she had knocked on the gate.

Quite suddenly, a young girl of about sixteen opened the door to step out for some chore. On seeing Lakhi Dasi she asked in a concerned voice—

"Why are you lying here, *Mai?* Is everything all right?"

"If your father or brother is at home, please send him out, my daughter!" said Lakhi Dasi, licking her dry lips.

"Do you have some work with him?" asked the girl simply. "You can tell me, if you like."

This was the first time that morning when someone had bothered to talk to Lakhi Dasi. Her eyes flooded at this unexpected sympathy from the young girl. "An old woman from Amarbari has just died. A few men for her last rites . . ."

"All right, I will get papa. You can talk to him," said the girl and went back inside.

After a few minutes the good man emerged and asked in a kindly voice—"Who is this old woman who has just died?"

"She was a widow," replied Lakhi Dasi, wiping her tears.

"That is all right but what was her caste? What community was she from . . .?"

"Oh *Baba!*" Lakhi Dasi's eyes distended. "Who can tell? The unfortunate Saptadal herself did not know this! At the age of ten she was dumped here by a relative from her in-laws' side. No member of the family ever came back to look for her."

"Then you should look elsewhere, mother. This is a *kulin* Brahmin household. Had the dead woman been a Brahmin I would certainly have done something for her deliverance. But for an old woman of an uncertain caste . . ."

Tears streamed from Lakhi Dasi's eyes. "We are poor and helpless women, *Baba*. It is our fate to suffer. I beg you with folded hands to help this woman reach the cremation ground. Once the fuss of Holi begins it will be impossible to find help."

"I can see this is a delicate matter, Mother. But you must excuse me. Had the dead woman been . . ."

"That she was a Brahmin by caste is not something I can say for sure. The eighty-year-old Saptadal herself did not know her caste. But you will earn great merit by arranging for her last rites."

Sobbing uncontrollably, Lakhi Dasi fell at the good man's feet as he shrank in horror—"Get away, let go of my feet! How dare you ruin this auspicious day with your copious tears! It's not for nothing that God has exiled you from home. You are paying for your karma. Didn't you find anything better than to go after me! Move along now, this minute, you understand?"

What was left to understand? Lakhi Dasi covered her eyes with the end of her torn sari, groped for her walking stick and started out, barefoot, on the dust-filled street.

At the same time, the master of the house went back in to vent his anger on his daughter—"You should have better sense, Geeta. You did not even enquire about the dead woman's caste. You should have asked her that little question and sent her on her way! A *kulin* Brahmin's daughter and you don't know the basics of social conduct?"

The girl kept silent in her father's presence. But later she went up to her mother who was frying *puris* in the kitchen and grumbled, "Papa is weird! On the question of the last rites of an old woman from Amarbari he just took off on caste and community."

"And what is wrong with that? Caste and community issues are important—from breaking bread and marrying daughters to shouldering the dead. But young girls these days think it's fashionable to turn up their noses at tradition," her mother chided Geeta.

Not one to give up easily, Geeta approached her brother who was two years older—"*Ai* Prashant! Will you do me a favor?"

"Speak!" said Prashant, positioning a brightly colored cap on his head and admiring his appearance in the mirror.

"An old woman from Amarbari has just died. Couldn't you get your friends to help with her cremation rites?"

"Are you mad?" said Prashant. "My friends must be in the thick of celebrations. Will I ask them to shoulder a corpse at this time? In any case, this kind of social service is best left to the elderly."

Geeta said not a word more to anyone after this. When her heart felt heavy she went up to the terrace to breathe in the cool, fresh air. She was a class ten student. Anasuya and Deepa who lived on either side of her house were not just her classmates but also her intimate friends. She called them both to the terrace and the three went into a huddle for a long time. Then she came down to the kitchen and announced to her mother, "I am going out to see my class teacher."

"At this hour? This is no time to visit your teacher!" Ma was puzzled.

"She has sent for Deepa, Anasuya and me. She said she'll tell us some important questions for the English exam," Geeta shrugged carelessly.

"Today? On Holi?"

"Holi will come and go but exams are not going to be held back on its account." Geeta was cross. "I have an English exam in two days' time. All three of us are so bad at English. The teacher knows this well. She's sent a message through Deepa that we should bring 500 rupees each and reach her house this evening. She will reveal the questions to us so that our futures may be redeemed!"

"Your father . . ."

"Don't talk to me about Papa. He objects to everything. He objected to my dropping English for Intermediate exams. Now he will object to my visiting the teacher and tomorrow he will object to my failing in English. In fact, his last objection will be the strongest. You know this, don't you?"

"When will you return?"

"These things take time, Ma! Only after she's taken the money from us will the teacher attempt to get the rest of the exam questions from the other teachers. Three to four hours at the least. But why should you worry? There are three of us going together and we will come back together."

Irritated to see her mother hesitate still, Geeta cried, "Look, Deepa and Anasuya are already here . . . now, are you giving me the money or will you have me repeat my first year of college?"

Stuffing five hundred-rupee notes into her purse, Geeta swiftly slipped out of the house. On reaching the main road the trio stopped a cycle rickshaw and climbed in, saying, "Take us to where we can buy all the items for a funeral."

"There is some shame in having to lie . . ." Deepa said seriously as she wiped her damp forehead.

"As girls, could we have stepped out of the house if we had told the truth?" Anasuya countered.

"Forget it. This is just the beginning. Our intentions are pure and so we must overlook the impurity of our means. Let's hope we can do something for those unfortunate women," Geeta said.

From that moment the women of Amarbari settled in the hearts of the three girls.

One by one, the old women had all returned to the ashram, failure darkening their eyes, and the sea of despair heaving in their hearts. Their pleas had borne no fruit. The appeal for the last rites of a widow of uncertain caste and community had been dismissed completely by all. Even wandering for hours in the narrow lanes of Vrindavan and beating their heads at every door had been to no avail.

The evening sky was turning dark and the fear of a sleepless night gradually swallowed the light of their consciousness. The cause of concern was not just the prospect of having to spend a night keeping vigil over a corpse but also the speed with which it was deteriorating in the summer heat. The women had no arrangement for slabs of ice. Nor was there any incense at hand to conceal the smell of death. The old women aged between sixty and one-hundred-and-five who found it difficult to bear the weight of their own underclothes could now do little except sit in silence around the body, their words and tears both spent. As for food— since afternoon not even a drop of water had passed their lips.

And somewhere nearby a group of men were swaying to the beats of drums and *mridangam*:

*Aaj Biraj mein Holi re rasia . . .*

The widows of Amarbari had played such Holi that day, their faces were discolored from the *gulal* of dust and grime and the darkness of grief.

Breaking the silence suddenly, Lakhi Dasi uttered a cry. "Krishna's land has bidden fare-well to goodness and humanity, Saptadal! For all our efforts we could not raise your bier today."

Ananda Dasi also broke down. "Was the weight of your lifeless body so great, my friend, that four men couldn't be found in all of Vrindavan to bear it?"

Ananda Dasi beat her shaven head. "Even a dead animal brings the butcher running to have it skinned. This dust which is your body could not find even that price, Sister."

The mourning would perhaps have gone on longer when suddenly a voice was heard: "Don't weep, *Maji*, we are here to help you."

*Help?*

Who has come to breathe life into these fading creatures?

The old women turned their blurry, sightless eyes towards the voice. Three young girls of about seventeen stood holding the items needed for the cremation.

"We have to prepare for the funeral procession urgently," said Geeta in a soft voice when she found the old women staring at her.

"But you . . ."

"We are your well-wishers, we'll take care of everything. All you need to do is gather your strength," Deepa reassured them. The old women stared in disbelief at this unexpected help from the Divine Mother.

"The cremation ground is quite some distance away, *Maji*. We must hurry." Anasuya touched Lakhi Dasi's shoulder in a gesture of intimacy that seemed to rouse her from a deep slumber.

Without another word the women got busy with the job at hand. Three young girls and a group of old women. They had never thought they'd find themselves doing a job which men had always kept them from doing on the grounds that they were too fragile. They prepared the body and raised the bier on their shoulders and were on their way to the cremation grounds.

Along with the three girls it was Lakhi Dasi who leant her shoulder to the task. To the chants of *"Ram naam satya hai,"* Saptadal embarked with great ceremony on her last journey.

Not an ordinary funeral procession, this was also at once a protest march by women against a selfish and insensitive patriarchy which shadowed the lives of women from the beginning to the end: destroying the female embryo after an ultrasound report and forbidding women to conduct the last rites of the dead. At least that is how it seemed to this small group.

Since the cremation ground was some distance, and the shoulders bearing the body delicate, they had to pause after every ten steps and exchange places. But not once did they lose heart. On reaching the ground the girls bought the wood for the cremation. They did not remember the verses from the Vedas and perhaps did not need them. Lakhi Dasi walked ceremonially around the pyre once and set it on fire. Within minutes the flames were licking the sky. Several pairs of eyes turned moist yet again.

Lakhi Dasi, who had been still as a statue this whole time, suddenly stirred. "I swear upon you, Saptadal," she cried, "from this day on no woman from Amarbari will look towards a man for her last rites. Instead of begging from door to door for help, we will now be cremated with pride by our own people, our last remains gathered and immersed in the sacred rivers."

Geeta who stood nearby also folded her hands—"Saptadal, this is not just your funeral pyre; this is Holika herself. You chose a very special day to die, Saptadal."

"Not one Holi in all of Vrindavan could compare with this," Deepa said softly.

Anasuya simply stood there, her palms pressed together.

## Ali Rasheed   *THE MALDIVES*

Ali Rasheed is a writer and filmmaker. He has written feature-length screen-plays in both English and Dhivehi, the language of the Maldives. He earned a First Class Honours B.A. in Film, Television and Radio Studies from Staffordshire University in the United Kingdom and has filmed and edited feature films, documentaries and music videos for over a decade. His works have been shown at international film festivals and broadcast on national television in the Maldives. Through the auspices of the Thomson Foundation of the U.K. he was able to undertake journalism training, and has won a British Council short story competition held for Maldivians writing in English. Ali Rasheed has travelled throughout the Maldives in connection with his work, and has backpacked and filmed in India, Tibet and Nepal, where he trekked four times up the 5,600-metre Kala Pattar at the foot of Mt. Everest/Chomolungma. His works include the filming and editing of a documentary on the making of *Firaaq,* the feature directorial debut of celebrated Indian actress and human rights activist Nandita Das.

# THE VISIT

THE KATHEEB OF KUDAFUSHI WAS IN A FOUL MOOD. He had slept very little that week. He had been trying, rather unsuccessfully, to convince people to slog day and night to decorate the island for an official visit. In the end, he and a few die-hard loyals had done all the work while the rest of the island slept.

It was also common knowledge that the Katheeb and his wife had had a bad row lately, and that divorce was imminent. In fact it had been imminent for years, for they had a major tiff at least once a month, not to mention the weekly, and sometimes daily, fights which were not considered as serious.

When the Katheeb entered the island office his face expressed all his troubles, the wife and the visit, and the temporary clerk, a pesky girl just out of school, was unable to suppress a giggle. He turned on her at once.

"You there! Copy all of last year's daily fish reports and add them up."

The temporary looked dismayed. "Do I have to copy them? I can add them up nicely without copying them."

"Copy them and then add them."

He stormed into his room. Temporary's face looked like a moon-less night. The radio telephone operator grinned. He had enjoyed every second of the exchange. He hated the temporary clerk and was glad of any misfortune that befell her.

The Katheeb yelled for him.

"Go and fetch that Saranfeena. Didn't I tell you yesterday that she was to be here at 7:30 sharp?"

Radio's face fell. If there was one thing he hated more than everything else about his job, it was summoning people to the office. He had never been able to bring anyone here at one whack. Usually it took at least three visits to successfully convince anyone that they had to report, and then they grumbled about it so much that he would almost wish he hadn't.

The women were infinitely more tiresome. Saranfeena hadn't even acknowledged his presence when he gave her the Katheeb's message yesterday. "I did tell her to come," he sulked to his boss.

"Then why isn't she here?"

"I've no idea. She didn't bother to reply when I asked her to come. You know what they're like, the women of this island."

"*Do* I?" the Katheeb glared suspiciously at the young man. "Well tell her again."

"It won't do any good. She doesn't like you."

"On your way! And don't come back without her."

As the radio telephone operator fled the office, he caught sight of the temporary clerk looking on with interest. It was clear that she had been listening. He was furious. "Better start adding up," he called, leaving. "Only 365 reports to go."

It took only three minutes to ride to Saranfeena's house on his perishing bicycle. The island was so small that it was almost no use owning a bike at all. It was impossible to have a decent ride. Kudafushi was less than one square kilometre. The village, with its sparse population, was in the centre. The island had a noticeable lack of young men; most had gone off to Malé or the tourist resorts for work. It was years since the island had been able to hold Friday prayers, which required a minimum attendance of 40 adult males.

Kudafushi had two mechanized fishing *dhonis,* at least they had been built for the purpose of fishing. They were anchored most of the year because people were reluctant to toil away at sea for a meager income. They only went out when they absolutely had to, and when there was no other way of getting emergency cash into the household. The island had once been famous for dried fish and *rihakuru.* In the days before mechanization, six sailing *dhonis* had gone fishing regularly. Fish-collecting vessels equipped with freezing holds did not exist back then. All the catch was cooked at home by women. Men would then take large stocks of dried fish to Ceylon on the large *odi.* The *odi* had been obliterated though, like the island's previous wealth. Now packers bought the catch straight off the local *dhonis* for scanty sums.

Unlike the radio telephone operator, Saranfeena, the President of the Women's Committee, had seen those glorious times. She came out of her house and looked at him with undisguised contempt. "You can tell the Katheeb from me that the women of this island are not his slaves."

Radio felt a spray of saliva on his face and backed away, alarmed. "But the office needs you and all the members of the Women's Committee to make the island look nice for the government dignitary who is coming."

"We've already done more than our share of the work," the President scoffed. "Tell the Katheeb to make the men do some work around here for a change!" Her massive bosom heaved in a frightening but fascinating manner.

"But they're out at sea in the *bokkuras,* catching fish for supper."

"Do you really think a couple of skinny *tholhis* will keep the island from starving? They're running away from work. I'm not fooled even if the island office is."

"But, but . . . I can't go back without you. You'll have to come."

"I'm the President of the Women's Committee, an elected leader, unlike the Katheeb, I might add—and I expect to be treated like one.

If the Katheeb wants me he can fetch me himself. Tell him not to send half-witted clerks." With that, the President turned her unyielding back on Radio and returned inside her palm hut.

"I'm not a clerk," he yelled after her, but it was no use. He got back on his creaking bicycle and rode off. Passing by Sameena's house, he decided to stop in for a chew. Sameena didn't look pleased to see him.

"Oh, it's you," she said. "I was just going out."

Radio lowered his lean frame onto an outdoor *joli* cot and stared at Sameena's figure appreciatively. She was light-skinned and comely, with just the right amount of roundness that gave softness and femininity to a woman. A picture of health and unflagging energy, he thought, as his eyes travelled upwards, stopping at her bosom.

"Bring out the chewing box," he said huskily.

Sameena hesitated for a moment before reluctantly going into the house. Radio paused comfortably to enjoy her rear view as much as the front. Sameena's mother, he knew, always insisted that she be nice to him. After all, his father owned the only decent shop on the island and it was obvious to everybody what the old lady had in mind. Sameena had already declared to her mother that she wouldn't mind owning the shop, but not if it came with the radio telephone operator.

She brought out the chewing box and placed it on Radio's lap. He felt a little shiver of excitement. "Where's your mother?"

"She's gone to make a *fanditha* for Saranfeena's back."

"What's the matter with it? I've just been to see her. She looked alright to me."

"Well, she isn't. She's been complaining about a pain in her back for days. She said it was because of all the work the island office was making her do for some official visit."

"Never mind Saranfeena's back. It's your parts I'm interested in. If you don't have any pain anywhere I'm happy."

"I do have a pain, in the neck. But it'll disappear eventually I hope."

"Perhaps I should massage it," Radio suggested. "I'm exceptionally good at that."

"No thanks," she said firmly. He had tried clawing at her before and she wasn't having any of it again. She shuddered as his long, clammy fingers folded the areca nut shavings into the betel leaf. Radio put it into his mouth and his eyes gleamed with pleasure and satisfaction as the juice dripped down his chin. He wiped the red-brown liquid with the back of his hand and looked hungrily at Sameena.

"Sit down here. You look sick. What are you standing for?"

"Sameena!" She heaved a sigh of relief as she heard her mother's shrill voice. Sakeena arrived busily, small and thin with large hands and feet. Radio looked at her frontage with distaste. Flat as a *murana roshi*, he thought; not at all like her lovely daughter.

"Saranfeena's having a bath," the mother scowled. "She's always bathing when I go there." Then Sakeena noticed Radio and her scowl disappeared immediately. "Sameena," she called, "why haven't you brought your guest anything to eat?" The radio telephone operator beamed at this. "We need to fatten you up, my dear boy. You're far too thin to marry my daughter. Why, she would break you in half the first night," she cackled. "Why, for that matter I would too!"

Radio felt a certain thrill at Sakeena's familiarity as well as repulsion. He imagined her as a mother-in-law, and his stomach turned at the thought. He wouldn't mind marrying Sameena, she had the most fulsome form on the island, but not if she came with Sakeena.

All this time Sakeena was oblivious to Radio's feelings toward her. It was a study in contrast, mirroring her daughter's very feelings for Radio. Sameena had absolutely no intention whatsoever of marrying Radio. She would marry anybody if they would only take her away from her mother and the radio telephone operator. She watched her mother fussing over him and marvelled at their amazing likeness, both of them scrawny and callous. Her father had died two years ago and she missed him even now. He had adored her from the first. Some people claimed he had often stopped her mother from beating her up when she was a child. Not that she didn't take the occasional smacking, they said. She had driven her mother crazy with her disappearances. Sometimes she would spend all day out with the boys, swimming, fishing and drinking coconuts from other people's trees. No matter how hard her mother scolded her, Sameena just wouldn't read the Koran or learn her prayers. The more her mother scolded her, the worse she got, and the more indulgent her father became. Some people said he'd stopped loving his wife then, if he had ever loved her in the first place.

As Sameena grew older, Sakeena drew her husband aside firmly. "She's becoming a woman now. It's not proper for a father to show so much affection for a grown-up daughter. It might lead to unspeakable things."

He died soon afterwards of a mysterious illness. Some people said Sakeena had put a spell on him to prevent the unspeakables she so dreaded. Sameena herself had become quieter and more disciplined. Sakeena's only wish now was to get her married off; indeed it was her burning desire. The radio telephone operator was a perfect match for any girl, she deduced. Why, he had everything a woman could possibly want—a government job, a retail shop, good looks and a bicycle. Admittedly, the bicycle creaked a bit, and he was a little on the thin side. But those were minor faults which could easily be rectified with a bit of Singer oil and fried food. In fact Radio was so attractive that Sakeena would have married him herself if she didn't have a grown-up daughter to look after.

Radio felt increasingly uncomfortable as he felt Sakeena's gaze on him and hastily got up to go. He would have brushed hard against Sameena but she neatly dodged out of his way as he went out. Walking back into the office he bumped into the Katheeb, who was hurrying out.

"Where've you been?" the Katheeb demanded. "It's been hours since you left. And where's Saranfeena?"

"She wouldn't come. I told you it was no use."

Strangely, the Katheeb didn't seem to mind. "He's coming tomorrow," he primped.

"Who is?"

"The high government dignitary of course. I'm not supposed to release his name, not yet. So I can't tell you who it is. Isn't it wonderful? A truly respectable person is at last about to grace this soil. Why I don't believe we've had a high-level visit in a decade."

"What's he coming for?" Radio asked cautiously.

"I've no definite idea. Undoubtedly he'll give a pious, morally beneficial speech to the entire population. I must beautify the school hall. I've waited all my life for this moment. The degeneration of this island will be reversed tomorrow! I shall ask for an electricity generator, an English teacher, a family health worker, new corrugated sheets for the roof of the mosque."

Radio felt an unexpected pang. "I hope he'll remember all that," he said.

"Of course he will. I shall assure him of the island's undying support for the government. And he will be fed the best meal he's ever had in his life. No less than forty fat chickens will grace our tables. When I get the island what it needs, I can resign for I will know that I have been of use to it."

Radio felt awkward and looked away. He didn't know what to say.

"I'm going out for a bit," the Katheeb announced. "Blow the conch. I want the entire island gathered here when I come back."

Radio was relieved to hear the familiar authority in the Katheeb's voice. He went in to fetch the conch shell. The temporary clerk was busy fiddling with something.

"What're you playing with now?"

She looked up at him. "It's the *durra*. I'm admiring the lacquer work. Most intricate."

Radio was shocked at her irreverence. The flat punishment baton was a symbol of ultimate authority! "Put it away at once," he demanded. "It's a good thing the magistrate didn't see you. What would he think if he knew you were playing with his *durra?*"

"Oh is that why he didn't come in this morning?" She ran her fingers over the heavy paddle. "I love these stud-things."

"You'll love them even more if you get the feel of them on your back-side. You know why it's used."

"Go and make Sameena pregnant! I hope you get squashed in the process." Giggling, the temporary went into the island court, which occupied one room of the island office, to put away the *durra*.

"Good-for-nothing lump of flesh."

"What a marvellously accurate description of Sameena!" she retorted from the court.

Radio went to the office locker and took out the conch. Then he went outside. A few people were sitting on the road, talking in the shade. He put the conch on his mouth and blew with all the might of his small lungs. A hoarse, windy sound wafted out of it. The people lifted their heads, stared at him, and then resumed talking. He gave two more blows and went in, out of breath. The clerk was back at her desk.

"Nobody will come," she remarked. "Nobody takes any notice of the conch anymore. They know it's only sounded to make them slave away or to take a donation from them to repair the mosque or the visitor's house or some such thing. You'll have to go round the village as usual and beg them to come. The conch has outlived its effectiveness, and not a bad thing either."

"You give that tongue of yours a rest or it'll drop off in a year."

"If it does it will have done more service to this world than your tongue, or any other part of you is ever likely to do."

The small room darkened as a huge shape blocked off the light coming in from the doorway. It was the President of the Women's Committee. She was dressed in a pink *digu hedun* with matching *bolu foti*. Her hands and neck glittered with ornaments. Radio looked at her in awe. He felt she would burst out of her dress any minute. He could almost hear the seams saying their last prayers. Did she and her husband still . . .?

Saranfeena looked at him sharply, as if she could read his thoughts. He looked away hurriedly. "Kindly tell the Katheeb that I wish to see him."

"He's not here. Come later." The temporary clerk was the only person in the island office who wasn't scared of Saranfeena. The President ignored her.

"Where's he gone?" she asked Radio.

"I don't know but I'm sure he won't be long."

"How dare he disappear after asking me to come here? I've a good mind to report this to the Department of Women's Affairs and have them appoint another Katheeb. Go out and find him. I can't wait here all day."

The radio telephone operator fled thankfully. He got on his bike and rode off to the Katheeb's house. The Katheeb's wife was sitting on the road in the shade of a breadfruit tree. Another woman was sitting behind her, removing nits from her hair. The Katheeb's partly deaf mother was also sitting in the shade, weaving a *fungi*.

"The problem with the island is that it hasn't got enough people. No wonder nobody's ever visited it," the Katheeb's wife was saying.

"You could say this island is like the country. Nobody outside it takes any notice of it," remarked the nit-remover.

"Yes, and the country is like the world. God's left it to destroy itself."

"How irreligious."

The Katheeb's mother took part in the conversation. "I think it's disgraceful that the island's team lost the match against Bodufushi last Eid. Bodufushi may have more people than this island, but what's the use of that if they're all fools?"

"They once said Friday prayers on a Thursday," added the lice-remover disdainfully.

"When I was on the team we never lost a single match," the Katheeb's mother declared.

The Katheeb's wife spied the radio telephone operator. "The Katheeb's not here," she said, "he hasn't come here since he left for work."

Radio rode off without a word, leaving the women staring after him.

"Rude, skinny thing," said the Katheeb's wife.

"I know what he's after," said her mother-in-law, lowering her voice. "He wants the Katheeb's job. I knew it the day he was employed. His father thinks just because he has a little money his family can rule this island. Don't they know my son and the ministers are like brothers?"

"His mother's worse," said the Katheeb's wife. "Never turns up to do her share on sweeping day, just because she was in some third-rate school in Malé for a few years."

"As if money can buy leadership. You can take it from me that they'll die wanting but not getting what they want," concluded her mother-in-law.

Happily, Radio hadn't a clue about his gloomy prospects as he rode back to the office, panting. There was no point in looking for the Katheeb in the hot sun. He could be anywhere on the island. There was nobody in the office. Perhaps they'd all gone out for mid-morning tea. He suddenly remembered it was call time and went to the communications set. He turned it on and the entire atoll squealed at him. He turned down the volume hurriedly.

The Katheeb burst out of his room. "Turn that thing off. Can't you see I'm busy with Saranfeena?"

Sure enough, through the half-opened door he could see a pink posterior protruding from the back of the chair.

"It's call time," he said stiffly. "Romiet, Papa Three. Romiet, Papa Three calling." Romiet was the code name for the capital island of the atoll. There was a squeal in response. Radio adjusted the tuning and called again. This time the answer was loud and clear. "Papa Three, Romiet. You can switch off. There's nothing for you."

The Katheeb snatched the mouthpiece. "Romiet, Papa Three. Any news about the visit?"

"He's changed his mind. He's not visiting you after all. He's visiting Bodufushi instead."

"But we've already slaughtered the chickens," the Katheeb said.

"I'm cutting you off now." The squealing stopped.

Saranfeena came out of the Katheeb's room. "So all my work was for nothing."

The Katheeb looked at her helplessly. "Perhaps he'll change his mind again tomorrow."

The President of the Women's Committee snorted, turning her back on them. Dismayed, the Katheeb and his Radio Operator watched in silence as Saranfeena's generous pink rump disappeared into sunshine.

# GLOSSARY

**aakondo:** purple flower or blossom used in Hindu rituals/*pujas*. It forms one of the five darts with which the God of Love is supposed to pierce the hearts of young mortals

**achar:** oily or salty Indian pickle of any kind (mango, lemon, pepper, etc.), usually spicy

**aiselu:** wild strawberries

**aloo tarkari:** potato curry

**amla:** citrus fruit, used for medicinal purposes

**anchal:** part of sari used to cover head and breast

**andarmahal:** the inner part or room of a home, usually for the women; male guests and outsiders are not allowed to enter

**annas:** Indian coins worth one quarter of a rupee

**asr:** evening, or evening prayer

**Aum Shanti:** a peaceful blessing

**Baba:** colloquial word for a senior or respected person (term of address)

**Bablu:** endearing nickname for a boy, means "small sir"

**babu:** Hindu title of address equivalent to Sir, Mr., Esq., or a native Indian clerk who writes in English

**badam:** almond, or almond oil

**Baishakh** (also *Vaisakh*): second month of the Hindu calendar, follows *Chaitra*

**bandha:** servant

**barolok:** wealthy, well-to-do

**bashi:** not fresh, going to be rotten

**bbaji:** deep-fried veggie snacks

**bel:** leaves of wood-apple fruit used in ritual offerings

**Bhagwan:** term for God or a spiritual teacher

**Bhaijan:** brother

**bhajans:** Hindu devotional hymns

**bhakris:** rotis, flatbread

**Bhanubhakta:** Nepali poet who translated the *Ramayana* from Sanskrit into Nepali

**bhavas:** refers to the emotive facial expressions and gestures used in classical South Indian dance

**Bhil:** tribal people of central India

**bideshi:** foreigner

**bidis:** cheap, hand-rolled cigarettes

**bighas:** measure of land, a third of an acre

**bikriwala:** market vendor of general house-hold items and simple jewellery

**biryani:** fragrant meat dish served over rice

**bokkura:** small rowboat

**bolu foti:** head-dress worn with *digu hedun*

**bou bhat:** reception party given by the groom's family after a wedding

**bukhari:** small coal-fired stove used in the Himalayas

**bulath:** betel nut leaf

**Chaitra:** first month of the Hindu calendar

**chapatti:** thin unleavened bread, similar to tortillas

**chhapra:** a kind of shanty or hut found in urban slums

**chowki:** string cot or bed

**chowki hawaldar:** low-level police officer

**chowkidar:** night watchman

**dacoity/dacoit:** banditry/robbery, bandit

**dal/daal:** lentils, pulses

**Deva:** India's great Mother Goddess

**dhonis:** small fishing boats

**dhoti:** voluminous cotton leggings worn by men

**digu hedun:** tight-fitting long dress, widely used as national dress

**doma:** betel nut, a digestive and mild stimulant

**dosais/dosas:** veggie or meat-filled crepe-pockets typical of South India and Sri Lanka

**durra:** flat baton used for flogging people for offenses such as fornication

**duva:** young girl

**fanditha:** magic spell

**fungi:** matting woven from dry coconut leaves and used for fences and thatched roofs

**gandharaj:** a flowering, scented tree

**Govind Maharaj:** a manifestation of Lord Krishna

**gram-devata:** traditional village deity

**gulal:** the powder (usually red) thrown and sprinkled by participants in the Holi festival

**guru:** teacher/master

**haldi:** turmeric

**halwa:** sweet sesame paste

**Hare Om:** healing mantra invoking Lord Vishnu

**hari:** cooking pot

**Holi:** Hindu festival of light and colours; celebrates the defeat of the demoness Holika

**Holika dahan:** lighting the Holi fire

**houri:** voluptuous, supernatural woman

**hurs:** heavenly girls of eternal youth and beauty

**Huzoor:** sir

**Id/Eid:** Muslim festive occasion at the end of Ramadan

**jadu-tona:** superstition, black magic

**jalebi:** deep-fried, curly sweet

**janaza:** funeral prayer service

**jhol:** light, spiced gravy

**ji:** denotes respect when used as a suffix to a person's name

**jinn:** genie, spirit

**joli:** garden or beach-side seat made of rope and sticks with a back-rest

**Kalema Tayyeba:** another term for the *Shahadat* or Testimony of Faith in Islam

**kantha:** embroidered quilt generally made with the old clothes of women

**Karna:** an important character from the *Mahabharata*, known for his generosity

**Katheeb:** head of the island

**khabar:** food

**khaini:** mild digestives, stimulants

**khatam-shafa:** a special prayer to God to have His mercy in any critical situation

**khukuri:** the national knife of Nepal and symbol of the far-famed Gurkha soldier. Used for defence, for kitchenware and for cutting wood.

**kira:** an apron of rectangular cloth wrapped around the body worn by women in the hills. The national dress of Bhutan, usually worn with a long-sleeved blouse.

**kishmish:** raisins

**korma:** Mughal thick curry with cream

**kulin:** of noble descent; respectable

**kurta:** long cotton shirt

**laddoo:** sweet deep-fried dough ball

**loban:** resin/incense used medicinally

**madal:** two-sided Nepali hand-drum

**madama:** orphanage

**madrassah:** Muslim religious school for boys

**mahajan:** moneylender

**Mahars:** sub-community within the Dalits

**mahattaya:** gentleman

**mahatturu:** gentlemen, "Sirs"

**mahrum:** person whom one is not permitted to meet for religious reasons

**Mahua:** plant from which rough home-brewed liquor is made

**Mai:** old mother or old lady

**Maji:** respectful term for mother

**maktab:** school where students are taught Qur'an and Islamic subjects. Also, a prayer and study room in larger, traditional homes.

**mandapam:** open-air temple pavilion

**manna:** heavy Sri Lankan knife for shredding coconut

**Mariai:** village goddess of pestilence formerly revered by Dalits, and in some areas still worshipped by them

**Mataji:** "My Mother"

**maulvi:** Sunni Muslim religious scholar/teacher

**mela:** large religious gathering

**moksha:** release from rebirth in the world; deliverance

**momo:** Tibetan steamed dumplings

**mridangam:** a musical instrument

**mudras:** sacred hand gestures, associated with ancient dance styles and some forms of meditation

**muezzin:** Muslim crier of prayers from minaret tower

**muji-jatha:** casual insult, similar to "motherf..."

**murana roshi:** toasted pancake

**muri:** puffed rice

**Mussalman:** Muslim

**nagra:** a type of trumpet or horn

**Namaskar/Namaste:** Hindu customary greeting; "I bow to the divine within you"

**nauzubillah:** "alas!"

**nona:** Lady

**nonala:** young lady

**odi:** large traditional wooden cargo vessel

**paan:** betel nut

**pagari:** cloth turban, can also be added to a Nepali pill-box hat

**panchayat:** local governance council

**paneer:** homemade cheese

**para:** neighbourhood

**pir:** older person, usually a spiritual teacher

**poee:** a type of bread commonly sold by Goa street vendors in the early morning

**polao/pulao:** rice dish

**pootham:** dark supernatural spirit

**puja:** religious ceremony

**pukka:** good, the right stuff

**purdah:** system of household seclusion of women

**puris:** deep-fried bread

**putha:** son

**Ram naam satya hai:** "the name of Ram is the only Truth"

**rambuttans:** sweet tree fruit

**rihakuru:** thick paste made from excessive cooking of tuna

**rishi munis:** sages, enlightened teachers with special powers

**roshgulla/rasgulla:** cheese dumpling dessert served with sweet syrup

**sag/saag:** spinach

**sambar:** thick South Indian veggie soup

**shahnazar:** literally "an imperial view." Moment in wedding ceremony when the bride and groom see each other's face.

**shalwar:** loose trousers; part of the traditional clothing of *Shalwar-Kamiz* (*kamiz:* shirt or tunic)

**shandesh:** Bengali fresh cheese dessert

**Shari'ah:** Islamic religious law

**Shudra:** last of the four castes, the working caste

**string-hoppers:** popular Sri Lankan/South Indian dish: steamed, curled rice noodle spirals

**sukuti:** dried meat/jerky

**surma:** cosmetic eye make-up/medicine

**tableeg:** meeting of the pious to propagate Islam and to gain religious knowledge

**tahajjud:** night prayer

**taka:** Bangladeshi currency

**taluka:** district, or an area grouping of villages

**tehsildar:** civil official, tax gatherer

**thana:** police station

**tholhi:** trumpet fish

**tip shoi:** thumb print used as the signature of an illiterate person

**tonga:** old-fashioned horse-drawn cart, also used as a taxi in isolated areas

**watte:** shanty complex

**zamindar:** Muslim-era term for a deputy-collector, still used in referring to an official supervising land use and taxation of a large region

**zaqqum:** tree that grows in hell; bitter fruit

**zohr:** prayer after mid-day

**zunka:** Maharashtra dish of lentils and onions

# ABOUT THE EDITOR

Trevor Carolan was born in Yorkshire, England. His family emigrated to British Columbia and he began writing professionally at age 17, filing dispatches from San Francisco's Haight-Ashbury music scene. He travelled in Britain, Europe and India before receiving an M.A. in English at Humboldt State University, California, in 1978. He served as literary coordinator for the XV Olympic Winter Games from 1986-88, and has since published 16 books, including works of fiction, poetry, memoirs, translations, and anthologies. His work has appeared in five languages and includes *Return to Stillness: Twenty Years With a Tai Chi Master* and *Giving Up Poetry: With Allen Ginsberg At Hollyhock,* a memoir of his acquaintance with the late poet. A longtime activist on behalf of international human rights and Pacific Coast watershed issues, he earned an interdisciplinary Ph.D. at Bond University, Queensland, Australia and teaches English at the University of the Fraser Valley near Vancouver, Canada. In 2009, Cheng & Tsui published his companion anthology to this present volume entitled *Another Kind of Paradise: Short Stories from the New Asia-Pacific.*

# ABOUT THE TRANSLATORS

**Priya Adarkar** was born in Mumbai in 1939. A writer and translator, she received an M.A. in English from Oxford University and is well-known for her translations of the Marathi language plays of Vijay Tendulkar.

**Joydeep Bhattacharya** was born in Lubeck and raised in Calcutta. A playwright, actor and director of Bengali group theatre, he formerly worked in finance before dropping out to live a more spiritual life. He also works in social welfare and lives in Singur, near Kolkata.

**A.J. Canagaratna** is a former professor of English at the University of Jaffna. A literary critic and translator, he lives in Jaffna.

**Mridula Nath Chakraborty** trained in English literature at Delhi University and completed her Ph.D. at the University of Alberta in Canada. Her research interests range from postcolonial literatures to global English and Bombay cinema. In 1997, she won the A. K. Ramanujan Award for translation from two Indian languages and has translated and co-edited, with Rani Ray, *A Treasury of Bangla Stories* (Srishti, 1999).

**Pratik Kanjilal** is publisher and co-editor of *The Little Magazine*. A translator and specialist in New Media, he worked earlier as Chief Operating Officer of Indian Express Online Media and with *The Indian Express, Business Standard* and *The Economic Times*. His awards include the first New York University Prize for Hyperfiction and the Sahitya Akademi Translation Prize. He lives in Delhi.

**Muhammad Umar Memon** is emeritus professor of Urdu, Persian and Islamic Studies at the University of Wisconsin–Madison. His collection of short stories, *Tareek Galee,* appeared in 1989. He has translated widely from English and Arabic into Urdu. His translations from Urdu include *The Essence of Camphor* and *Snake Catcher,* both by Naiyer Masud, and several other collections of short stories. General editor of the Oxford University Press, Pakistan Writers Series, he is also editor of the *Annual of Urdu Studies.*

**Shabnam Nadiya** is a writer and translator. She works as a senior director in the Bengal Foundation, an organization for music, arts and literature in Dhaka.

**Ira Raja** is an assistant professor in English at the University of Delhi, India, and a postdoctoral fellow at La Trobe University, Australia. She has edited *Endless Winter's Night: An Anthology of Mother-Daughter Stories* (Women Unlimited, 2010); *Grey Areas: An Anthology of Indian Fiction on Ageing* (Oxford University Press, 2010); and with John Thieme, *The Table Is Laid: Oxford Anthology of South Asian Food Writing* (Oxford University Press, 2007).

**Jai Ratan** is a veteran translator and literary commentator. He has offered to readers in English some of the best Urdu writing from the Indian subcontinent. His honours include the Sahitya Akademi Translation Prize. He lives in Delhi.

**Antara Dev Sen** is the Founding Editor of *The Little Magazine*. A columnist, critic and translator, she worked earlier as Senior Editor of *The Hindustani Times* and Senior Assistant Editor of *The Indian Express*, among other assignments, including stints as a copywriter and private investigator. She is based in Delhi.

**Sheila Sengupta** is a freelance translator based in Delhi. Her published translations include Sunil Gangopadhyay's poetry collection *Murmur in the Woods* and his novel *Ranu O Bhanu*. Her work has appeared in *Indian Literature, The Journal of the Poetry Society (India), Parabaas*, and *Bengal Partition Stories: An Unclosed Chapter* (Anthem Press, UK).

# CREDITS

"His Father's Funeral," by Neeru Nanda. From *If.* Rupa and Company, New Delhi, 2008. Reprinted by permission of the publisher.

"Arjun," by Mahasweta Devi. First published as "Arjun" in Bangla in *Dainik Bartaman,* 1984. This translation in English by Mridula Nath Chakraborty first published in Meenakshi Sharma, ed. *The Wordsmiths,* by Katha, 1996; and in *The Bell and Other Stories,* by Katha, 2000, New Delhi.

"Nina Awaits Mrs. Kamath's Decision," by Salil Chaturvedi. Published in *First Proof 4,* Penguin, New Delhi, 2008. Reprinted by permission of the author.

"I Won't Ask Mother," by Kunzang Choden. From *Tales In Colour and Other Stories,* Zubaan, New Delhi, 2009. Reprinted by permission of the author and publisher.

"Law and Order," by Sushma Joshi. From *New Nepal, New Voices,* Sushma Joshi and Ajit Baral, eds. Rupa and Company, New Delhi, 2008. Reprinted by permission of the publisher.

"Emancipation," by Hasan Manzar. This translation in English by Muhammad Umar Memon published in *Requiem and Other Stories,* Oxford University Press, Pakistan, 1998. Reprinted by permission of Muhammad Umar Memon.

"The Dispossessed," by Kunthavai. This translation from the Tamil story "Peyarvu" by A.J. Canagaratna with Antara Dev Sen published in *The Little Magazine, Favourite Fiction II,* New Delhi, 2007. Reprinted by permission of the publisher. TLM: www.littlemag.com/about/about.html.

"Bablu's Choice," by Ela Arab Mehta. This translation by the author with Devina Dutt and Pratik Kanjilal. Published in *The Little Magazine, Favourite Fiction II,* New Delhi, 2007. Reprinted by permission of the publisher. TLM: www.littlemag.com/about/about.html.

"Libations," by Usha Yadav. Originally published in Hindi as "Tarpan," *Hans,* April (2001): 73-79. This translation by Ira Raja, 2010. Reprinted by permission of the author and translator.

"The Visit," by Ali Rasheed. Published by permission of the author.

# CHENG & TSUI
## CONTEMPORARY ASIAN LITERATURE SERIES

### DIGITAL GEISHAS AND TALKING FROGS
A collection of short fiction from celebrated Japanese authors, several making their English-language debut.

### THE LOTUS SINGERS
South Asia's most dynamic literary voices contribute compelling stories about a rapidly changing region.

### ANOTHER KIND OF PARADISE
Well-crafted stories from literary traditions rarely translated into English; includes works from Burma, Thailand, and Cambodia.